Raniero

MARY
MIRROR OF THE CHURCH

Translation by Frances Lonergan Villa

A Liturgical Press Book

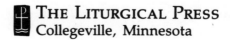 THE LITURGICAL PRESS
Collegeville, Minnesota

Cover design by Ann Blattner.

Cover icon from *Great Panagia* (all holy) (13th century) Tretjakov Gallery, Moscow.

This book was originally published in Italian by *Editrice Àncora* under the title *Maria: Uno Specchio per la Chiesa*.

5	6	7	8	9

Library of Congress Cataloging-in-Publication Data

Cantalamessa, Raniero.
   [Maria. English]
   Mary : mirror of the Church / Raniero Cantalamessa ; [translation by Frances Lonergan Villa].
      p.   cm.
   Translation of: Maria.
   Includes bibliographical references.
   ISBN 0-8146-2059-0
   1. Mary, Blessed Virgin, Saint—Theology. 2. Catholic Church-
-Doctrines. I. Title.
BT613.C2813   1992
232.91—dc20   92-12402
                                            CIP

As each has received a gift,
employ it for one another,
as good stewards
of God's varied grace
(1 Pet 4:10)

For my Protestant brethren,
from whom I have received much,
even in writing this book
on Mary

Contents

Part Three
MARY, MIRROR OF THE CHURCH
AT PENTECOST

Mary, A Letter Written by the Finger of the Living God

The Apostle Paul, who wrote so many beautiful letters to the Christians, now reveals the existence of another type of letter to us, a letter, he said, "written not with ink but with the Spirit of the living God, not on tablets of stone but on tablets of human hearts" (2 Cor 3:2-3).

In this sense Mary, too, is God's letter, in that she is part of the Church. She is particularly and singularly so because she is not simply a member of the Church like others but the very figure of the Church, or the Church in her nascent state. Indeed, she is a letter written not with ink but with the Spirit of the living God; not on tablets of stone, as in the old Law, and neither on parchment nor papyrus, but on the tablet of her heart, the heart of a mother and believer. A letter for all of us, whether we are learned or not. Tradition embraced this idea and considered Mary "a waxed tablet" upon which God was able to write what he wished (Origen), or "a wonderful new book" in which the Holy Spirit alone wrote (St. Epiphanius), or "the book in which the Father wrote his Word" (Byzantine liturgy).

We wish to read this letter of God's for a practical and edifying purpose: that of sketching a path to holiness totally modeled on God's mother. It is not, therefore, a treatise on Mariology or a series of conferences on Mary but a pilgrimage of listening and obedience to God's Word following Mary's example. I believe that Mary can say to each one of us what the apostle said to his followers in Corinth: "Be imitators of me, as I am of Christ" (1 Cor 11:1).

Mary is not often referred to in the New Testament. Nevertheless, we can notice that she was present at all three of the events that form the Christian mystery: the incarnation, the paschal mystery, and Pentecost. The incarnation, when the person of the Redeemer, God and man, was formed; the paschal mystery, when he worked our redemption by destroying sin and renewing life; Pentecost, when the Holy Spirit was given to make salvation in

9

the Church operative and relevant. Mary was present at all three of these events. She was present at the incarnation because it came about in her. Her womb, said the Fathers of the Church, was the loom or workroom where the Holy Spirit wove the Word's human form, the thalamus where God united himself to humanity. She was present at the paschal mystery, because it is written: "Standing by the cross of Jesus was Mary his mother (John 19:25). And she was present at Pentecost, because it is written that the apostles "with one accord devoted themselves to prayer, with Mary the mother of Jesus" (Acts 1:14). Following Mary in each of these fundamental steps will help us to really and resolutely follow Christ so that we can live his entire mystery.

To do this, we are necessarily obliged to mention almost all the main theological and exegetical problems that have arisen about Mary, and it would be better to explain immediately the criteria I am following in this book. The main lines are those traced by Vatican Council II in the chapter on Mary in *Lumen gentium*. The text explains Mary's two fundamental roles, mother and figure: Mary, mother of Christ and figure of the Church. This concept, which includes Mary in the discourse on the Church, is here integrated with another view, which tries to see Mary's role in the light of what the council said about the Word of God in *Dei Verbum*. First and foremost, Mary is a chapter of God's Word. She is spoken of in the canonical books in the New Testament; her primordial place is revelation, that is to say, Scripture. The council emphasized a well-known principle concerning revelation, that it is "realized by deeds and words."[1] St. Gregory the Great said, "At times God admonishes us with words, at other times with deeds."[2] "Deeds too are words!" exclaimed St. Augustine.[3] We already find in the prophets silent symbolic deeds, full of deep meaning in the history of salvation, and there are in the Bible whole lives and people who are prophetic and exemplary in themselves, like Abraham. These are of interest for what they did and were and not only for what they said. In this way the prophet is a forewarning sign of what is to happen to the people, the figure and model of what they must do: "Ezekiel will be a sign for you; you will do just as he has done" (Ezek 24:24). Mary participates in this. She is not God's word just because of what she says in Scripture or because of what is said of her but also for what she does and is. Her simple presence by the cross is a sign, and how full of meaning it is!

10

There is a big advantage in seeing Mary there in her primordial place, or *Sitz im Leben,* which is Scripture, and in starting from that point, guided by tradition, to deepen our knowledge of her. In fact, the time has come to make Mary a source of unity and reconciliation among Christians and no longer a topic of discussion and division. Mary appears as the sign of a Church not yet divided, not even in Jews and Gentiles, and therefore as the strongest possible call to unity. This ecumenical purpose we wish to follow is greatly favored by starting to study Mary from the Bible instead of starting with formal principles, theological theses, or the dogmas. The dogmas were formulated to explain the Bible and not vice versa. They are the exponent, not the basis. When dogma is the basis and Scripture the exponent, the dogmatic affirmation is placed first and biblical verses are used to demonstrate the argument, often far from the context and in a subordinate role as proof *ex Scriptura.* When Scripture is the basis, the starting point is God's Word, and in expounding its meaning the dogma is reached as the true interpretation given by the Church. This is the way truth came down to us.

One of the not always unjustified suspicions that has kept our Protestant brothers far from Mary is that in speaking of her and exalting her role, the Church in fact speaks of herself and exalts herself.[4] When we read Mary's life in the light of God's Word, this suspicion becomes groundless: with Mary, it is not the Church speaking of herself but God speaking to the Church. This is the conviction with which we shall start our spiritual journey of conversion and holiness with Mary: that through Mary, God speaks to the Church and to each one of us. That she is a "pregnant" word of God. Of Mary alone can it really and not only figuratively be said that she is pregnant with the Word. She is a pregnant word of God also in that the few words and verses referring to her in the Gospels are extraordinarily charged with meaning and resonance. In an analogic sense we could apply to her the category of the visible word *(verbum visibile)* that St. Augustine used for the sacraments. That's precisely why, as we shall see, her guidance is so practical and close to us. We can say of her what is generally said of God's Word: "It is not in heaven, that you should say, who will go up for us to heaven, and bring it to us. . . . Neither is it beyond the sea. . . . But the word is very near you" (Deut 30:12-14).

The criterion followed to throw light on the person and role

11

of Mary in the history of salvation is what I call the method of analogy from below. It consists in trying to state Mary's role precisely, starting not from above, as it were—from the persons of the Trinity or from Christ—to then adapt our findings to Mary by the method of reduction but, on the contrary, starting from below—from events and figures in the history of salvation—to then apply them *a fortiori* to Mary. This principle will be clearer when we have actually applied it in our spiritual journey.

In passing from our considerations on Mary to the Church, the concept of Mary as figure of the Church will be useful. This concept was used by the Fathers of the Church and newly taken up by Vatican Council II. It essentially indicates two things: something that is *behind* us, as the beginning or first flowering or even archetype of the Church, and, at the same time, something that stands *before* us, as a model and perfect example to imitate. It is not a category unknown to the Protestant world, and is therefore, ecumenically speaking, of considerable value. When commenting on Luke 2:19 ("Mary kept all these things, pondering them in her heart"), Luther wrote in a discourse on Christmas Day, 1522: "Mary is the Christian Church. . . . The Christian Church keeps all God's words in her heart and connects them, that is to say, she confronts them among themselves and with the Scripture."[5] For Luther, too, Mary keeping the word of God was the figure of the Church.

I preferred to use the term "mirror" rather than "figure" in the title and elsewhere because it is easier to comprehend and less bound to a certain type of technical language in biblical exegesis. It is also more suggestive and almost makes the idea plastic. But the significance is the same in both cases. Mary is a mirror of the Church in two ways: to reflect the light she herself receives, as a mirror does with the light of the sun, and because she is such that the Church can and must mirror herself in Mary to make herself beautiful for her heavenly Spouse. In this case too, we are only applying to Mary in a more particular sense what is said in general of God's Word, that it is a mirror (see Jas 1:23).

To say that Mary is the figure or mirror of the Church means in practical terms that after having first considered a word, an attitude, or an event in the Madonna's life, we then ask ourselves what this means for the Church and each one of us. What should we do to practice what the Holy Spirit wished to communicate to us through Mary? The best answer we can give is not *devotion* to Mary but *imitation* of her. It will therefore be a very simple and practical spiritual journey, a kind of spiritual exercises guided by Mary. Exercises, because each meditation will suggest something to be done and not only to be understood. St. James said of the mirror of God's Word: "For if anyone is a hearer of the word and not a doer, he is like a man who observes his natural face in a mirror; for he observes himself and goes away and forgets what he was like. But he who looks into the perfect law, the law of liberty, and perseveres, being no hearer that forgets but a doer that acts, he shall be blessed in his doing" (Jas 1:23-25). The same must be said for the word, or special letter, that is Mary.

Besides making use of the Bible, the Fathers, tradition, and theology, to read this letter of God we shall often refer to particular poets who have sung the mysteries of our faith or spoken of God. Why? Isn't there already a risk when talking of Mary of indulging in fancy or feeling? The reason is simple. It is a question of reawakening and giving voice to truths of faith and the old Christian dogmatic terminology so often ruined from overuse. The philosopher Kierkegaard said that the old Christian dogmatic terminology is like an enchanted castle where the most beautiful princes and princesses rest in a deep sleep—it needs only to be awakened, brought to life, in order to stand in its full glory,[6] and no one is better able to do this than poets. A true poet is sometimes a sort of inspired prophet. There is great need today for inspiration so as not to succumb when speaking of the truths of faith and explaining Scripture to an arid philological virtuosity or dead speculation. Modern philosophy sensed this. Heidegger, after struggling in vain to grasp the being of things, at a certain point in his life abandoned the project halfway and turned his attention to the poets, saying that it was in them that being furtively showed itself. A point, this, that we theologians should carefully consider. Theology welcomed every type of suggestion from this philosopher except this particular one, perhaps the most fruitful, open as it is to the Christian doctrine on grace.

In writing these pages, the contemplation of certain icons of the Mother of God were of invaluable help to me. It seemed that everything I was saying about her was already written on them and in an infinitely better way. I have inserted a few of these icons into the book, which place Mary before our eyes and spirit in the three events of the incarnation, the paschal mystery, and Pente-

13

cost, in the hope that their contemplation will assist us in "reading" Mary, this wonderful letter written by God's Spirit.

It is obvious that our greatest help will not come from the poets or iconographers but from the Holy Spirit who "wrote" the Word in Mary and who made her a word of God for the Church. Mary, too, as part of God's Word, is symbolized in that scroll "written within and on the back, sealed with seven seals" (Rev 5:1). Only the Lamb can break its seals by his Spirit and reveal the meaning to whom he wishes. Let us begin our reading of God's word, Mary, with the hope and prayer that God will deign to reveal to us what the Spirit is saying to the Church today through the Virgin Mary, the Mother of God.

NOTES

1. Vatican Council II, *Dei Verbum* 2.
2. St. Gregory the Great, *Homilies on the Gospels,* XVII, 1 (PL 76, 1139).
3. St. Augustine, *Sermons* 95, 3 (PL 38, 582).
4. See K. Barth, *Church Dogmatics,* I, 2 (English trans. I, 1936, p. 143f.).
5. Luther, *Sermons on the Gospels (Kirchenpostille)* (ed. Weimar 10, 1, p. 140).
6. See S. Kierkegaard, *Journals,* II A 110 (ed. H. V. Hong and E. H. Hong, Indiana University Press, Bloomington and London, IV, 1975, entry 4774).

Part One

Mary, Mirror of the Church in the Incarnation

Chapter I

"Full of Grace"

Mary guides the Church in discovering God's grace

1. *"By the grace of God, I am what I am"*

God's living letter, Mary, begins with the word "grace," a word so meaningful as to enclose in itself, like a seed, Mary's whole life. When the angel appeared to her, he said, "Hail, full of grace," and then again, "Do not be afraid, Mary, for you have found grace with God" (Luke 1:28-30).

When the angel greeted Mary, he did not address her by name but simply called her "full of grace" or "filled with grace" *(kecharitomene);* he didn't say, "Hail Mary," but "Hail, full of grace." Mary's truest identity is in grace.

Mary's grace is undoubtedly in function of what the angel then went on to announce to her, that is, her role as the Messiah's mother, but it is not only this. Mary isn't just a mere passive function for God. She is first and foremost a person, and it is as a person that she is so dear to God from all eternity.

Thus Mary is the real living manifestation of that grace that comes first in the relation between God and his children. Grace is the meeting point between creatures and their Creator. The Bible also portrays God as being full of grace (see Exod 34:6). God is full of grace in an active sense, as he who *fills* with grace; Mary, and after her every other person, is full of grace in a passive sense, as she who is *filled* with grace. In between them there is the mediator, Jesus Christ, who is "full of grace" (John 1:14) in both the active and passive sense: as God and head of the Church, he gives grace, and as man, he is filled with the Father's grace, and he increases in grace (see Luke 2:52). Grace is God "leaning forward" and stooping toward man. It is the convex angle that fills the concavity of the human longing for God. St. John says that "God is love" (1 John 4:8), and outside the Trinity, this is the same as saying that God is grace. In fact, it is only within the Trinity,

17

in the relationships of the divine persons among themselves, that God's love is nature, that is, need; in every other case it is grace, a gift. The fact that the Father loves the Son is neither grace nor gift but a paternal need—in a certain way it is a duty—whereas his love for us is, instead, pure grace, a freely given and unmerited gift.

The God of the Bible not only gives grace but is grace. It has been pointed out that the words of Exodus 33:19, "I will be gracious to whom I will be gracious," are in line with and, so to say, explain Exodus 3:14, "I am who I am." The same is true of Exodus 34:6. "The Lord passed before him and proclaimed, 'The Lord, the Lord, a God merciful and gracious, slow to anger and abounding in steadfast love.' " Besides being "he who exists for himself," the biblical God is also "he who exists for us," that is to say, he is grace.

Now, as I have already mentioned, Mary is a kind of living icon of God's grace. Speaking of Christ's humanity, St. Augustine said: "On what basis did Christ's humanity merit being incorporated by the Father's eternal Word in the unity of his person? What good work of his warranted this? What had he done prior to this, what had he believed, or asked, to be raised to such unique dignity?" "Try to find the merit, try to find the justice, reflect and see if you can find anything but grace."[1]

These words throw a particular light on Mary's whole person. With greater reason we may ask, what had she done to merit the privilege of giving the Word his humanity? What had she believed in, asked for, hoped in or suffered, to be born holy and immaculate? In this case too, try to find the merit, the justice, anything you want, and see if you can find in her, at the beginning, anything but grace! In all truth can Mary apply the apostle's words to herself and say, "By the grace of God, I am what I am" (1 Cor 15:10). A full explanation of Mary, her greatness and beauty, is to be found in grace. As Péguy has said, there comes a time when we can no longer content ourselves with our own patron saint, nor with the patron saint of our town, and not even with the greatest of patron saints; we must go back to the one who is most acceptable and closest to God, "to the one who is Mary because she is full of grace."[2] Simple and profound words! Mary is Mary because she is full of grace. To say she is full of grace is to say all there is to say of her.

2. *What Is Grace?*

What is grace? Let us take the common meaning, which we can all understand. What does the word "grace" mean to us? The most common meaning is beauty, graciousness, amiability (the French word *charme* is derived from the same root, *charis*, grace). But this is not its only significance. It can also mean favor, mercy, good will.

In biblical language we find the same double meaning. God says, "I will be gracious to whom I will be gracious, and I will show mercy on whom I will show mercy" (Exod 33:19). It is clear that in this verse grace signifies absolute gratuitous favor, freely given and unmotivated, the same meaning that is to be found in Exodus 43:6, where we read that God "abounds in grace and faithfulness, keeping his favor for thousands." "You have found grace in my sight," God said to Moses (Exod 33:12), precisely as the angel said to Mary, "You have found grace with God." In this case, too, grace denotes favor and benevolence.

Alongside this principal meaning, the Bible gradually unfolds a second meaning, where grace denotes a quality inherent in the person, at times seen as the effect of divine favor and which makes the person beautiful, attractive, and amiable. Thus, for example, it the *grace* poured upon the lips of the regal spouse, the fairest of the sons of men (see Ps 45:3), and a good wife is said to be as "fair as a hind, *graceful* as a fawn" (Prov 5:19).

It is possible, as I have mentioned, to see a link between the two things, at least in the actual meaning if not in the terms themselves. It is because God passed by the maiden symbolizing Israel and loved her and made a covenant with her that God's grace caused her to grow more and more beautiful until she rose to be a queen (see Ezek 16:8 ff.). In any case, no mention is made anywhere in the Bible of the opposite, that beauty and goodness attract or provoke the divine favor. The beauty of a person depends on God's favor and not God's favor on the beauty of a person.

Turning back to Mary now, we can see that the angel's greeting reflects these meanings of grace. Mary found grace, favor, with God; she is full of divine favor. As water fills the sea, so grace fills Mary's soul. What grace did Moses, the patriarchs, or the prophets find in God's eyes compared to Mary? Who else was the Lord more with than with her? God wasn't in her just through power or providence but also in person, through his presence. God didn't only give Mary his favor but all of himself in his Son. "The Lord is with you!" When said of Mary, these words hold a different meaning than for any other person. What other election had a higher purpose than Mary's, which concerned the very incarnation of God?

As a consequence of all this, Mary is full of grace in the second significance too. She is beautiful, of a beauty we shall call holiness; all beautiful *(tota pulchra)* the Church calls her in the words of the canticle (see Song 4:1). As Mary has received grace, she is also graceful. Superbly bringing together the two meanings of grace, Péguy, the poet mentioned earlier, said that Mary "is full of grace, because she is full of grace," that is, she is full of beauty and grace because she is full of divine favor and election. Mary is beautiful because she is loved.

This grace, consisting in Mary's holiness, has in itself a quality that places it above the grace possessed by any other person, both in the Old Testament and the New. It is uncontaminated grace. The Latin Church expresses this in the title "Immaculate," and the Orthodox Church in the title "All Holy" *(Panaghia).* One emphasizes the negative aspect of Mary's grace, the absence of all sin, even of original sin, whereas the other emphasizes the positive aspect, the presence of all virtue in her and the splendor that comes from this.

The Church, too, is called to be "without spot or wrinkle or any such thing, that she might be holy and without blemish" (Eph 5:27). But as Péguy said, "What has been saved, defended with all one's might, renewed, achieved, is not the same as what has never been lost. A whitened page will never be a white page, nor a whitened canvas a white canvas, just as a soul made white will never be a white soul."[3] The Church is freed from all stain; Mary is preserved from all stain. The Church has wrinkles that will, one day, be smoothed out; Mary, by God's grace, has nothing that needs to be smoothed.

However, I don't wish to pause too long on this secondary meaning of grace, which constitutes Mary's so-called store of grace. In fact, preaching on grace also needs to be renewed in the Spirit, and this consists in replacing, all the time, in the foreground, the original significance of grace, that which concerns God before man, the giver before the receiver of grace. It consists in "giving God's power back to him." When talking of the title "full of grace" with which the angel addressed Mary, it is easy to make the mistake of insisting more on Mary's grace than on God's grace. The title "full of grace" was the privileged starting point and basis for defining the dogmas of the Immaculate Conception, the Assumption, and almost all of Mary's other privileges. All of this constitutes progress where the faith is concerned. But once this has been understood, we must move back to the original meaning, which talks to us more of God than of Mary, more of him who gives grace than of her who receives it, because this is exactly what Mary herself wants. Without this reference, grace might gradually and imperceptibly indicate its opposite, which is merit.

The same grace of God that filled Mary is also Christ's grace *(gratia Christi)*. It is "the grace of God which was given in Christ Jesus" (1 Cor 1:4), the favor and salvation that God now grants humankind through Christ's redeeming death. Mary is on this side of the great ridge; it is not the water flowing from Mount Moriah or Mount Sinai that touches Mary but that flowing from Mount Calvary. Her grace is the grace of the new covenant. In defining the dogma of the Immaculate Conception, the Church declared that Mary was preserved from sin, "in view of the merits of Jesus Christ, our savior."[4] In this sense she is really, as Dante said, "the daughter of her Son."[5]

In Mary we contemplate the newness of grace in the New Testament with respect to the old covenant; in her there was a leap in quality. St. Irenaeus asked himself, "What did God's Son bring that was new when he came into the world?" and he answered, "He brought every newness by bringing himself."[6] God's grace no longer consists in some gift or other but in the gift of himself; it doesn't consist in some favor of his but in his presence. And this fact is so new that we can now say, "The grace of God has appeared for the salvation of all men" (Titus 2:11), as if, in comparison, what had existed before had not even been grace but-just a preparation for it.

St. Paul, the cantor of grace, teaches us that the first thing we must do in answer to God's grace is to give thanks: "I give thanks to God always for you because of the grace of God" (1 Cor 1:4). In the Greek language in which he wrote, the word "thanksgiving" *(eucharistein)* is formed from the very word "grace" *(charis)*. Man's thanks must follow God's grace. To give thanks doesn't mean to pay back a favor or give in exchange the same as one has received. Who could give God something in exchange? Actu-

21

ally, to give thanks means to acknowledge grace, to accept its gratuity, not to wish "to ransom ourselves or give to God the price of our life" (Ps 49:8). That's why it is such a fundamental religious attitude. To give thanks means accepting ourselves as debtors, as dependents on God, letting God be God.

This is what Mary did in her *Magnificat:* "My soul magnifies the Lord . . . , for he who is mighty has done great things for me." The Hebrew language doesn't have a special word that signifies "giving thanks" or "thanks." When he wanted to thank God, the biblical worshiper praised him, exalted him, and proclaimed his wonders with great enthusiasm. Perhaps that's why the *Magnificat* doesn't contain the word "thanks," whereas it does contain the words "magnify" and "exult." But even if the word itself is not used, the corresponding sentiment is not missing. Mary truly gave God's power back to him. She took nothing of its gratuity from grace. She attributed to God's favor, to grace, the great thing that was taking place in her and attributed no merit to herself. The *Panaghia,* or *All Holy* icon, venerated especially in Russia, is the icon that best expresses all of this. The Mother of God is standing in an upright position with her arms raised in an attitude of total surrender and acceptance. The Lord "with her" is depicted as a princely child, visible in the center of her bosom. Her expression is one of wonder, silence, humility, as if she were saying, "See what the Lord has done for me, when he turned his gaze on this, his humble servant!"

3. *"By grace you have been saved"*

It is now time to recall the guiding principle formulated in the Prologue: that Mary is the figure and mirror of the Church. What does the fact that Mary's story begins with the word "grace" signify for the Church and for each one of us? It signifies that for us, too, at the beginning, there is grace, the freely given election of God, his inexplicable favor, his coming down to us in Christ and giving himself to us for the sake of pure love. It signifies that grace is the first principle of Christianity.

The virgin-mother Church, too, received her annunciation. And the greeting the divine messenger addressed to her was "Grace and peace to you, from God the Father and from Jesus Christ!" That's how the letters of the apostles, not only Paul's but John's as well, almost invariably begin (see John 1:3). Let us listen to one of these greetings so as to savor to the full its force and sweetness: "Paul, called by the will of God to be an apostle of Christ Jesus, and our brother Sosthenes. To the Church of God which is at Corinth. Grace to you and peace from God our Father and the Lord Jesus Christ. I give thanks to God always for you because of the grace of God which was given you in Christ Jesus" (1 Cor 1:1-4).

The words "grace" and "peace" are not just a greeting, they contain news; the implicit verb doesn't just signify "be" but "is." We announce to you that you are in God's grace, in his favor, that God's peace and favor exist for you because of Christ! Paul, above all, never tired of announcing God's grace to believers and of keeping this feeling alive in them. He believed that the ministry he received from Christ was "to testify to the Gospel of the grace of God" (Acts 20:24). The word "grace" summarizes on its own the whole Christian message and the entire Gospel, which is, in fact, the word of his grace (see Acts 14:3; 20:32). In order to find again the force of newness and consolation hidden in this message, we need to become pure of hearing, like those for whom the Gospel was first intended. Theirs was an "epoch of anguish." Pagan man was desperately looking for a way out from that feeling of condemnation and distance from God in which he found himself, in a world considered to be a "prison," and he did this in various cults and philosophies. To get an idea, let us think of a man condemned to death who has been living in oppressive uncertainty for years, who jumps with fear at the sound of every footstep outside his cell. What would he feel if a friend unexpectedly turned up waving a sheet of paper and shouting, Reprieved, reprieved; you have been reprieved! He would suddenly feel a new man, the world would look different and he would feel as if he were born again. The apostle's words must have had a similar effect on those listening to him: "There is therefore now no condemnation for those who are in Christ Jesus!" (Rom 8:1). St. Paul spoke of grace as one who, having overcome dreadful difficulties, had at last found refuge in a safe harbor: "Through him [Christ] we have obtained access to this grace in which we stand" (Rom 5:2).

For the Church, just as for Mary, grace represents the deep core of its reality and the root of its existence: what makes it what it is. The Church, too, must therefore confess: By the grace of

God, I am what I am. According to Christian metaphysics based on the concept of grace, "to be is to be loved" (G. Marcel). Man can find no other explanation of his being if not in the love God loved him with and, loving him, created him. On a supernatural level, this is also true of the Church. Salvation, at the root, is grace and doesn't come from man's will: "For by grace you have been saved through faith; and this is not your own doing, it is the gift of God" (Eph 2:8). In the Christian faith, therefore, the gift comes before the commandment. And it is the gift that gives rise to duty and not vice versa. That is to say, it is not the law that generates grace but grace that generates the law. In fact, grace is the Christian's new law, the law of the Spirit.

This is such a simple and clear truth that we often tend to forget it, so we should constantly have it before us as something new. It is not sufficient that others before me should have proclaimed this truth, lived it, and that I should have read their writings on grace. If I have never experienced it, never been blinded by the light of this truth at least for an instant, it's as if it were nonexistent for me.

Mary, therefore, principally proclaims to the Church that all is grace. Grace is the distinctive of Christianity in the sense that grace distinguishes Christianity from every other religion. From the point of view of moral doctrine or dogma or works done by followers, there may be, at least partially, similarities and equivalences. The works done by certain followers of other religions may even be better than those of many Christians. It is grace that creates the difference because grace is not a simple doctrine or idea; it is first and foremost a reality, and as such, either it exists or it doesn't exist. It is grace that gives value to works and life and distinguishes between what is human and divine, momentary and eternal. Grace exists in Christianity because it has a source, or center of production: the redeeming death of Christ and the reconciliation he brought about. The founders of other religions just gave an example, but Christ did much more; he gave grace. Seen on the outside, all electric copper wires look the same. But if one of them is a live wire, then what a difference between it and the others! Whoever touches it gets a shock, a thing the other, similar wires do not cause.

The greatest heresy and foolishness of nonbelieving modern man is the belief that he doesn't need grace. In the present-day technological culture we witness the elimination of the very idea of God's grace from human life. This is radical Pelagianism of modern mentality. Psychoanalysis is a typical example: the belief is that it is sufficient to enable a patient to reason about his neuroses and guilt complexes for him to get better, without any need of any God-given grace, which cures and renews. Psychoanalysis is confession without grace. If grace is what gives value to a human being and raises it beyond time and corruption, what is a man or a woman without grace, if not an empty man and an empty woman?

Modern man is rightly shocked by the blatant differences that exist between rich and poor, between those who have too much and the hungry. But he isn't troubled by the infinitely more dramatic difference between those living in God's grace and those without God's grace. Pascal formulated the principle of the three orders, or greatness, in the world: the order of the body, the order of the intellect and genius, and the order of holiness and grace. Between the order, or greatness, of the body—riches, beauty, and physical strength—and the superior greatness of the intellect and genius, there is an infinite distance: the first one cannot add anything to or take anything from the second. But, Pascal added, there is an "infinitely more infinite distance" between intellect and grace.[7] This third greatness is higher than any other, as distant as the heaven is from the earth. This is the greatness that makes Mary so outstanding over all other creatures. In this objective sense, based on the absolute superiority of grace over nature, Mary is the most sublime of creatures, after Christ.

To disregard grace or foolishly believe we don't need it is, therefore, the same as condemning ourselves to being incomplete; it is to remain in the first or second human order without even suspecting that an infinitely higher order exists.

4. *"I prefer it whole!"*

At the beginning of the Church, grace was the sun illuminating Christian preaching. To make it so again we must reestablish what it is and restore it to its proper meaning, and as we shall see, a deep conversion is needed to do this.

In a well-known medieval book on spirituality, we find a sort of cry of rebellion. For a spirit in search of the living God but ensnared, as it were, by the numerous distinctions and definitions of God, his perfections and attributes proposed by the theology of the time, the unknown author advised him to reject all distinctions and subtleties and cry out from the depths of his soul, "I prefer it whole!"[8] We must do the same where grace is concerned.

In the history of the Church grace has been subjected to numerous distinctions and subdivisions, which have impoverished and broken it down. We speak of actual grace and habitual grace, of sanctifying grace, sufficient or efficacious, of the grace of state and the state of grace, this last meaning the state of not having unconfessed grave sins on one's conscience.

Grace began to lose the extraordinary depth of meaning it had in the New Testament when, due to the error of the Pelagians, it was seen above all as a necessary help to man's weak will to help him keep the law and not to sin (the so-called prevenient grace) and then, when it became a habit to talk of it almost only in the context of contraposition, that of grace and freedom, nature and grace, grace and law, grace and merit. The light was gradually diffracted into its various colors and faded.

All this was the result of a process that was in itself positive and inevitable and was useful in emphasizing the richness and treasures of the grace of Christ, which the human mind can only grasp in part and through distinctions. It is just as natural for man to distinguish and analyze things as it is for a prism to break up light and refract it into diverse colors. But as soon as the need for contemplation is felt, it becomes necessary to see the whole, not the fragments. Contemplation, in fact, exists only in relation to something as a whole. Explanations tend to distinguish the parts, whereas contemplation tends to see the object as a whole. What is true of contemplation is also true in a different way of evangelization. You cannot evangelize by preaching subtle distinctions of grace. The gospel of grace is quite another thing to a long list of opinions and doctrines on grace!

The sign of the unity of grace is precisely the word "grace," which must be understood in the widest and most comprehensive way possible found in the Bible itself, just as for us the best sign of the living reality of God is the simple word "God," uttered lovingly in prayer, just as it is.

Among Christians, two fundamental lines of thought were formed and still exist concerning grace. One comes from the distinction made between intrinsic grace and extrinsic grace. The traditional Churches, both Catholic and Orthodox, see grace as a real participation in the nature and life of God. The Reformation Churches, instead, see it more or less strictly, as an imputation of justice, which leaves man in himself what he is, a sinner, rendering him just not in himself but only in the eyes of God *(simul iustus et peccator)*. The Protestant view considers grace almost exclusively in the original sense of freely given favor, a sovereign and unilateral act of God, whereas the Catholic and Orthodox view also considers it in the second sense of beauty and a sanctifying gift creating a state of grace in the person.

The second diversification derives from the distinction between uncreated grace and created grace. It accounts for a distinction between catholics and orthodox within the framework of the above-mentioned common interpretation. In orthodox theology, grace is the presence of God himself in the soul where he dwells through the Holy Spirit who transforms and divinizes man, whereas in catholic theology, especially after the Council of Trent, it is principally a created quality, sanctifying grace, which makes the personal presence of the Holy Spirit possible. But the difference, in this case, lies more in what is stressed and in the perspective than in the content of the doctrine itself which they share, especially if one looks at great theologians like Saint Thomas.

As I have said, we must again find the basic unity underlying all these distinctions, each of which emphasizes an aspect of grace that needs all the other aspects if it is not to remain biased and incomplete. Nowadays we are beginning to realize that the different way other Christian traditions have of explaining certain mysteries, such as the Trinity or the real presence in the Eucharist, is not a threat to our way. Instead, it is often a providential enrichment and completion, so long as we abandon the pretext of wanting to explain the "formal reason" or the exact way in which the Christian mysteries are realized. In the last few decades the change of attitude and the dialogue among Christians have caused many of the barriers that existed over grace to fall. The day no longer seems far off when we shall no longer be divided over grace. Even the Lutheran principle of being "just and sinner at the same time" *(simul iustus et peccator)* is compatible with Catholic and Orthodox tradition, so long as *simul* is understood in the sense of "at the same time," and not also in the sense of "under the same aspect," or "in the same way." Seen in this light, it helps in understanding a Christian experience that even in justified man there remains a basis of sinful egoism. All told, this principle means nothing if not that the old self and the new self live, in fact, together in different degrees in a baptized person.

As I have said, the light of grace broke into various colors. But light is still beautiful even when distributed among its colors, so long as the colors remain together, as in the spectrum or in a rainbow. The light of grace can shine in all its fullness even if each Christian Church only brings out one particular aspect, so long as it doesn't despise or reject the other aspects dear to other Christian Churches.

In contemplating Mary, we can once again discover the synthesis and unity of faith. She is the icon of undivided grace, grace that is still whole. As we have seen, grace in her indicates both the fullness of divine favor and the fullness of personal holiness; it indicates the very presence of God in the strongest way imaginable, both physical and spiritual; and it indicates the effects of this presence, which makes Mary what she is, Mary. No other person is like her even if they possess the same Spirit that sanctified her.

5. *The Beauty of the Princess*

A reawareness of the importance of grace over all things can help us to cultivate a right attitude toward the Church. The Church is disregarded and rejected by many because they see it only as a human organization with its laws, its rites, and the incoherence of its ministers. In the effort to rectify this error we often just reinforce it, because we remain on the same level as the adversary, which is not the level of grace but always and only the level of works. I am convinced that the Church today suffers enormously and loses many of her members and much of her attraction because she is not seen as being "full of grace," offering it to mankind, but as a human organization made up of rites, laws, doctrines, ministers who are men about whom we could spend a lifetime talking of their incoherences and faults. We are thus under the illusion that we know what the Church is, whereas, in fact, we only see its outer appearance. Sometimes, as I have mentioned, Church members just increase this ambiguity. In fact, on what are discussions within the Church based? On God's grace? More often than not they are based on who supports whom, on party lines, on external alliances. Each one tries to judge events in a way that will always be somehow to his own advantage or in line with the ideology he practices. So the grace of God is side-tracked, and the Church becomes the target of easy criticism.

The Church and the entire Christian life can be presented in two ways. One is through *apologetics and controversy* and consists in defending the Church by hitting back at the accusations of her enemies. The other is the *kerygmatic way,* or through preaching, and consists in serenely preaching the gospel of grace, certain that it contains an intrinsic power that goes beyond us and them and that, on its own, has the power "to destroy strongholds, arguments, and every proud obstacle to the knowledge of God" (2 Cor 10:4 f.). Christian life can be illuminated in two ways, just like an ancient cathedral. It can be illuminated from the outside by floodlighting it from suitable points, as is done for certain historical monuments in cities today, or from the inside, opening doors and windows and letting the light within be diffused. Both ways can be good, but while the first just emphasizes the historical and human aspect of the Church—the walls of the building—the second emphasizes its intimate and divine aspect, which is grace. It is not enough to illuminate the institution; the mystery of the Church must also be illuminated. Apologetics is necessary; there are even saints among the apologists. We must not discard it therefore, but we must remember that on its own it is not sufficient.

As I have mentioned, the second way is to let the grace within the Church diffuse itself and that is, its capacity to forgive and its divine power, through its own means: preaching, prayer, forgiveness, love, gentleness. This way exacts faith because we must believe that the grace of God is present and acts in the Church, so as to be able to trust in it and not in our own explanations. When this is the case, we can almost see the effect with our own eyes. God's Word touches man's heart like a sword and brings him to his knees in a way that would never have happened if we had gone on trying to explain something for a whole day.

There is the same difference between the two ways of looking at the Church as there is between looking at the window of a well-known medieval cathedral from the outside and looking at it instead from the inside, against the light. In the first case you can only see pieces of dark glass held together by strips of equally dark lead. In the second case, when you look at the stained-glass windows from within the cathedral, a whole spectacle of colors, shapes, and harmony meets the eye, leaving you breathless. I personally experienced this one day when I visited the cathedral of Chartres.

From the beginning, the Fathers of the Church applied to Mary and the Church this verse of a psalm which, in the text known to them, says, "The beauty of the princess comes from within [*ab intus*]" (Ps 45:14).⁹ The beauty and power of the Church also come from within, from grace, of which she is full and which she ministers. Grace is in the Church like a pearl in an oyster. The difference is that in the case of the Church it is not the oyster that produces the pearl, it is the pearl that produces the oyster. The Church doesn't generate grace, it is grace that generates the Church.

In the second century there lived a Christian named Abercius whose sepulchral inscription was found in the last century and is considered to be the "queen of Christian inscriptions." On it, in veiled terms—these were times of persecution—Abercius set down the most beautiful experience of his life. He was widely traveled, and one day the "great Pastor," Jesus, had led him to Rome. What could Abercius have possibly seen in Rome that made such a strong impression on him to last to the end of his life? He had seen "the royal palace and the queen dressed in gold"; he had seen "a people with a splendid seal," baptism. He had contemplated the mystery of the Church, her hidden grace. He too applied, implicitly, Psalm 45 to the Church, where mention is made of the princess with "gold-woven" robes, whose beauty comes from within and who, with her companions, enters "the palace of the king." Without doubt, human misery existed in the Church of Rome then too, but Abercius saw beyond it.

6. *Grace Is the Beginning of Glory*

This rediscovery of grace, in which Mary is guiding us, doesn't only change our way of considering the Church in general but also the way of considering our own lives. It holds a personal and urgent appeal to conversion. For many persons, the religious problem is reduced to the question of whether life hereafter, or something after death, exists or not. The only thing that holds them back from definitely breaking all ties with faith and the Church is this doubt: And if there should really be something after death? Consequently, it is thought that the main function of the Church is to lead men to heaven, to meet God, but only after death. This type of faith is easy prey to the criticism of those who see life hereafter as an escape and an illusory projection of unfulfilled desires. However, this criticism has very little to do with genuine preaching on grace, which is not just an anticipation but is also the actual presence and experience of God. The doctrine of grace is, therefore, the only doctrine that can change this sad situation.

A well-known theological principle states that "grace is the beginning of glory."[10] What does this mean? It means that grace somehow makes eternal life present in this life; it makes us see and savor God even in this life. It is true that "in hope we were saved" (Rom 8:24), but "in hope" doesn't principally mean in expectation, in anticipation, but also, and even more so, as a first flowering. Christian hope is not the turning of the soul toward something that might happen or that one wants to happen; it is a form of possession, however temporary and imperfect. "Whoever has the seal of the Spirit and hopes in the resurrection, already has what he is waiting for."[11]

Grace is God's presence. The two expressions "full of grace" and "the Lord is with you" are almost the same. God's presence within us is now realized in Christ and through Christ. He is the Emmanuel, the God-with-us. New Testament grace can be defined in St. Paul's words, "Christ in us, the hope of glory" (Col 1:27). Seen in this light, there is an analogy and a symbol between the Christian life and Jewish betrothal, that is, in Mary's situation at the time of the annunciation. She was already Joseph's spouse by right; no one could break the nuptial agreement or separate her from her spouse. But she wasn't living with him yet. That's what the time of grace is like with respect to the time of glory and the time of faith with respect to the time of vision: we already belong to God and Christ even if we are not fully and permanently living with him.

The fact that grace is the beginning of eternal life is a deeply rooted conviction in tradition that must be revived in Christians so that they will not be content to live only in the hope, or doubt, of eternal life. As St. Basil said, "We already possess the first flowering of this life (life hereafter in Christ); we are already in it, and we are living now completely in God's grace and gift."[12] And Cabasilas wrote, "Right from now it is granted to the saints

31

not only to dispose themselves to get ready for eternal life, but to live and work in it." The same author compares the life of grace to the life of an embryo in its mother's womb: "This world carries in its womb the new man created according to God's will, until, molded, shaped and made perfect, he is born into that perfect world which never ages. Just like the embryo which, while still in its dark and fluid existence, nature is preparing for its future life in the light . . . , so it is with the saints."[13] With respect to eternal life, a Christian is, in fact, something more than just an embryo. An embryo in its mother's womb doesn't receive any ray of light from this world, whereas the future life has overflowed into us and mingles with our present life; the Sun of Justice, Christ, has risen for us; the heavenly oil, the Holy Spirit, has been poured into our hearts and is already spreading its perfume; and we have been given the bread of angels, the Eucharist, to nourish us. This signifies that grace is the beginning of glory.

The words of Blessed Elizabeth of the Trinity express the same vision: "I have found heaven on earth because heaven is God and God is present in my soul. Everything was illuminated for me the day I understood this and I want to communicate this secret to all those I love."[14] It is, as we can see, a question of ecumenical conviction common to both the Orthodox and Catholic Churches. In virtue of grace, "hereafter" is "here within" for us.

Nonbelievers think that this is all an illusion and not a reality. To them, reality is what can be experienced. They don't think that God can seem infinitely more real than anything visible in the world around us. Try to pray, try to have faith, try to accept your sufferings, try to experience what it means to live in communion with others, and then you will be able to tell me if all of this is still an illusion or if, instead, it is not more real in your eyes than what you used to call reality.

7. *Do Not Accept the Grace of God in Vain*

As I have said, the discovery of grace also implies conversion. It makes us face the question, what have I done with God's grace? What am I doing with it? I am reminded of the question a blind, young Jewish girl asks a Christian boy who has both sight and the light of grace in one of Claudel's dramas: "But you who can see, what do you do with the light?"[15]

St. Paul put us on our guard when he said, "Working together with him, then, we entreat you not to accept the grace of God in vain" (2 Cor 6:1). The grace of God can actually be accepted "in vain"; it can fall on deaf ears, and this is a dreadful situation. We can waste grace, and this occurs when we don't correspond to grace; when we don't nourish grace so that it can produce its fruits, the fruits of the Holy Spirit, the virtues; when, as the apostle said, "you presume upon the riches of the kindness and forbearance and patience of God, without knowing that God's kindness is meant to lead you to repentance" (Rom 2:4). In this way we accumulate wrath upon ourselves for the day of judgment.

Even in the apostle's day there were those who thought it possible to live at one and the same time in grace and in sin. To them he replied: "What shall we say then? Are we to continue in sin that grace may be abounding? By no means!" And again he exclaimed: "Are we to sin because we are not under law but under grace? By no means!" (Rom 6:1-2, 15). It would be a monstrosity because it would mean answering grace with ingratitude, it means wanting to make life and death coexist.

The worst case of receiving grace in vain is to lose it, to live in sin, in the dis-grace of God. This is really a dreadful situation because it is a premonition of eternal death. In fact, if God's grace is the beginning of glory, to be in the disgrace of God is the beginning of damnation. To live in God's disgrace is to already live as damned; it means to suffer in this life the torment of the damned even if you are not yet able to recognize and experience the torment in question. You should not live in God's disgrace even for one night—it's too risky. "Do not let the sun go down on your anger," Scripture warns us (Eph 4:26), but it is more important still that the sun does not go down on God's anger. St. John Bosco persuaded one of his boys, who had sinned to repent by placing a note on his pillow that night on which he had written, "And if you were to die tonight?"

To willfully live without God's grace is like being dead a second time, and, alas, how many corpses there are in our streets and squares! They are often the picture of vitality and youth and yet they are dead! A well-known atheist was asked one day how he felt deep within his heart and what he was feeling now at the end of his life. He replied, "I have lived all my life with the strange feeling that I was traveling without a ticket." I don't know what he really meant by this, but his answer is certainly true. To live without God, refusing his grace, is like traveling without a ticket with the risk of being discovered at any moment and being forced to get off. It reminds us of what Jesus said to the man at the wedding feast who had no wedding garment, who was speechless and cast out (see Matt 22:11 f.).

We must therefore have a sound sense of fear and awe at the responsibility that the grace of God gives us. We mustn't only protect it, we must also cultivate it and increase it because it is possible to grow in grace, as is said of Jesus himself. St. Paul said, "By the grace of God I am what I am," and he added, "and his grace toward me was not in vain" (1 Cor 15:10). His grace flowered. He was the great preacher of grace, but he also greatly cultivated it. He teaches all Christian preachers that the first message in Christianity must be the message of grace, but that in order to be able to preach it, grace must be experienced and lived. A priest pretending to administer grace to others while he himself receives it in vain is a tragedy for the Church. It is true that the sacraments act in their own right and confer grace notwithstanding the unworthiness of whoever is administering them, but experience proves that their efficacy is generally quite limited: people are not converted, they do not change their way of living. A person living in sin cannot help others free themselves of sin.

8. *Mary of Grace*

The message of grace is also charged with consolation and courage, which we must find before ending our reflections. Mary was invited by the angel to rejoice because of grace and not to fear because of the same grace. We, too, are invited to do the same. If Mary is the figure of the Church, then this invitation is addressed to each believer: "Rejoice, full of grace!" and then: "Do not be afraid, for you have found grace with God!"

Grace is the main reason for our joy. In the Greek of the New Testament the words "grace" *(charis)* and "joy" *(charà)* are almost confused: grace is what gives joy. To rejoice because of grace means to seek joy in the Lord (see Ps 37:4) and in no one else but him, to let absolutely nothing come before God's favor and friendship. Grace is also the main reason for our courage. When

St. Paul besought the Lord about the thorn in his flesh, God replied, "My grace is sufficient for you" (2 Cor 12:9). The grace or favor of God's is not, in fact, like man's, which is so often forgotten in the hour of need. God is both grace and faithfulness (see Exod 34:6); his faithfulness "is firm as the heavens" (Ps 89:2). All may forsake us, even our mother and father, a psalm says, but God will always gather us up (see Ps 27:10). And so we may say, "Kindness and faithful love pursue me every day of my life" (Ps 23:6).

We must do our utmost each day to renew contact with the grace of God that is in us. It is not a question of being in contact with a thing or an idea but with a person, for, as we have seen, grace is simply "Christ in us, hope and glory." Through grace we can have even in this present life "a certain spiritual contact" with God, which is much more real than anything we could have through speculation on God.[16] Each one has his own means and way of establishing this contact with grace, like a kind of secret way that he alone knows. It might be a thought, a memory, an interior image, a word of God's, an example received. Each time, it's like going back to the source and heart, and feeling grace being rekindled. St. Paul, too, reminded his disciple Timothy to rekindle the grace of God that was within him (see 2 Tim 1:6).

In the introduction to this pilgrimage toward holiness, we said that we would be contemplating the various steps in Mary's life so as to then put them into practice and imitate them in our own lives, because our aim is to do some spiritual exercises and not just simple spiritual conferences. Now, at the end of this first step, or chapter, in Mary's life, which is grace, what exercise should we do? An exercise in faith, gratitude, and wonder. We must believe in grace, believe that God loves us, that he really looks on us with favor, that we have been saved by grace, that the Lord is also with us, though not in the same way that he was with Mary. We should accept the words uttered by God through his prophet as being said to each one of us: "But you, Israel, my servant, Jacob, whom I have chosen . . . fear not, for I am with you, be not dismayed, for I am your God" (Isa 41:8-10). Fear not, for you have found grace!

We have seen what is the first duty, rather the first need felt by the person receiving grace: to give thanks, which in the Bible signifies to bless, to exalt the Giver, showing him great love and admiration. Let us therefore say in the words of the psalms, "How precious is your steadfast love, O God!" (Ps 36:7); "It is better than life" (Ps 63:3).

We shall, indeed, have done a wonderful exercise and made a great discovery, the discovery of our life, if we have even glimpsed what God's grace is in this meditation.

In certain Catholic countries there are numerous towns, cathedrals, and sanctuaries where Christians venerate Mary under the title of "Holy Mary of the graces." It is one of the titles most loved by Christians who, on certain occasions, crowd to one of the pictures or statues thus depicting her. Why don't we go a step further and discover an even more beautiful title, a more essential one: "Holy Mary of grace" (not graces)? Why don't we ask Mary to obtain grace for us before asking her to obtain graces? The graces we ask of her and for which we light candles and make solemn promises and novenas are generally material graces for this life; they are what God gives in abundance to those who first of all seek the kingdom of God. What joy we would give Mary in heaven and what progress we would make in devotion to her if, without disdaining the title "Holy Mary of the graces," we were to honor her and invoke her as God's Word has revealed to us: "Holy Mary of grace"!

NOTES

1. St. Augustine, *On the Predestination of the Saints,* 15, 30 (PL 44, 981); *Sermons,* 185, 3 (PL 38, 999).
2. Ch. Péguy, *The Porch of the Mystery of the Second Virtue,* in *Oeuvres Poétiques Complètes,* Paris, Gallimard, 1975, p. 573.
3. Ch. Péguy, *The Mystery of the Saints Innocents,* in *Oeuvres Poétiques Complètes,* cit., p. 804.
4. Denzinger-Schönmetzer, *Enchiridion Symbolorum,* Herder, 1967, no. 2803.
5. Dante Alighieri, *Paradiso,* XXXIII, 1.
6. St. Irenaeus, *Against the Heresies,* IV, 34, 1 (SCh 100, p. 846).
7. B. Pascal, *Pensées,* no. 793, Brunschwicg.
8. *The Cloud of Unknowing,* ch. 7 (trans. into modern English by C. Wolters, London, 1978, p. 55).
9. St. Jerome, *Letter* 107, 7 (PL 22, 874).
10. St. Thomas Aquinas, *Theological Summa,* II-IIae, q. 24, a. 3, 2.
11. St. Cyril of Alexandria, *Commentary on the Second Corinthians,* 5, 5 (PG 74, 942).
12. St. Basil of Caesarea, *Homilies,* 20, 3 (PG 31, 531).
13. N. Cabasilas, *Life in Christ,* I, 1-2 (PG 150, 496).

14. Bl. Elizabeth of the Trinity, *Letter,* 107, to M.me De Sourdon (year 1902).
15. P. Claudel, *Le Père humilié, act I, sc. 3, in Théâtre,* II, Paris, Gallimard, 1956, p. 506.
16. St. Augustine, *Sermons,* 52, 6, 16 (PL 38, 360).

Chapter II

"Blessed Is She Who Believed!"

Mary, full of faith

Mary is God's living letter, and a "reading" of this letter will give us insight into God's "style." She is the living example of God's way of acting in the history of salvation. Tertullian wrote: "Nothing disconcerts the human mind as much as the simplicity of the divine works when compared to the great effects they obtain. . . . How miserable is human incredulity to deny God his qualities of simplicity and power!"[1] He was referring to the greatness of the effects of baptism and to the simplicity of the external means and signs used, which are just a little water and a few words. The opposite, Tertullian added, to what takes place in human and idolatrous undertakings, where the greater the result desired, the greater the show, the setting, and the expense involved.

The same principle applies to Mary and the coming of the Savior into this world. Mary is the example of the divine disproportion between what can be seen exteriorly and what is taking place within. To all appearances, what was Mary in her own village? Certainly she did not stand out in any way. To her relatives and the other village people she was, probably, simply "Myriam," a modest young girl, well behaved but not outstanding. It is well to keep this in mind so as not to risk transforming her by projecting her, as has so often been done in iconography and popular devotion, into an ethereal and disincarnate dimension, she who is the mother of the "incarnate" Word! When talking of her we must always keep in mind the two characteristics of God's style, simplicity and magnificence. In Mary the magnificence of grace and calling coexist with the most absolute simplicity and reality.

In this spirit, let us approach the second chapter of the living letter Mary, the chapter of faith.

1. *"Behold, I am the handmaid of the Lord"*

Elizabeth welcomed Mary with great joy and exclaimed, "Blessed is she who believed there would be a fulfillment of what was spoken her from the Lord" (Luke 1:45). The evangelist St. Luke used the episode of the visitation to bring to light the secret of Nazareth, which could become known only by being put into words.

The wonderful thing that took place in Nazareth after the angel's greeting was that Mary "believed," and thus she became the "mother of the Lord." There is no doubt that the word "believed" refers to Mary's answer to the angel: "Behold, I am the handmaid of the Lord; let it be to me according to your word" (Luke 1:38). In these few simple words, the greatest and most decisive act of faith in history took place. Mary's answer represents the "summit of all religious behavior before God, because it expresses, to the highest degree, both a passive willingness and active readiness, the deepest void that accompanies the greatest fullness."[2] Origen said that it's as if Mary were saying to God, "Behold, I am a tablet to be written on: let the Writer write whatever he wills, let the Lord of all things do with me as he wishes."[3] He compared Mary to the wax writing tablet used in his day. Nowadays, we might say that Mary offered herself to God as a clean page on which he could write whatever he wanted.

Mary, too, questioned the angel: "How can this come about? I know no man" (Luke 1:34), but she did so in a very different spirit from that of Zechariah. She didn't seek for an explanation to help her understand, she only wanted to know how to carry out God's will. She asked how she was to behave and what she would have to do, as she didn't know man. Thus she shows us that it is not right to want to understand God's will at all costs in certain cases or to know the reasons for some apparently absurd situations, but that it is right, instead, to ask for God's light and help in order to carry out his will in these cases.

Mary's *fiat* was total and unconditioned. It comes spontaneously to compare Mary's *fiat* with those that resounded at other crucial moments in the history of salvation: to God's *fiat* at the beginning of creation and the *fiat* of Jesus in the redemption. All three express an act of will, a decision. The first one, the *fiat lux!* is the divine yes of God—divine in nature and divine in the person uttering it; the second one, the *fiat* of Jesus in Gethsemane, is the human act of God—human because issued by a human will, divine because this will belongs to the person of the Word; Mary's *fiat* is the human yes of a human being. Its entire value lies in grace. Before Christ's decisive yes, everything that stands for human consent in the work of redemption is expressed in Mary's *fiat*. "In an instant that will exist for all time and remain for all eternity, Mary's word was the word of humankind and her 'yes' was the Amen of all creation to God's 'yes' " (K. Rahner). It's as if God were once again challenging created freedom through her, offering it a chance of redemption. This is the deep meaning of the Eve-Mary parallelism, so meaningful to the Fathers of the Church and all tradition. "Eve, when she was still a virgin, accepted the serpent's word and gave birth to disobedience and death. Instead, Mary, the Virgin, accepting with faith and joy the good news given by the angel Gabriel, answered: 'Let it be to me according to your word.' "[4] "That which Eve had bound through her unbelief, Mary loosened through her faith."[5]

From Elizabeth's words "Blessed is she who believed" we note that early in the Gospel Mary's divine maternity is not just considered in the physical sense but, much more so, in a spiritual sense, based on faith. This is what St. Augustine based himself on when he said: "The Virgin Mary gave birth believing what she had conceived believing. . . . When the angel had spoken, she, full of faith *(fide plena),* conceiving Christ in her heart before she did so in her womb, answered: 'Behold, I am the handmaid of the Lord, let it be to me according to your word.' "[6] The fullness of faith on Mary's part corresponds to the fullness of grace on God's part, the *fide plena* to the *gratia plena.*

2. *Alone with God*

At a first glance, Mary's act of faith was easy and could even be taken for granted. She was to become the mother of a king who would reign forever in the house of Jacob, mother of the Messiah! Wasn't this the dream of every Hebrew girl? But this is a rather human and worldly way of reasoning. True faith is never a privilege or an honor; it means dying a little, and this was especially true of Mary's faith at that moment. First of all, God never deceives and never surreptitiously extorts consent from his children by concealing the consequences from them of what they are taking on. We can see this in every great calling on God's part. He forewarned Jeremiah: "They will fight against you" (Jer 1:19), and to Ananias he said of Saul: "I will show him how much he must suffer for the sake of my name" (Acts 9:16). Would he have acted differently only with Mary for a mission such as hers? In the light of the Holy Spirit that accompanied God's call, she certainly sensed that her path would be no different from that of all other "chosen ones." In fact, Simeon soon put this foreboding into words when he told her that a spear would pierce her soul.

But even on a simply human level Mary found herself in complete solitude. To whom could she explain what had taken place in her? Who would believe her when she said that the child she was carrying in her womb was the work of the Holy Spirit? This was something that had never taken place before and would never take place again. Undoubtedly Mary was well aware of what the law exacted if the signs of virginity were not found in a young woman at marriage: she would be brought to the door of her father's house and be stoned to death by the men of her city (see Deut 22:20 f.). Nowadays we are quick to talk about the risk of faith, and we generally mean the intellectual risk, but Mary faced a real risk! In his book on the Madonna, Carlo Carretto told us how he came to understand Mary's faith. When he was living in the desert, he had heard from some Tuareg friends of his that a young girl in the encampment had been betrothed to a young man but she had not gone to live with him as she was too young. Carretto had associated this fact with what Luke said of Mary. So, two years later, finding himself in the same encampment, he asked about the girl. He noticed a certain embarrassment among his interlocutors, and later one of them, secretly approaching him, made a sign to him: he held his hand to his throat in the characteristic gesture of the Arabs when they want to say, "Her throat has been slit." It had been discovered that she was with child before the marriage, and her death was necessary for the honor of the family. Then he thought of Mary again, of the pitiless glances of the people of Nazareth, of the knowing winks, and he understood Mary's solitude, and that same night he chose her as his traveling companion and the mistress of his faith.[7]

If believing is "going forward along a path where all the warning signs say: 'turn back, turn back!' "; if it's like "finding oneself in the open sea which is seventy leagues deep beneath you"; if believing is "doing something that will throw you completely

41

into the arms of the Absolute'' (all images of the philosopher Kier-kegaard); then, undoubtedly Mary was the believer par excellence who can never be equaled. She really found herself completely thrown into the arms of the Absolute. She is the only one to have believed in a "situation of contemporaneity," that is to say, she believed while the event was taking place and prior to any confir-mation by the event or by history.[8] She believed in total solitude. Jesus said to Thomas: "Have you believed because you have seen me? Blessed are those who have not seen and yet believe!" (John 20:29). Mary was the first to have believed without having seen.

Mary believed on the spot; she never hesitated or suspended judgment. On the contrary, she committed her whole self at once. She believed she would conceive a son by the Holy Spirit. She didn't say to herself, Now we shall see what will happen; time will show if this strange promise is true and comes from God; she didn't say to herself, "If it is to be it will be." That's what any other person would have said according to common sense and reason. But not Mary; Mary believed. If she hadn't believed, the Word would not have become flesh in her and Elizabeth could not have greeted her as the mother of the Lord.

In a similar situation, almost in triumph and amazement, Scrip-ture tells us that Abraham, who was promised a son even though he was advanced in years, "believed the Lord; and he reckoned it to him as righteousness" (Gen 15:6). And with what greater triumph can we now say that of Mary! Mary had faith in God, and it was reckoned to her as righteousness—the greatest act of righteousness ever fulfilled on earth by a human being, after that of Jesus, who is, however, also God.

St. Paul said that "God loves a cheerful giver" (2 Cor 9:7), and Mary uttered her yes cheerfully. The verb Mary used to ex-press her consent and which is translated by *fiat* or by "let it be done" is in the optative mood *(génoito)* in the original text. It doesn't just express a simple resigned acceptance but a living de-sire. It's as if she were saying, I, too, desire with all my being what God desires; let his wish be fulfilled quickly. Indeed, as St. Augustine said, before conceiving Christ in her body she conceived him in her heart.

Mary didn't use the Latin word *fiat*; neither did she use the Greek *génoito*. What did she use then? Which word or expres-sion? What did a Jew say for "so be it"? He said "Amen!" If we reverently try to go back to the *ipsissima vox,* that is, to the exact word Mary used—or at least to the word that existed on this point in the Hebrew source used by Luke—it must really have been the word "amen." "Amen"—a Hebrew word whose root means solidity, soundness—was used in the liturgy as an answer in faith to God's word. Each time in the Vulgate where *fiat, fiat* appears at the end of certain psalms (in the Septuagint version, *génoito, génoito)* the original Hebrew, which Mary knew, is *amen, amen!*

The use of "amen" acknowledges what has been said as being firm, stable, valid, and binding. Its exact translation when it is in answer to God's word is, "It is so, may it be so." It indicates both faith and obedience; it acknowledges that what God says is true and submits to it. It is saying yes to God. This is how Jesus himself used it: "Yea, Amen, Father, for such was thy gracious will" (Matt 11:26). Rather, he is the Amen personified (see Rev 3:14), and that is why we utter the amen through him, to the glory of God (see 2 Cor 1:20). Just as Mary's *fiat* precedes that of Jesus in Gethsemane, so her amen precedes that of the Son. Mary, too, is a personified amen to God.

3. *A Nuptial Yes*

The beauty of Mary's act of faith lies in the fact that it is the nuptial yes of a bride to her bridegroom, uttered in total freedom. Mary is the sign and the first flowering of the nuptials between God and his people, foretold by the prophets. Therefore the prophet's words are applied to her: "I will betroth you to me for ever. . . . I will betroth you to me in steadfast love" (Hos 2:16f.). Faith is the wedding ring of these nuptials and God's corresponding part is faithfulness.

Mary's yes is not just a human act, it is also divine because it was prompted in Mary's inner soul by the Holy Spirit himself. It is written of Jesus that "through the eternal Spirit he offered himself without blemish to God" (Heb 9:14). Mary, too, offered herself to God in the Holy Spirit, that is to say, she was moved to act by him. The Holy Spirit, promised to her by the angel when he said, "The Holy Spirit will come upon you . . . ," was not just promised to her so that she could conceive Jesus in her body but also conceive him in faith, in her heart. If she was "filled with grace" it was above all to enable her to accept, in faith, the message she was about to receive. If we cannot even say "Jesus is Lord!" (1 Cor 12:3) without the Holy Spirit, what should we think of Mary's *fiat,* on which, in a certain sense, the incarnation depended and therefore the very existence of the Lord? That's how great obediences are always accomplished, starting with Christ's obedience: God, through the Holy Spirit, fills a heart with love, and this love moves the person to do what God wants. Love becomes a law, the law of the Spirit. God doesn't force his will on us but he gives us love. It has been rightfully said that love doesn't permit that anyone loved should not love in return (Dante). This explains Mary's surrender; she felt loved by God, and this love urged her to give herself entirely to God. We find a similar experience in the life of St. Thérèse of the Child Jesus when she offered herself to God for all time: "It was," she wrote, "a kiss of love: I felt loved and said: I love you and give myself to you for all eternity."[9]

Yet Mary's *fiat* was a free act; rather, it was the first really true free act since the beginning of the world, because true freedom does not consist in doing or not doing what is good but in freely doing what is good; freedom to freely obey and not freedom to obey or not obey God. "Didn't Christ possess a free will and wasn't it all the more free the less it could serve sin?"[10] This freedom is in the image of God's freedom, which doesn't consist in being able to do good and evil. God cannot but want and do good; he is, so to say, thus obliged by his very nature, and yet who is freer than God?

There is an analogy in this to what took place in biblical inspiration: "Men moved by the Holy Spirit spoke from God," Scripture tells us of those who wrote the books of the Bible (2 Pet 1:21). And yet we know that their speech was free, divine and human at the same time. This is all the more true of Mary: moved by the Holy Spirit, Mary spoke and said yes to God. That's why her yes was both divine and human: human by nature, divine by grace.

Mary's faith was therefore an act of love and docility; it was free even if it was prompted by God and was as mysterious as the ever-mysterious meeting point between grace and freedom. Herein was Mary's true personal greatness and her blessedness, confirmed by Christ himself. "Blessed is the womb that bore you and the breasts that you sucked!" (Luke 11:27), declared a woman in the Gospel. The woman called Mary blessed because she bore *(bastasasa)* Jesus; instead, Elizabeth called her blessed because she believed *(pisteusasa)*. The woman called the bearing of Jesus in the womb blessed; Jesus called the bearing of himself in the heart blessed: "Blessed are those who hear the word of God and keep it," he said. In this way Jesus helps the woman and all of us to understand where the true greatness of his mother lies. Who, in fact, "kept" God's words better than Mary, of whom Scripture twice says, "She kept all these things in her heart" (see Luke 2:19, 51)?

A well-known Protestant exegete wrote: "There can be no doubt that, though the key-word 'faith' occurs only once in them, it is the problem of faith which lies at the back of the stories about Abraham."[11] This is literally true, point by point, also of Mary. There is no doubt that for Mary too, faith was at the base of everything, even if, where she was concerned, the word "faith" was uttered only once, by Elizabeth.

We should not, however, end our brief meditation of Mary's faith under the impression that she believed only once in her life, that there was only one great act of faith in it. To do so would be to miss the essential point. God's ways of acting follow a very different logic from what we are used to imagining. God doesn't deal with his human partners, subject as they are to development and faith, in a mechanical way. Everything is not decided from the beginning with a promise and an acceptance, after which all becomes clear and easy. What is made clear in an instant at the beginning by the Holy Spirit may no longer be clear later on. Faith can be tried by doubt, not doubt about God but about oneself: Am I right? Maybe I've misunderstood? And what if I've been misled? And if it wasn't God talking? God's way of acting remains mysterious, and what agony we must undergo before resigning ourselves to living in mystery!

How often, after the Annunciation, must Mary have been martyrized by the apparent contrast between her state and all that was written and known about God's will in the Old Testament and about the very figure of the Messiah! How often must Joseph—yes, Joseph!—have assured and comforted her, telling her she had not sinned, that there was no fault in her, and that she was innocent and had not deceived herself, repeating to her, all told, what he himself had learned from the angel in a dream: "Do not fear . . . , that which is conceived in her is of the Holy Spirit" (Matt 1:20).

The Second Vatican Council made us a great gift when it affirmed that Mary, too, walked in faith; rather, she "advanced" in faith, that is to say, she grew in faith and became perfect in it.[12] Just as to a lesser degree in the case of certain souls called by God in special ways, walking in faith for Mary meant a martyrdom of conscience, of having no defense against the evidence of the facts other than the Word of God, interiorly heard once and after that revived by human intermediaries. In certain moments, Joseph's role in relation to Mary was similar to the role of a spiritual director, or simply of a good spiritual father in certain cases, that is, to protect and repeat in every crisis the certainty once given him by God, believing and hoping against all evidence.

If Jesus was tempted, it would be strange if Mary, who was so close to him in everything, were not. St. Peter says that faith is tested by fire (see 1 Pet 1:7), and Revelation tells us that "the dragon stood before the woman who was about to bear a child that he might devour her child when she brought it forth" (Rev 12:4, 13). It's true that the woman before whom the dragon stood indicates the Church. But how could Mary still call herself the figure of the Church if she, above all, hadn't to some extent experienced battle and temptation from the devil, as this aspect is so relevant in the life of the Church? Mary, too, like Christ, was "in every respect tempted as we are, yet without sinning" (Heb 4:15). Yet without sinning!

4. *In Mary's Wake*

The wake left on the surface of the water by a lovely ship gradually spreads until it disappears altogether and merges with the horizon, but it started with the point of the ship itself. The same is true of the wake of believers who make up the Church. It begins at a certain point, and this point is Mary's faith, her *fiat*. In everything else—in prayer, suffering, humility, charity itself—the point or beginning can only be Jesus Christ, who is the first flowering, the head from which the whole body develops. When we go back up the great stream of prayer that flows in the Church, who do we find at the springhead? We find Jesus praying, Jesus entrusting his prayer to his disciples in the Our Father. This is not the case of the other great stream, faith. Mary's faith existed even before the apostles' faith.

Faith, together with its sister, hope, is the only thing that does not begin with Christ but with the Church, and therefore with Mary, who was its first member in the order of time and importance. Jesus cannot be the subject of the Christian faith because he is its object. The New Testament never attributes faith and hope to Jesus. The Letter to the Hebrews gives us a list of those who had faith: "By faith Abel. . . . By faith Abraham. . . . By faith Moses" (Heb 11:4 ff.). Jesus is not included! Jesus is called the "founder and perfecter of faith" (Heb 12:2), the one on whom our faith depends from beginning to end, but not one of the believers, even the first. And it's easy to understand why. Faith is a relation between God and man as person to person, but Jesus is God and man in the same person. He is the person of the Word, who cannot relate to the Father through faith because he relates to him through nature. We cannot talk of faith and hope concerning Jesus, and if there are those who do so today, it can only be in an analogous and broader sense or in the sense only of faith—trust—unless we say that God and man constitute, in Christ, two different persons, or only one person but human and not divine.

By the mere fact of believing we therefore find ourselves in Mary's wake, and we now want to look more deeply at what following in her wake really means. From reading what concerns Mary in the Bible, we can see that the Church, right from the Fathers, has followed a criterion that can be expressed thus: *Maria, vel Ecclesia, vel anima:* "Mary, or rather the Church, or rather the soul." The meaning is that what is said especially of Mary in Scripture is universally meant for the Church, and what is universally said of the Church is meant personally for each believer. Keeping to this principle, let us now see what Mary's faith has to say first of all to the Church as a whole and then to each one of us. Just as we did with grace, let us first stress the ecclesial or theological implications of Mary's faith and then the personal or ascetical implications. In this way, the Madonna's life will not just be useful in developing our private devotion but will also give us a deeper understanding of God's Word and of the Church's problems, and this should also make us joyfully accept the difficulties we might come across in this first step.

First of all, Mary talks to us of the importance of faith. There can be no sound or music if there is no ear to hear it, no matter how many melodies or sublime chords fill the air. There is no grace, or at least grace cannot work, if there is no faith to accept it. Just as the rain cannot germinate anything unless it falls on soil that absorbs it, so it is with grace if it doesn't fall upon faith. It is through faith that we are sensitive to grace. Faith is the basis for everything; it is the first and the best among the good works. This is the work of God, that you believe, Jesus said (see John 6:29). Faith is so important because it alone maintains the gratuity of grace. It doesn't try to invert the order, making God a debtor and man a creditor. That's why it is so dear to God, who makes almost everything depend on faith in his relations with man.

Grace and faith: this is how the two pillars of salvation are placed. Man is given two feet to walk on or two wings to fly with. It is not, however, a question of two parallel things, almost as if grace came from God and faith from us and that salvation thereby depends equally on God and us, on grace and freedom. Heaven help the person who thinks that grace depends on God but faith depends on me; together God and I bring about salvation! We would once again have made God a debtor, somehow depending on us and who must share the merit and glory with us. St. Paul banished all doubt when he said, "By grace you have been saved through faith, and this [that is, faith, or more generally, being saved by grace through faith, which is the same thing] is not your own doing, it is the gift of God, lest any man should boast" (Eph 2:8 ff.). We have seen that Mary's act of faith was also prompted by the grace of the Holy Spirit.

What interests us now is to throw light on some aspects of Mary's faith that could lead today's Church to greater belief. Mary's act of faith was very personal, unique, and can never be repeated. It was trust in God and the total entrusting of herself to God. It was a person-to-person relation. This is called *subjective* faith. The emphasis is on believing rather than on what is believed. But Mary's faith was also very *objective*. She didn't believe in a subjective, personal God, detached from everything, who revealed himself only to her in secret. She believed, instead, in the God of the Fathers, the God of her people. She saw in the God who revealed himself to her the God of the promises, the God of Abraham and his descendants. She humbly felt part of the host of believers and became the first believer of the new covenant, just as Abraham was the first believer of the old covenant. The *Magnificat* is full of this faith based on Scripture and of references to the history of her people. Mary's God was a God of exquisitely biblical characteristics: Lord, Almighty, Holy, Savior. Mary would not have believed the angel if he had revealed a different God to her, one whom she could not have recognized as the God of her people Israel. Also in her external life Mary conformed to this faith. She subjected herself to all that the Law prescribed: she had the child circumcised, she presented him in the Temple, she underwent the rite of purification, and she went up to Jerusalem for Passover.

There is a great lesson in all of this for us. Faith, like grace, has throughout the centuries undergone the phenomenon of analysis and division, so that we have innumerable forms and subforms of faith. Our Protestant brethren, for example, give more value to the first aspect—subjective and personal—of faith. Luther wrote, "Faith is a living and bold trust in God's grace"; it is a "firm trust."[13] In some trends of Protestantism, as in Pietism, where this tendency is carried to the extreme, dogmas and the so-called truths of faith are of very little importance. An interior personal attitude toward God almost exclusively prevails.

Instead, in the Catholic and Orthodox tradition, the problem of right faith and orthodoxy has always been of great importance right from ancient times. The problem of what was to be believed very quickly prevailed over the subjective and personal aspect of believing, that is to say, over the act of faith. The treatises of the Fathers called "On Faith" *(De fide)* do not even mention faith as a subjective act or as trust and abandonment, but they are concerned with defining the truths to be believed in communion with the whole Church in opposition to the heretics. After the Reformation and as a reaction to the unilateral emphasis on faith-trust, this tendency became more emphasized in the Catholic Church. "Believing" principally meant adhering to the belief of the Church. St. Paul said that man believes with the heart and he confesses with his lips (see Rom 10:10), but the confession of the right faith has often prevailed over believing with the heart.

In this case, too, Mary urges us to find again the "whole," which is much richer and much more beautiful than each single part. A simple subjective faith, a faith that is abandonment to God in one's inner conscience, is not sufficient. It is easy to reduce God to one's own measure this way. This happens when we form our own idea of God, based on our own personal interpretation of the Bible or on the interpretation of our own narrow circle, and then adhere to this with all our strength, even fanatically, without realizing that we believe more in ourselves than in God and that our unshakable trust in God is nothing other than an unshakable trust in ourselves.

However, a simply objective and dogmatic faith is not enough if it fails to lead to an intimate I-you personal contact with God. It can easily become a dead faith, belief through a third person or institution, which fails as soon as there is a crisis, no matter what the reason, between one's faith and one's personal relation with the institution of the Church. In this way, a Christian can easily reach the end of his life without ever having made a free and personal act of faith, which alone justifies the name "believer."

It is necessary, therefore, to believe personally, but in communion with the Church; we must believe in communion with the Church, but personally. The dogmatic faith of the Church doesn't take from personal faith or from the spontaneity in believing, rather, it preserves it and allows us to know and embrace an immensely greater God than the God of our own limited experience. There is no one, in fact, who is able to embrace through his own act of faith all that can be known about God. The faith of the Church is like a great wide-angle lens, which, in a particular panorama, makes it possible to see and photograph a much wider view than that of the simple lens. In uniting myself to the faith of the Church, I make the faith of all those who have gone before me mine: that of the apostles, the martyrs, and the Doctors of the Church. The saints, as they could not take their faith to heaven with them, where they no longer need it, left it in heredity to the Church.

The words "I believe in God the Father Almighty" contain incredible power. My small "I" united and joined to the great "I" of the whole mystical body of Christ, past and present, makes a sound more powerful than the roaring of the sea and makes the very foundations of the reign of darkness tremble.

5. *Let Us Too Believe!*

Let us now go on to consider the personal and ascetic implications that spring from Mary's faith. After affirming in the above-mentioned text that Mary, "full of grace, gave birth believing what she had conceived believing," St. Augustine explained what he meant: "Mary believed and what she believed was fulfilled in her. Let us, too, believe so that what was fulfilled in her may also be to our advantage."[14]

Let us, too, believe! The contemplation of Mary's faith urges us to renew, above all, our personal act of faith and abandonment to God. This is the spiritual exercise we should do at the end of this second step as we follow in the Madonna's wake. We are God's edifice, God's temple. The undertaking of our sanctification is like "the building of a spiritual house" (1 Pet 2:5); we are "built for a dwelling place of God in the Spirit" (Eph 2:22). But who would build on land that has not been freely given and does not belong to the builder? We know that anything built under such conditions would automatically belong to the owner of the land and not to whoever put up the building. God cannot build his temple in us or make us into a holy dwelling place if we have not first given him ownership of the land, and this takes place when we give God our freedom through an act of faith and consent, with a complete and total yes.

The land is our own freedom, land that must first be broken, turned over and dug. That is why it is so vitally important to say to God, once in life, let it be done, *fiat,* as Mary did. This is an act enveloped in mystery because it involves grace and freedom at the same time; it is a form of conception. The soul cannot do it alone; God helps, therefore, without taking away freedom. It has been said that "God must allow the soul to go back to nature. But first he unexpectedly makes the soul secretly taste a grain of pomegranate. The grain of pomegranate is the soul's consent, almost unknown and unacknowledged, an imperceptible thing in the midst of the carnal inclinations and yet, it decides the soul's destiny forever."[15] If we were to carefully probe into the story of each soul that has reached the summit of holiness or is definitely advancing toward it, this grain of pomegranate is almost always to be found.

What should we do then? The answer is simple: after praying, so that our prayer does not remain superficial, say to God, using the very words Mary used: Here I am, I am the servant of the Lord: let it be done to me according to your word! I am saying amen, yes, my God, to your whole plan. I give you myself!

At the beginning I recalled the three great *fiats* in the history of salvation: God's *fiat* at creation, Mary's at the incarnation, and that of Jesus in the paschal mystery. There is a fourth *fiat* in the history of salvation, which shall be said every day to the end of time, the *fiat* of the Church and believers who in the Our Father say to God, *Fiat voluntas tua:* "Your will be done!" By saying this *fiat* we unite ourselves, like Mary, to the great *fiat* of Christ, who in Gethsemane said the same words to the Father: "Your will be done" (Luke 22:42).

We must, however, remember that Mary pronounced her *fiat* willingly and joyfully. How often do we repeat the word with poorly hidden resignation and, tight lipped, murmur, "If it cannot be avoided, well then, let your will be done!" Mary teaches us to say it in a different way. Knowing that God's will is infinitely more beautiful and richer in promises than any of our own plans, and knowing that God is infinite love and nourishes "plans for welfare and not for evil for us" (see Jer 29:11), let us say, full of desire and almost impatiently, as Mary did: Let your will of love and peace be fulfilled in me, O God!

In this way the meaning of human life and its greatest dignity is fulfilled. To say yes, amen, to God does not decrease man's dignity, as modern man often thinks; instead, it exalts it. And what is the alternative to this amen said to God? Modern philosophy itself, especially the existential stream, has clearly demonstrated man's need to say amen, and if it is not said to God, who is love, it must be said to something else that is simply a cold and paralyzing necessity: to destiny or fate. The philosophical alternative to faith is fatalism. The most renowned philosopher of this century, after stressing at a certain point that the only unconditioned and insuperable possibility that belongs absolutely to man is death and that his very existence is nothing other than "living-for-death," said that the only means man has of living a genuine existence is to accept his destiny. Freedom, here, consists in making a virtue of necessity, in choosing and accepting responsibility for the actual situation one is in, and in remaining steadfast in this. Man's destiny is decided by the history and the community he belongs to and cannot be other than a repetition of what has already been. Man reaches completeness in his love of fate *(amor fati),* accepting and actually loving what has taken place and what will inevitably take place.[16] This is a return to that type of "mysticism of consent," which, with Cleanthes, pagan stoic religiosity reached before Christ. It is an unreserved abandonment to fate and the necessity of all things. And this is not just the voice of one isolated philosopher; all atheistic existential thought leads to this terrible ideal of the love of fate. The freedom that was to be safeguarded has become a pure acceptance of necessity. The words of Jesus have been completely fulfilled: "Whoever would save his life will lose it" (Mark 8:35). Whoever would save his freedom will lose it.

As I have said, man cannot live and fulfill himself without saying amen, yes, to someone or something. But how different and oppressive is this pagan amen compared to the Christian amen said to him who created you and which is not just cold and blind necessity but love. How different is abandonment to fate from the abandonment to the Father expressed by C. de Foucauld in this prayer: "My Father, I abandon myself to you. Do with me what you will. Whatever you do with me, I thank you. I am ready to accept anything so that your will may be fulfilled in me and in all your creatures. I desire nothing else, my God, with all the love of my heart because I love you. And the exigency of this love is that I place myself wholeheartedly in your hands, with infinite trust, because you are my Father."

6. *"The righteous shall live by his faith"*

We are all called to imitate Mary's faith, but especially pastors and those in any way called to transmit the faith and the Word to others. The righteous, God says, shall live by his faith (see Heb 2:4; Rom 1:17), and this is true in a special way of pastors. My priest, God says, shall live by his faith. He is the man of faith. A priest's "specific weight" depends on his faith. His influence on others will be determined by his faith. A priest's, or pastor's, task among his people is not simply that of distributing the sacraments and of service, but it is also that of enkindling faith and being a witness to it. He will really be one who guides and leads souls to God to the extent to which he believes and has given his freedom to God, as Mary did.

The essential thing that the faithful sense immediately in a priest or in a pastor is whether he believes or not, whether he believes in what he is saying and in what he is celebrating. Whoever is seeking God through a priest will realize this immediately. Whoever is not seeking God through him may easily be deceived and, in turn, deceive the priest himself, making him feel important, clever, and with-the-times, whereas in fact he, too, may be empty, like the man without grace we mentioned in the last chapter. Even a nonbeliever who approaches a priest with a searching spirit immediately understands the difference. What can provoke him and cause him to positively query his way of life are not, generally speaking, the most gifted discussions on faith but simple faith itself. Faith is contagious. Just as contagion does not take place by simply talking about or studying a virus but by coming into contact with it, so it is with faith.

The power of God's servant is in proportion to the strength of his faith. We sometimes suffer or maybe complain to God in prayer because people abandon the Church, they go on sinning, and because we talk and talk without results. One day the apostles tried unsuccessfully to cast out a demon from a young boy. After Jesus had cast it out the disciples came to Jesus in private and said: " 'Why could we not cast it out?' And Jesus said to them, 'Because of your little faith' " (Matt 17:19-10). Every time I have faced a pastoral failure or a soul has gone away without my being able to help, I have felt the disciples' question loom in my mind: "Why could we not cast it out?" and the answer in my inner self is always the same: "Because of your little faith!" And I keep silent.

As we have said, the world, like the sea, is furrowed by the wake of a beautiful ship, which is the wake of faith, started by Mary. Let us be part of this wake. Let us, too, believe, so that what was fulfilled in her will be fulfilled in us. Let us invoke the Madonna with the sweet title of *Virgo fidelis:* Virgin most faithful, pray for us!

NOTES

1. Tertullian, *On Baptism,* 2, 1 f. (CC 1, p. 277).
2. H. Schürmann, *Das Lukasevangelium,* Freiburg in Br., 1982, ad loc.
3. Origen, *Commentary on the Gospel of Luke,* Fragment 18 (GCS 49, p. 227).
4. St. Justin Martyr, *Dialogue with Trypho,* 100 (PG 6, 709).
5. St. Irenaeus, *Against the Heresies,* III, 22, 4 (SCh 211, p. 442).
6. St. Augustine, *Sermons,* 215, 4 (PL 38, 1974).
7. See C. Carretto, *Blessed Are You Who Believed,* London, Burns & Oates, 1982, p. 3 f.
8. S. Kierkegaard, *Training in Christianity,* I, 4 (trans. W. Lowrie, Princeton University Press, 1972, p. 66 f.

9. St. Thérèse of Lisieux, *Autobiographical Manuscripts,* A f. 35 (trans. R. Knox, London, Fontana Books, 1960, p. 82).
10. St. Augustine, *The Predestination of the Saints,* 15, 30 (PL 44, 981).
11. G. von Rad, *Old Testament Theology,* I, London-Edinburgh, Oliver & Boyd, 1963, p. 171.
12. Vatican Council II, *Lumen gentium* 58.
13. Luther, *Preface to the Epistle to the Romans* (ed. Weimar, Deutsche Bibel 7, p. 11); *On Good Works* (ed. Weimar 6, p. 206).
14. St. Augustine, *Sermons,* 215, 4 (PL 38, 1074).
15. S. Weil, *Intuitions préchrétiennes,* Paris, La Colombe, 1951, p. 11 f.
16. See M. Heidegger, *Being and Time,* London, SCM Press, 1962.

Chapter III

"You Will Conceive and Bear a Son"

Mary, Mother of God

The steps we are taking in Mary's wake correspond quite faithfully to the historical development of her life as we know it from the Gospels. It can already be observed in this first part that we are not just generally contemplating Mary in the mystery of the incarnation. The meditation on Mary "full of grace" took us back to the moment of the annunciation, that of Mary, who believed; to the moment of the visitation; and now, that of Mary, Mother of God, to Christmas.

It was at Christmas, in fact, and not before, at the moment in which "she gave birth to her first-born son" (Luke 2:7), that Mary truly and fully became the Mother of God. The title "mother" is not like any other title that can be given to a person without, however, affecting the very being of the person. To become a mother, a woman goes through a series of experiences that leave their mark forever and modify not only her physical appearance but her very awareness of herself. It is one of those things that takes place once and forever. At the moment of ordination, we were told, "Once a priest, a priest forever," because of the character that ordination impresses on the soul, according to Catholic doctrine. This is even more true of a woman: once a mother, a mother forever. In this case the character is not the invisible mark left by the event on the soul; it is a creature, a child, destined to live eternally beside its mother and to proclaim her such.

When talking of Mary, Scripture constantly stresses two fundamental acts, or moments, which correspond to what common human experience considers essential for a real and full maternity to take place—to conceive and to give birth. "Behold," the angel said to Mary, "you will conceive in your womb and bear a son" (Luke 1:31). These two moments also exist in Matthew's account: that which was conceived in her was of the Holy Spirit, and she would bear a son (see Matt 1:20 f.). The prophecy of Isaiah in which all of this had been foretold used the same expression: A "young woman shall conceive and bear a son" (Isa 7:14). Now you can see why I said that it was only at Christmas, when Mary gave birth to Jesus, that she became in a full sense the Mother of God. The title "Mother of God" *(Dei Genitrix)*, used by the Latin Church, places more emphasis on the first of the two moments, on the moment of the conception; whereas the title *Theotokos,* used by the Greek Church, places greater emphasis on the second stage, on the giving birth (*tikto* in Greek means "I am giving birth"). The first moment, the conception, is common to both the father and the mother, while the second, the giving birth, belongs exclusively to the mother.

Mother of God: a title that expresses one of the greatest mysteries and, for human reason, one of the greatest paradoxes in Christianity. It is a title that has filled the liturgy of the Church with wonder. The Church, recalling the moment when the glory of God came in a cloud to dwell in the temple (see 1 Kgs 8:27), exclaims: "That which the heavens cannot contain, has become man in your womb!"[1] The title "Mother of God" is Mary's oldest and most important dogmatic title, since at the Council of Ephesus in 431 it was defined by the Church as a truth of faith to be believed by all Christians. It is the basis of all Mary's greatness. It is the principle itself of Mariology. Because of it, Mary is not just an object of devotion in Christianity but also an object of theology, and that means that she is part of the discourse on God himself, because God is directly involved in the divine maternity of Mary. It is also the most ecumenical of her titles, not just historically because it was defined in an ecumenical council, but also practically, because it is the only title shared and accepted without distinction, at least in principle, by all Christian denominations.

We shall approach the dogma of Mary Mother of God in three different ways or methods, which together should give us a better understanding of the basis of Marian doctrine. We shall historically reconstruct this dogma and make it a contemplation on faith and then apply it practically to our lives.

1. "If anyone doesn't believe that Mary is the Mother of God. . .": A Historical Glance at the Formation of Dogma

In the New Testament Mary is never explicitly given the title "Mother of God." However, there are certain affirmations, which in the light of careful meditation by the Church under the guidance of the Holy Spirit, will later prove to hold this truth *in nuce*. As we have seen, Mary conceived and bore a son who was the Son of the Most High, holy, and Son of God (see Luke 1:31-32, 35). It results, therefore, from the Gospels that Mary was the mother of a son whom we know to be the Son of God. In the Gospels she is commonly called the mother of Jesus, the mother of the Lord (see Luke 1:43), or simply the mother or his mother (see John 2:1-3). In the development of the faith, the Church itself must be clear about who Jesus is before knowing who Mary was the mother of. Mary certainly didn't become the Mother of God at the Council of Ephesus in 431, just as Jesus didn't become God at the Council of Nicaea in 325, which defined him as such. He was God before that. That was the moment when the Church, in the process of developing and making explicit her faith under the pressure of heresy, became fully aware of this truth and defended it. It's like what happens when a new star is discovered: it is not born when its light first reaches the earth and is observed by someone. It had probably existed for thousands of years. A council definition is the moment in which the light is placed on the candelabrum, which is the creed of the Church.

In the process leading to the solemn proclamation of Mary Mother of God, there are three great stages I shall now mention.

MARY'S PHYSICAL MATERNITY: THE ANTI-GNOSTIC PERIOD

At the beginning and while the battle against Gnosticism and Docetism dominated, Mary's maternity was seen almost only in its physical aspect. These heretics denied that Christ possessed a real human body or, if he did possess one, that this human body was born of a woman or, if it was born of a woman, that it was really part of her flesh and blood. There was the necessity, therefore, of strongly affirming that Jesus was Mary's son and the "fruit of her womb" (Luke 1:42) and that Mary was the true and natural mother of Jesus. In fact, some of these heretics acknowl-

edged that Jesus was born of Mary but not that he was conceived in Mary, that is to say, that he was not of her flesh. According to them, Christ was born *through* the Virgin but not
of the Virgin: "Having been placed in Mary from heaven, it
was more like a passage than a real birth, through her and not
of her, as if the Virgin were a passage and not a Mother."[2]
Mary "didn't carry Jesus in her womb as her son but as her
guest."[3]

In this most ancient phase, Mary's maternity serves to demonstrate the true humanity of Jesus more than anything else. It was
at that time and in such an atmosphere that the article of the Creed
"born [or incarnated] by the Holy Spirit of the Virgin Mary" was
formulated. At the beginning this simply meant that Jesus was
both God and man: God insofar as he was generated by the Spirit,
that is to say, by God, and man insofar as he was generated according to the flesh, that is to say, of Mary.

MARY'S METAPHYSICAL MATERNITY:
THE PERIOD OF GREAT CHRISTOLOGICAL CONTROVERSIES

In the most ancient stage, during which Mary's real or natural
maternity was being affirmed against the Gnostics and Docetists,
the title *Theotokos* appeared for the first time. From then on,
it was the use of this title that brought the Church to the discovery of a deeper divine maternity, which we could call "metaphysical maternity." It was the time of the great Christological
controversies of the fifth century, when the main problem concerning Jesus Christ was no longer that of his true humanity but
that of the *unity* of his person. Mary's maternity was no longer
seen in reference to the human nature of Christ but, more rightfully, in reference to the one person of the Word made man. And
as this one person, generated by Mary according to the flesh, was
none other that the divine person of the Son, she, in consequence,
was seen as the true Mother of God.

Here the example of what happens for every human maternity is advanced. A mother gives her child its body and not its
soul, which is infused directly by God. Yet I don't call my mother,
mother of my soul but simply my mother, the mother of my
whole self, because my body and soul form one nature or reality in me. Thus likewise, Mary must be called the Mother of

God even if she only gave Jesus his humanity and not his divinity, because in him humanity and divinity form only one person.

There is not just a physical relation between Mary and Jesus. There is also a metaphysical relation, and this places her on a vertiginous height, creating a unique relation between her and the Father. At the Council of Ephesus, this became a permanent conquest of the Church. "Anyone," a council text reads, "who doesn't confess that God is truly Emmanuel and that, therefore, the Blessed Virgin, having generated according to the flesh the Word of God made flesh, is the *Theotokos,* he is anathema."[4] It was a time of great jubilation for the people of Ephesus, who awaited the Fathers outside the council room and accompanied them to their dwelling places with torchlights and hymns. Such a proclamation caused an explosion of veneration to the Mother of God that has never decreased, neither in the West nor the East, which is manifested in liturgical feasts, icons, hymns, and in the numerous churches dedicated to her.

MARY'S SPIRITUAL MATERNITY: THE WEST'S CONTRIBUTION

There was still another depth to be discovered in Mary's divine maternity besides the physical and metaphysical ones. In Christological controversies, the title *Theotokos* was valued more in function of the person of Christ than of Mary, even if it is a Marian title. The logical consequences concerning the person of Mary and, in particular, her singular holiness, were still to be drawn. *Theotokos* was in danger of becoming a tool of conflict between opposing theological trends instead of being an expression of the Church's faith and devotion to Mary. This is clear from a particular detail that must be mentioned. Cyril of Alexandria had fought relentlessly for the title of *Theotokos* once the controversy had exploded, and he was now the strident voice among the Fathers of the Church in the general esteem given to Mary's holiness. He was one of the few to attribute weaknesses and faults to Mary, especially to Mary beneath the cross. Following Origen, Cyril couldn't believe that a woman, even if she were the mother of Jesus, could have possessed faith and courage greater than the faith and courage of the apostles, who, even though men, wavered at the moment of the passion.[5] Words, these, that spring from the general disesteem toward women in the ancient world, and they show how pointless an acknowledgment of Mary's physical or metaphysical maternity would be if her spiritual maternity weren't also acknowledged, that is to say, a maternity of the spirit other than that of the body.

This was the big contribution made by Latin authors and especially by St. Augustine. Mary's maternity was seen as a maternity in faith, one that was also spiritual. It was the epopee of Mary's faith. As regards the words of Jesus, "Who is my mother?" Augustine's answer attributed to Mary to the highest degree the spiritual maternity that comes from doing the Father's will: "Did, perhaps, the Virgin Mary not do the Father's will, she who in faith believed, in faith conceived, who was chosen so that man's salvation would be born of her and who was created by Christ before Christ was created in her? Certainly, the holy Mary did the Father's will and therefore, it is a higher thing for Mary to have been Christ's disciple than to have been Christ's Mother."[6]

Mary's physical and metaphysical maternity was now crowned by the acknowledgment of a spiritual maternity, or a maternity of faith, which makes Mary the first and holiest child of God, the first and most docile disciple of Christ, the creature who, St. Augustine continued, "for the honor due to the Lord must not even be mentioned when sin is spoken of."[7] Mary's physical or "real" maternity, because of the exceptional and unique relationship it created between her and Jesus and between her and the whole Trinity, was and will remain from an objective point of view the greatest honor and a privilege that cannot be equaled, but this is true precisely because it finds a subjective counterpart in Mary's humble faith. It was certainly a unique privilege for Eve to be the "mother of all the living," but because she lacked faith it was of no avail to her, and instead of being blessed, she became unfortunate.

2. *"Daughter of your Son!"*:
A Meditation on the Mother of God

Let us now approach the second aspect of the dogma on Mary's divine maternity, the contemplative aspect. Contemplation doesn't lie in the search for truth but in enjoying the truth discovered, in relishing all its richness and depth. It has been written that the old Christian dogmatic terminology is like "an enchanted castle where the most beautiful princes and princesses rest in a deep sleep; it needs only to be awakened, brought to life, in order to stand in its full glory."[8] The dogma on Mary's divine maternity is one of these; it is up to us now to awaken it with the help of the breath of the Holy Spirit, which always gives back life to dead bones. Just as the sun rises every day in all its radiance as if it were the first day of creation and fills man's eyes with its light, so it should be with the truths of faith if they are to be efficacious.

Certain Eastern icons like the *Virgin of Vladimir* or *Our Lady of Tenderness* are insuperable ways of contemplating the Mother of God, and it would be a great help to keep them before our eyes during this meditation. There should be a deep similarity between an icon of the Mother of God and a sermon on the Mother of God. Both must make the ever-old and ever-new mystery of faith present, one to the eyes, the other to the ears. The iconographer collects himself, prays, and fasts, not to create something new and original or to present a subjective point of view but to enable himself to fix the invisible reality in color. The preacher must do the same. He must awaken the mystery and make it a living reality. That's why he keeps to tradition, puts together an inheritance, and transmits it. If he quotes the Fathers of the Church, poets, or philosophers, he doesn't do so for the sake of erudition but because the living words of God can only be transmitted in a live environment, and tradition and culture make up this environment. The icon and the sermon complete each other. Words need the help of color, as I am doing at this moment, but also color needs the help of words. At the top or at the side of every icon of the Mother of God there is a caption, usually abbreviated, that says, "The Mother of God." What is the reason for this strange iconographic rule? Does the iconographer think, perhaps, that Mary could be mistaken for another woman? No, the caption is not put there to identify the figure, which would not really be necessary, but to proclaim a truth of faith in words too. It is a profession of faith. It means that we believe that this woman is the Mother of God!

Let us now try to gaze on the Mother of God with a free, penetrating, loving, and still look (that is to say, contemplate) with, if possible, an icon before our eyes. We shall gradually discover the richness contained in the title "Mother of God." It will talk to us of Jesus, God, and Mary.

"MOTHER OF GOD": IT TALKS TO US OF JESUS

At the beginning the title "Mother of God" concerned Jesus more than Mary. As we have seen when outlining the history of the title, it proves first of all that Jesus is true *man:* "Why do we say that Christ is man if not because he was born of Mary who was a human creature?"[9] And not only that he is man in essence but by existence, because he wished to share not only man's nature in a general way but also his experience. He lived the human condition in all its reality. Before our "imitation of Christ," there has been Christ's imitation of man. The poet imagined God explaining this to us: "You often speak—says God—of the imitation of Jesus Christ. Which is the imitation, the faithful imitation of my son made by men. . . . But after all you must not forget how my son begun himself with this singular imitation of man. Singularly faithful. Pushed to a perfect identity. When he so faithfully, so perfectly imitated to be born. And to suffer. And to die."[10] The most difficult aspect to accept of Christ's imitation of man was, precisely, at first, his being conceived by a woman and born of her. To one of the above-mentioned heretics who shuddered at the idea of a God "coagulated in a womb, delivered in pain, washed and clothed," Tertullian replied, "The fact is that Christ loved man and together with man he loved the way man comes into the world."[11] And addressing the heretic, he added, "You shudder at this natural subject of veneration that the birth of a man and the suffering of a woman in childbirth constitutes, and yet, how were you born?"

The title "Mother of God" attests, secondly, that Jesus is *God.* It is only possible to call Mary "Mother of God" if Jesus is seen not just as a man, even as the greatest of prophets, but as God too. Otherwise Mary could be called the mother of Jesus, or of Christ, but not of God. The title "Mother of God" can no longer be justified and becomes blasphemous as soon as we no longer acknowledge God made man in Jesus. If we think about it, it is the only title that can prevent all ambiguity about Christ's divinity because it is a sentinel that is placed there by nature itself and not just by philosophical and theological reasoning (as is the title *homoousios*). You can call Jesus "God," meaning, as unfortunately happens even in our time, many different realities for "God": God by adoption, God by indwelling, or God for the sake of saying so. But in this case, you can no longer go on calling Mary "the Mother of God." She is the Mother of God only if Jesus was God at the moment she gave him birth. What takes place after that no longer concerns the mother as such. We cannot say that Mary is the Mother of God if our definition of God differs from the Church's definition at Nicaea and Chalcedon.

Finally, the title "Mother of God" attests that Jesus is both God and man *in the same person*. Rather, this was the reason for which the Fathers of the Council of Ephesus adopted it. It expresses the deep unity between God and man realized in Jesus and how God bound himself to man and united man to himself in the most profound unity that exists, that is to say, the unity of the person. The Fathers used to say that Mary's womb was the "bridal chamber" where the nuptials between God and humankind took place, the "loom" where the robe of the union was woven, the "workroom" *(ergastérion)* where the union between God and man came about.[12]

Once again if, as the heretics condemned at Ephesus thought, humanity and divinity had been united in Jesus in a union that was purely moral and not personal, Mary could no longer be called the Mother of God but only the mother of Christ: *Christotokos* and not *Theotokos*. "The Fathers did not hesitate to call the blessed Virgin the 'Mother of God' and this was certainly not because the nature of the Word or the divinity had its origin in her but because it was from her that the sacred body was born, endowed with a rational soul to which the Word is united to the point of forming one only person."[13] Thus, the title "Mother of God" is also a sort of bulwark of defense against both the ideologization of Jesus, which would make of him an idea or a personage more than a true person, and the division of humanity and divinity in him, which would put our salvation at risk. It was Mary who anchored God to earth and humanity; it was Mary who, by her divine and very human maternity, made God the Emmanuel, God among us, for all time. She made Christ our brother.

"MOTHER OF GOD": IT TALKS TO US OF GOD

The title "Mother of God" also speaks to us of God. It is not only a Mariological and a Christological title but also a theological one. It reveals the true nature of God the Father, the Son, and the Holy Spirit. Actually, this is the most useful and relevant aspect to stress today, just as that of Christ was the most useful and relevant one against the great controversies in the fifth century. In fact, the problem is more radical today than it was then; it concerns God in the widest meanings of this name more than the single aspects of the Christian mystery. The problem is no longer Monophysism but atheism.

What does this title of Mary's tell us about God? It tells us first of all about *God's humility*. God wanted to have a mother! And just think that the human mind has reached the point where certain scholars find it strange and almost offensive that a human being should have a mother, because this means total dependence on someone else; it means that we are not self-made and cannot completely plan our existence ourselves.

Man has always looked heavenward in search of God. He tries to build through his own ascetic or intellectual efforts a sort of pyramid, thinking that at the top of it he will find God or his equivalent, which in some religions is Nothingness. And he doesn't realize that God descended and overturned the pyramid; he placed himself at the base to take onto himself everything and everyone. God silently entered the womb of a woman. It is really the case to say that this is credible precisely because it is crazy; it is certain precisely because it is impossible; it is divine precisely because it is not what man would do.[14] What a contrast to the god of the philosophers, what a comedown for human pride, and what an invitation to humility! God comes down into the very heart of matter *(mater* comes from *materia)* in the most noble sense, indicating concreteness and reality. The God who became flesh in a woman's womb is the same God who comes to us in the heart of matter, in the Eucharist. It is a unique economy and a unique style. St. Irenaeus was right in saying that he who doesn't comprehend God's birth of Mary cannot comprehend the Eucharist either.[15] All of this proclaims better than any words could that the Christian God is grace and that this grace is received by gift and not by conquest.

In choosing to reveal himself to us through a maternity, God reminded human foolishness—which sees evil where it doesn't exist and doesn't see it where it exists—that everything is pure; he proclaimed the holiness of what he created. He not only sanctified and redeemed nature in the abstract but also human birth and the holy reality of existence. Above all, God revealed the dignity of woman as such. "When the time had fully come, God sent forth his Son, born of woman" (Gal 4:4). If Paul had said, "born of Mary," it would only have been a biographical detail. By saying "born of woman" he gave this fact an immense and universal significance. It was woman, every woman, that was raised in Mary to this unbelievable height. Here, Mary was the woman. Nowadays we speak a great deal about women's rights, and this is one of the most beautiful and encouraging signs of the time. But how late we are in respect to God! He acted before any of us. He conferred such an honor on woman as to dumbfound us and make us reflect on how much there is still to be done on this point.

"MOTHER OF GOD": IT TALKS TO US OF MARY

The title "Mother of God" finally tells us about Mary, too. Mary is the only one in the world who could say to Jesus what his heavenly Father said to him: "You are my son; I have begotten you!" (see Ps 2:7; Heb 1:5). St. Ignatius of Antioch, in all simplicity and almost unaware of the tremendous dignity he was giving a human creature, said that Jesus is "of God and of Mary."[16] It's like saying that a man is the son of a particular man and woman. Dante Alighieri managed to contain the dual paradox (virgin and mother; mother and daughter) in one verse: "Virgin Mother, daughter of thy Son!"[17]

The title "Mother of God" is sufficient in itself to establish the greatness of Mary and to justify the honor attributed to her. Catholics are sometimes reproached for exaggerating the honor and importance they attribute to Mary, and, we must admit, the reproach has often been justified, at least for the way she has been honored. But we never think of what God did. By making her the Mother of God, he so honored her that no one could possibly honor her more even if he possessed, as Luther said, as many tongues as there are blades of grass: "In the title Mother of God, all honor is included; no one could say anything greater of her, or to her, even if he had as many tongues as there are blades of grass or stars in the sky or grains of sand in the sea. We must let our hearts reflect on what it means to be the Mother of God."[18]

The title "Mother of God" places Mary in a unique relationship with each person of the Trinity. St. Francis of Assisi expressed this in a prayer: "Holy Virgin Mary, among all the women of the world there is none like you. You are the daughter and hand-maid of the most high King and Father of heaven; you are the mother of our most holy Lord, Jesus Christ; you are the spouse of the Holy Spirit. Pray for us to your most holy and beloved Son, our Lord and Master."[19]

The title "Mother of God" is eternal and irreversible because irreversible is the incarnation of the Word. As in the heavenly Jerusalem Christ's glorified humanity exists, so his mother exists and is acknowledged and honored as such. If Jesus was not ashamed to call us his brethren (see Heb 2:11 f.), he is certainly not ashamed to call Mary his mother! He doesn't need to deny he had a mother to prove who he is and his divine independence, like some of the great contemporary champions of human freedom.

The title "Mother of God" is still today, for all Christians, the meeting point or the common base from which to begin to find an agreement on Mary's place in the faith. It is the only ecumenical title in the sense that it is recognized by all the Churches. We have already seen what Luther thought. On another occasion he wrote: "The article affirming that Mary is the Mother of God has been in force in the Church from the beginning and the Council of Ephesus did not define it as being new because it is a belief that had already been asserted in the Gospel and Holy Scripture. . . . These words (Luke 1:32; Gal 4:4) strongly affirm that Mary is the Mother of God."[20] In a formula of faith composed after his death we find: "We believe, teach and confess that Mary . . . is rightly called, and truly is, the Mother of God."[21] Zwingli wrote, "In my opinion Mary is rightly called the Genitrix of God, *Theotokos,*" and the same Zwingli elsewhere called Mary "the divine *Theotokos,* chosen even before she could have faith."[22] Calvin, in his turn, wrote, "Scripture explicitly tells us that he who is to be born of the Virgin Mary will be called the Son of God (Luke 1:32) and that the same Virgin is the Mother of our Lord."[23]

The title "Mother of God," *Theotokos,* is therefore the title we must always go back to, distinguishing it as Orthodox Christians do from the other innumerable Marian names and titles. If it were taken seriously by all the Churches and made the most of, besides being theoretically acknowledged it would suffice to create a basic unity around Mary, who instead of being a cause of division among Christians would become one of the most important factors of Christian unity, a maternal help "to gather into one the children of God who are scattered abroad" (John 11:52). Notwithstanding the infinite difference between Mary and the Holy Spirit, I would like to say to our Protestant brethren, still so prejudiced in Mary's regard (through our fault, too, as I have mentioned), what a Father of the Church exclaimed at a certain point to his contemporaries, urging them to overcome their doubts and hesitations in proclaiming the full divinity of the Holy Spirit: "For how long more shall we hide the light under the bushel? It is time now to place it on the candelabrum so that it may be a light for all the Churches, for all souls, for the whole world."[24] During the Council of Ephesus a certain bishop addressed the council Fathers, saying: "Let us not deprive the Virgin Mother of God of the honor that the mystery of the Incarnation conferred on her. My beloved brethren, is it not absurd to honor together, at Christ's altars, the ignominious cross that held him and make it shine in the Church and then deprive the Mother of God of her honor, who, in view of the great benefit to come of it, welcomed the divinity?"[25]

3. *Mother of Christ: The Imitation of the Mother of God*

Our method of advancing in our pilgrimage in Mary's wake consists in contemplating the single steps she took so as to then imitate her in our own lives. How can we imitate the Madonna as the Mother of God? Is it possible for Mary to be the figure of the Church, her model, on this point too? Not only is it possible but there have been those, for example, Origen, St. Augustine, St. Bernard, who went so far as to say that without imitation Mary's title would be of no value to us: "What use would it be to me that Christ was born once of Mary in Bethlehem if he were not born of faith in my soul too?"[26]

We must remember that Mary's divine maternity was fulfilled on two levels: physical and spiritual. Mary is the Mother of God not only because she carried him in her womb but also because she first conceived him in her heart in faith. We cannot, of course, imitate Mary in the first sense by giving birth to Christ again, but we can imitate her in the second sense, that of faith.

It was Jesus himself who first gave the Church the title "Mother of Christ" when he declared, "My mother and my brethren are those who hear the word of God and do it" (Luke 8:21; see Mark 3:31 ff.; Matt 12:49). St. Augustine wrote:

> I understand that we are Christ's brethren and that the holy and faithful women are Christ's sisters. But how can we be mothers of Christ? Yes, of course, let us dare to call ourselves mothers of Christ! I have, in fact, called you all his brethren and should I hesitate to call you his mother? I hesitate much more to deny what Christ affirmed. Well, then, my beloved, observe how the Church, and this is obvious, is the spouse of Christ; it is a more difficult thing to understand that it is the mother of Christ, but this is also true. The Virgin Mary preceded the Church as her figure. I ask you how could Mary be the mother of Christ if not because she gave birth to the members of Christ? You, to whom I am speaking, are members of Christ: who gave you birth? I hear the voice of your hearts answering "Mother Church!" This holy and honored mother, like Mary, gave birth and is virgin. . . . The members of Christ give birth, therefore, in the Spirit, just as the Virgin Mary gave birth to Christ in her womb: in this way you will be mothers of Christ. This is not something that is out of your reach; it is not beyond you, it is not incompatible with you; you have become children, be mothers as well.[27]

This belief has been applied by tradition on two complementary levels. In one case, as in St. Augustine's text, this maternity is realized in the Church as a whole, insofar as she is a universal sacrament of salvation; in the other case, this maternity is realized in each single person or soul who believes. Vatican Council II follows the first view: "The Church. . . becomes herself a mother, for by her preaching and by baptism she brings forth to a new and immortal life children who are conceived of the Holy Spirit and born of God."[28] But the personal application to each soul is even clearer: "Each soul that believes, conceives and brings forth the Word of God . . . . If, according to the flesh, the Mother of Christ is one alone, all should bring forth Christ, according to the Spirit, when they accept the word of God."[29] As an Eastern Father said, "Christ is always mystically born in the soul by taking flesh from those who are saved and making the soul a virgin mother."[30] A medieval writer synthesized all these points of view:

> Mary and the Church are one mother and many mothers; one virgin and many virgins: both mother, both virgin. Both one

and the other conceive without concupiscence by the same Spirit; both one and the other give God a progeny without sin. One, without any stain of sin, brought forth the Head of the body; the other, in the remission of all sin, brings forth the body of the Head. Both are the mother of Christ, but neither one brings forth the whole without the other. That is why, in Scripture divinely inspired, what is universally said of the Virgin Mother Church, is said, in a special way, of the Virgin Mother Mary; and what is said in a special way of Mary is intended, in a general sense, of the Virgin Mother Church. . . . Finally, every faithful soul, spouse of the Word of God, mother, daughter and sister of Christ, is seen to be, in her own way, a fertile virgin. God's Wisdom itself, which is the Father's Word, therefore applies to the Church what is especially said of Mary and individually of every soul that believes.[31]

4. *How to Conceive and Bring Forth Christ Again*

Let us now see how to apply the title "Mother of God" to each one of us. Let us see how we can really become mothers of Christ. We have come to the spiritual exercise of this meditation.

Jesus himself told us how we become his mother. It happens in two ways: by hearing the Word and by practicing it. Let us just think again of how Mary became a mother: by conceiving Jesus and giving him birth. There are two types of unfulfilled maternities, two ways in which a maternity can be terminated. One is by abortion, when a child is conceived but not given birth to because the fetus dies either through natural causes or the sin of man. Up to recently this was the only known cause of an unfulfilled maternity. Today, there exists another type, which consists in giving birth to a child without having conceived it. This is the case of babies conceived in test tubes and then placed in the womb, and in the distressing and squalid case where the uterus is lent, even hired out, to develop human beings conceived elsewhere. In this case the child the woman gives birth to is not hers and has not first been conceived "in the heart before being conceived in the body." (As we have seen, there were, curiously enough, in ancient times, heretics who thought something similar of Mary. According to them Mary had "kept" Jesus in her womb more than given him birth, whose flesh was of a heavenly origin; she had been more a "passage" than a mother for him.)

70

Unfortunately, these two sad possibilities exist on a spiritual level too. Those who conceive Jesus without giving him birth are those who accept the Word without practicing it; those who have one spiritual abortion after the other, making proposals to convert that are then systematically forgotten and abandoned halfway; those who see the Word like someone glancing hurriedly at himself in a mirror and then forgetting what he looked like (see Jas 1:23-24). In a word, those who have faith without works. On the contrary, those who give birth to Christ without having conceived him are those who do many works, even good works, that are not done with the heart for love of God and good intentions but rather from habit, hypocrisy, the seeking of one's own glory or interests, or simply for the satisfaction that doing something gives. In a word, those who have works but not faith.

We have therefore finally come to the *problem of good works.* After talking about the grace of God and man's answer, faith, it is now time to mention works. Let us see what the continuation of Paul's text on grace and faith has to tell us: "For by grace you have been saved through faith; and this is not your own doing, it is the gift of God—not because of works, lest any man should boast. For we are his workmanship, created in Christ Jesus for good works, which God prepared beforehand, that we should walk in them" (Eph 2:8-10). We are God's workmanship: this is the essential point. The good work is what God himself did in Christ. God, however, saved us in Christ, not so that we would remain inert and passive, or worse still, in sin, but so that we would be capable of doing in our turn, through grace and faith, the good works he had prepared beforehand for us, which are the fruits of the Spirit, Christian virtues: mortification, works of charity, prayer, active zeal for the spreading of the kingdom.

At this point our spiritual journey ends and is, in itself, an abortion if we refuse to accept this law, if we don't seriously examine the problem of putting the Word into practice, if we don't ever pass from contemplation to the imitation of Christ. We have seen that it is not enough to simply do good works. These works are "good" only insofar as they spring from the heart, if they are conceived for God's love and in faith. In a word, if the intention prompting us is right. Scripture tells us that "whatever does not proceed from faith is sin" (Rom 14:23).

This synthesis of faith and good works is another of the syntheses being made with great difficulty among Christians, after

71

the age-old controversies between Catholics and Protestants. On a theoretical and theological level an accord has almost been reached. We know that we shall not be saved *because* of our good works, but neither shall we be saved *without* them. We know that we are justified through faith but that it is precisely faith that prompts us to do good works, if we don't want to be like the first son of the parable, who immediately said yes to his father when he asked him to go and work in the vineyard but then did not go (see Matt 21:28 ff.).

The synthesis between faith and works, reached on a theological level, must now be put into daily practice. Having to start somewhere, the philosopher Kierkegaard advises us to start with works and explained why: "The principle of works is more simple than the principle of faith," he said.[32] In fact, to reach a state of genuine faith presupposes the existence of a spiritual life and a pureness of spirit that is extremely difficult to reach, so difficult that there are not many in any generation who come so far; whereas it is easier to start with doing something, even if imperfectly. It is much easier to believe if, by doing something, we deny ourselves. Kierkegaard went on to say: "A scoundrel is treated this way—quite simply: May I see your works? If he comes and protests that in his hidden inwardness he is willing to sacrifice everything, in his hidden inwardness he longs to sit and sing hymns and fast in the stillness of a monastery, while outwardly he keeps profit and cuts quite a figure in society, then we say to him—this is the simplicity of it—no, my good friend, we want to see your works. Alas, but for us men this is surely needed!" Luther did discover the principle of justification by faith: this is true, but— the same philosopher, himself a Lutheran, continued—we forget that he did so after devoting years of his life to the most strenuous discipline in a cloister and there is no guarantee that without this noviciate he would have come to it. Many today want to begin where Luther ended.

5. *The Two Feasts of the Child Jesus*

We have considered the negative case of unfulfilled maternity for lack of faith or works. Let us now consider a fulfilled maternity that makes us similar to Mary. St. Francis of Assisi beautifully summed up what I want to stress: "We are mothers of Christ when we carry him in our hearts and bodies through divine love and a pure and sincere conscience; we bring him forth through works which must be a shining example to others. . . . O, how blessed and dear, how pleasant, humble, peaceful, sweet, amiable and desirable above all things to have such a brother and such a son as Our Lord Jesus Christ!''[33] The saint was telling us that we conceive Christ when we love him in all sincerity of heart and uprightness of conscience and we give him birth when we do works that show him to the world. This echoes the words of Jesus: ''Let your light so shine before men, that they may see your good works and give glory to your Father, who is in heaven'' (Matt 5:16).

St. Bonaventure, a disciple of St. Francis, developed this thought in a tract *The Five Feasts of the Child Jesus.* In his introduction he related how one day, while in retreat on Mount La Verna, he remembered that the holy Fathers had said that the soul devoted to God, by grace of the Holy Spirit and the power of the most high God, can spiritually conceive the blessed Word and firstborn Son of the Father, bring him forth, give him a name, seek him and adore him with the Magi, and finally, happily present him to God the Father in his temple.[34]

Of these five feasts of the Child Jesus to be lived by the soul, we are particularly interested in the first two: the conception and birth. St. Bonaventure said that a person conceives Jesus in his soul when, dissatisfied with his life, prompted by holy inspiration, and filled with holy fervor, he resolutely breaks away from his old habits and sins; he is, as it were, made spiritually fertile by the grace of the Holy Spirit, and he conceives the proposal to lead a new life. Christ has been conceived! Once the blessed Son of God has been conceived, he is born in the heart, as long as the person, after making the right discernment, seeking the right advice, and invoking God's help, immediately puts his holy proposal into practice and begins to act on what has been developing in his mind but which he disregarded for fear of failure. However, the proposal must be carried out immediately, it must bring about an outward visible change, if possible, in our way of living and in our habits. If the proposal isn't put into practice, then Jesus has been conceived but is not born. This is one form of the many spiritual abortions that take place. The second feast of the Child Jesus, Christmas, will never be celebrated! It is one of the many postponements that have perhaps marked our lives and one of the main reasons why so few reach holiness.

If you decide to convert and become one of the poor and humble who, like Mary, seek only God's grace and not to please others, then you really need to arm yourself with courage. You'll have to face two types of temptation. St. Bonaventure warned us: the "worldly" people in your environment will be quick to tell you that you've undertaken the impossible, you'll never succeed, you won't have the necessary strength, your health will suffer; these things are not suitable for you, you're compromising your good name and the dignity of your position. Once you've overcome these problems there will be others caused by people who are probably devout and religious but who really don't believe in the power of God and his Spirit. These will tell you that if you begin to live in a certain way—giving much time to prayer, avoiding useless gossip, doing good works—you will soon be considered a saint, a devout spiritual person, and as you well know that you have not yet reached this stage, you'll end up deceiving people, a hypocrite, bringing upon yourself the wrath of God, who sees into the heart. Your answer to all these temptations is faith: "Behold, the Lord's hand is not shortened that it cannot save" (Isa 59:1), and in fury with yourself, exclaim, as Augustine did on the eve of his conversion: "If these and those can do it, why not I?"[35]

As I've just mentioned St. Augustine, I should like to end this chapter with some words of his that may spur us on to imitate the Mother of God: "His Mother carried him in her womb, may we carry him in our hearts; the Virgin became pregnant with the Incarnation of Christ, may our hearts become pregnant with faith in Christ; she brought forth the Savior, may our souls bring forth salvation and praise. May our souls be not sterile, but fertile for God."[36]

NOTES

1. *Ancient Christmas Responsory.*
2. Tertullian, *Against the Valentinians,* 27, 1 (CC 2, p. 772).
3. Tertullian, *On the Flesh of Christ,* 21, 4 (CC 2, p. 911).
4. St. Cyril of Alexandria, *First Anathema against Nestorius,* in *Enchiridion Symbolorum,* cit., no. 252.
5. See St. Cyril of Alexandria, *Commentary on the Gospel of St. Luke,* XII, 19, 25–27 (PG 74, 661 f.).
6. St. Augustine, *Sermons,* 72 A (Denis 25), 7 (*Miscellanea Agostiniana* I, p. 162).

7. St. Augustine, *On Nature and Grace,* 36, 42 (CSEL 60, p. 263).
8. S. Kierkegaard, *Journals,* II A 110 (ed. H.V. Hong, cit., IV, entry 4774).
9. Tertullian, *On the Flesh of Christ,* 5, 6 (CC 2, p. 881).
10. Ch. Péguy, *The Mystery of the Holy Innocents,* in *Oeuvres Poétiques,* cit., p. 692.
11. Tertullian, *On the Flesh of Christ,* 4, 3 (CC 2, p. 878).
12. See St. Basil, *Homily "In Christi generationem,"* 3 (PG 31, 1464); Proclus of Constantinopolis, *Homily on the Mother of God* I (PG 65, 681).
13. St. Cyril of Alexandria, *Letter II to Nestorius* (PG 77, 448).
14. See Tertullian, *On the Flesh of Christ,* 5, 4 (CC 2, p. 881).
15. St. Irenaeus, *Against the Heresies,* V, 2, 3 (SCh 153, p. 34 f.).
16. St. Ignatius of Antioch, *Letter to the Ephesians,* 7, 2.
17. Dante Alighieri, *Paradiso* XXXIII, 1.
18. Luther, *The Magnificat* (ed. Weimar 7, p. 572 f.).
19. St. Francis of Assisi, *The Office of the Passion* (St. Francis of Assisi, *Writings and Early Biographies,* ed. M. A. Habig, Chicago, 1983, p. 142).
20. Luther, *On the Councils and the Church* (ed. Weimar 50, p. 591 f.).
21. *The Formula of Concord, of the Year 1577,* art. 8, 7 (*The Book of Concord,* ed. and trans. Th. G. Tappert, Philadelphia, Fortress Press, 1959, p. 488).
22. H. Zwingli, *Exposition of Christian Faith,* in Zwingli, *Hauptschriften der Theologie* III, Zurich, 1948, p. 319; *Account of Faith (Fidei ratio),* 6.
23. Calvin, *Institutes of the Christian Religion,* II, 14, 4 (London, SCM Press, 1961, I, p. 486 f.).
24. St. Gregory of Nazianzus, *Discourses,* 12, 6 (PG 35, 849).
25. Acacius of Melitene, *Sermon at the Council of Ephesus* (PG 77, 1472).
26. See Origen, *Commentary on the Gospel of Luke,* 22, 3 (SCh 87, p. 302).
27. St. Augustine, *Sermons* 72A (Denis 25), 8 (*Miscellanea Agostiniana,* I, p. 164).
28. *Lumen gentium* 64.
29. St. Ambrose, *Commentary on the Gospel of Luke,* II, 26 (CSEL 32, 4, p. 55).
30. St. Maximus Confessor, *Commentary on the "Our Father"* (PG 90, 889).
31. Isaac of Stella, *Sermons,* 51 (PL 194, 1863).
32. S. Kierkegaard, *Journals,* XI 2 A 301 (ed. cit., III, entry 2543).
33. St. Francis of Assisi, *Letter to All the Faithful, I (Writings,* cit., p. 96).
34. See St. Bonaventure, *The Five Feasts of the Child Jesus* (ed. Quaracchi, Grottaferrata, 1949, p. 207 f.).
35. St. Augustine, *Confessions,* VIII, 8, 19.
36. St. Augustine, *Sermons,* 189, 3 (PL 38, 1006).

Part Two

Mary, Mirror of the Church
in the Paschal Mystery

Chapter IV

"O Woman, What Have You to Do with Me?"

Mary teaches us self-denial

We must admit that the New Testament doesn't tell us much about Mary, at least not as much as we would expect, considering the place the Mother of God was to acquire in the Church. However, an attentive study will show us that Mary figures in the three most important stages constituting the mystery of salvation. In fact, there are three precise stages that together form the great mystery of redemption: the incarnation of the Word, the paschal mystery, and Pentecost. The incarnation was the moment in which the Redeemer himself was formed, God and man, who as man can represent us and struggle for us and as God, what he does is of infinite and universal value, enabling him to save all mankind. The paschal mystery was the moment in which the person of the Redeemer, as he is, that is to say, both human and divine, carried out the decisive act of salvation, destroying sin by his death and renewing life by his resurrection. Finally, Pentecost was the moment in which the Holy Spirit, descending on the Church and then through baptism on each believer, makes Christ's redeeming act relevant and operative. There wouldn't be the Christian mystery, or it would be something essentially different from what it is, if even one of these three moments hadn't existed.

As I have said, we see on reflection that Mary was present at all three of these fundamental events. She was certainly present at the incarnation, which actually took place in her. Mary was present at the paschal mystery, because it is written that standing by the cross of Jesus was his mother (see John 19:25). Finally, she was present at Pentecost, because it is written that the Holy Spirit came upon the apostles while they were with one accord devoted to prayer together with Mary, the mother of Jesus (see Acts 1:14). Mary's presence in these three key moments of our

79

salvation cannot have been by mere chance. They guarantee her a unique place beside Jesus in the work of redemption. Mary was the only one of all mankind to witness and take part in all three of these events.

On this second part of our journey let us follow Mary in the paschal mystery and allow her to guide us to a deeper understanding of Easter and participation in Christ's sufferings. May Mary take us by the hand and encourage us to follow her along this way as she tells us, like a mother talking to her children gathered round her, "Let us also go, that we may die with him" (John 11:16). In the Gospel, these words were uttered by Thomas, but it was Mary who lived them.

1. *She Learned Obedience from What She Suffered*

In Jesus' life, the paschal mystery didn't begin when he was seized in the garden, and its duration wasn't just the Holy Week. His whole life, from the moment John the Baptist greeted him as the Lamb of God, was a preparation for Easter. According to St. Luke's Gospel, Jesus' public life was a slow and relentless journey toward Jerusalem, where he would accomplish his exodus (see Luke 9:31). The baptism in the Jordan anticipated Christ's Passover because the Father's word had then revealed to Jesus that he would be a suffering and rejected Messiah, just like the servant of God mentioned in Isaiah.

Parallel with the journey of the new obedient Adam, the journey of the new Eve developed. For Mary too, the paschal mystery began rather early. Simeon's words on the sign of contradiction and the sword that would pierce her heart had already been a premonition, which Mary kept in her heart together with all the other words. Our step forward in this meditation is to follow Mary during Jesus' public life and to see her as our model during this period.

What happens normally when a soul called to sanctity has been filled with grace? What happens when that soul has generously said yes in faith and has willingly started to do good works and cultivate virtue? What happens after the moment of initial grace, when it seems that, at times, God can even be seen and touched? A period of purification and deprivation follows. The dark night of faith arrives. And we shall see that in this period of her life,

Mary is our guide and model precisely in how we should behave when it is "pruning time" in our lives. In his encyclical *Redemptoris mater*, written for the Marian Year, the Holy Father, John Paul II, rightly applied to Mary's life the big category of the *kenosis*, with which St. Paul explained the earthly event of Jesus: "Christ Jesus, though he was in the form of God, did not count equality with God a thing to be grasped, but emptied [*ekénosen*] himself" (Phil 2:6-7). "Through faith," the Pope wrote, "Mary was fully united to Christ in his deprivation. . . . Beneath the Cross she partakes, in faith, in the mystery of this terrible despoliation."[1] This deprivation was consummated beneath the cross, but it had started much earlier. Even in Nazareth and especially during Jesus' public life she advanced in her pilgrimage of faith. It is obvious that even then "she suffered in her heart and was in a sort of dark night of faith."[2]

All of this renders the events concerning Mary extraordinarily meaningful for us; it restores Mary to the Church and to mankind. We must joyfully acknowledge the great development there has been in devotion to Mary, which those of us who have lived the time spanning Vatican Council II cannot but be aware of. Before the council, the fundamental category through which Mary's greatness was explained was that of privilege, or exemption. It was thought that she had been exempted not only from original sin and corruption (privileges the Church defined in the dogmas on the Immaculate Conception and the Assumption), but it was even believed that Mary had been exempted from the pangs of childbirth, from fatigue, doubt, temptation, ignorance, and (worse still) even from death. In fact, some believed that Mary didn't die before being assumed into heaven. All these things, it was reasoned, are consequences of sin, but Mary was sinless. They didn't realize that instead of associating Mary with Jesus, they were totally dissociating her from him who, although he was without sin, had wanted to experience all these things: fatigue, sorrow, anguish, temptation, and death for our sake. All of this was reflected in the iconography on the Madonna, in the way she was depicted in statues, paintings, and pictures, generally as a disincarnate and idealized creature of a beauty that was often purely human and that any woman would love to possess, a Madonna, all told, who seems to have barely touched the earth.

Nowadays, since Vatican Council II, we no longer try to explain Mary's unique sanctity so much through privilege as through faith. Mary advanced in her pilgrimage of faith.[3] This doesn't diminish Mary's greatness; rather, it increases it beyond measure. Before God, the spiritual greatness of a person in this life is not in fact measured so much by what God gives, as by what God asks of the person. And as we shall see, God asked a lot of Mary, more than of any other person, more even than he asked of Abraham.

In the New Testament there are very powerful statements about Jesus. One of these says that "we have not a high priest who is unable to sympathize with our weaknesses, but one who in every respect has been tempted as we are, yet without sinning" (Heb 4:15); another statement tells us that "although he was a Son, he learned obedience through what he suffered" (Heb 5:8). If Mary followed her son in his *kenosis,* these words, due distinctions made, apply to her also and are the key to understanding her life. Although she was the mother, Mary learned obedience through what she suffered. Was Jesus perhaps not obedient enough in childhood or did he not know what obedience was, so that he had to learn it through what he suffered later on? No, "learn" in this context means what "know" generally means in the Bible, that is to say, the practical meaning of "experiencing" or "relishing." Jesus practiced obedience and grew in it because of what he suffered. An ever-greater spirit of obedience was necessary to overcome ever-greater trials and temptations, to the supreme trial of death. Mary, too, learned obedience and faith; she grew in them through what she suffered, so that with all confidence we may say of her that we have a mother who is able to sympathize with our weaknesses, our fatigue, and our temptations, one who was tempted as we are, yet without sinning.

2. *Mary in the Public Life of Jesus*

In the Gospels there are references to Mary which, in the past when the idea of privilege dominated, created a certain sense of uneasiness among believers and which now, instead, seem to be milestones in Mary's pilgrimage in faith and which we have no reason to disregard or smooth over with convenient explanations. Let us now briefly look at these texts.

Let us start with the loss of Jesus in the Temple (see Luke 2:41ff.). In emphasizing that Jesus was found "after three days," Luke was, perhaps, already alluding to the paschal mystery of the death and resurrection of Christ. At any rate, this was certainly the beginning of a paschal mystery of deprivation for the mother. In fact, what did he say to her when they found him? "How is it that you sought me? Did you not know that I must be in my Father's house?" What mother would not be able to understand what Mary felt in her heart at these words! "How is it that you sought me?" Words that placed a different will between Jesus and Mary, an infinitely more important will, making every other relationship secondary, even his filial relationship with her.

Later on, Mary is mentioned at Cana in Galilee right at the beginning of Jesus' public life. We know the facts. What did Jesus answer when Mary discreetly asked him to intervene? "O woman, what have you to do with me?" No matter how we try to explain these words they still sound harsh and mortifying. Once again they seem to place a distance between Jesus and his mother.

All three of the Synoptics relate this other episode, which took place during Jesus' public ministry. One day while Jesus was preaching, his mother and his brethren came to talk with him. Just like any mother, his mother was probably worried about his health, because the lines preceding recount that he could not even eat because of the crowd (see Mark 3:20). A small detail to note: Mary, his mother, had to beg even for the right to see him and talk with him. She didn't take advantage of being his mother to push her way through the crowd. Instead, she remained standing outside, and it was others who went to Jesus and said, "Your mother is outside asking for you." But here too, the important thing is what Jesus said: "Who are my mother and my brethren?" (Mark 3:33). We already know what he then went on to say. Let us place ourselves—let the mother of any priest whatever place herself—in Mary's shoes, and we shall be able to sense the humiliation and suffering these words caused her. We now know that they were words of praise rather than reproach for his mother, but she didn't know it, or at least, she didn't know it at that moment. For her they held only the bitterness of refusal. There is no mention of Jesus going out to talk to her. More likely than not Mary had to go away without seeing her son or speaking with him.

Another day, St. Luke relates, a woman in the crowd raised her voice in an enthusiastic outburst toward Jesus, exclaiming, "Blessed is the womb that bore you, and the breasts that you sucked!" A compliment that would be enough on its own to make any mother happy, but Mary, if she was present or came to hear of it, couldn't dwell on these words long enough to relish them because Jesus hastened to correct the woman at once and said, "Blessed rather are those who hear the word of God and keep it" (Luke 11:27-28).

Let us look at one last example. At a certain point in his Gospel, St. Luke mentions "Jesus' female followers," some holy women, and he named them, who had been blessed by him and who "provided for him out of their means" (Luke 8:2-3), that is to say, they looked after his and the apostles' material needs, preparing meals for them, washing or mending their clothes. How does this concern Mary? In the fact that she was not mentioned among these women, and we all know how much a mother longs to do these little things for a son, especially if he is consecrated to the Lord. It was the total sacrifice of the heart.

Such a precise and coherent series of facts and words cannot be there just by pure chance. Mary, too, had to go through her *kenosis*. Jesus' *kenosis* consisted in this: instead of asserting his divine rights and prerogatives, he deprived himself, becoming a servant and appearing before all as a man just like any other man. Mary's *kenosis* consisted in the fact that, instead of asserting her rights as the Messiah's mother, she let herself be deprived and appeared before all as a woman just like any other woman. The fact that he was God's son didn't spare Christ all kinds of humiliations, just as the fact of being God's mother didn't spare Mary all kinds of humiliations. Jesus said the Word is what God prunes with and cleans the branches: "You are made clean by the Word" (John 15:3), and this is the way he "pruned" his mother. Was this not, perhaps, precisely the sword that would one day pierce her heart, as Simeon had predicted?

Mary's divine maternity was also a human experience; there was a carnal aspect to it in the positive sense of the word. Jesus was her carnal son just as we say two brothers of the same mother are carnal brothers. That son was her son, her only treasure and her only support in life. But she had to renounce all that was humanly exciting in her calling. Her son himself saw to it that she gained no earthly benefit from her motherhood. Although she was his mother, she followed Jesus as if she were not. Once his ministry had started, Jesus had nowhere to rest his head, and Mary had nowhere to rest her heart.

To her already great material poverty Mary added a spiritual poverty to the highest degree. This spiritual poverty consisted in accepting total deprivation of all privileges, in not being able to count on anything, neither on the past nor the future nor revelations nor promises, as if these were not her affair and had never taken place. St. John of the Cross called this the "dark night of the memory," and in talking about it he explicitly mentioned the Mother of God.[4] It consists in forgetting oneself—or better, in being unable to recall the past, no matter how much one tries—and in straining forward only toward God and living in pure hope. This is the true and radical poverty of spirit, which is rich only in God and even then is rich only in hope. St. Paul said it is living "forgetting what lies behind" (Phil 3:13).

Toward his mother Jesus behaved like a clear-minded and demanding spiritual director who, having sensed he is dealing with an exceptional soul, doesn't allow the soul to waste time or to dwell on a lower level amidst natural sentiments and consolations. If he too is a holy man, he draws the soul on without rest toward total deprivation in view of union with God. Jesus taught Mary self-denial. He directs all his followers in all centuries through his Gospel, but he directed his mother personally and orally. On the one hand, he let himself be led by the Father by means of the Spirit wherever the Father wanted: into the desert to be tempted, onto the mountain to be transfigured, to Gethsemane to sweat blood. He said, "I always do what is pleasing to him" (John 8:29). On the other hand, Jesus led Mary in the same "race" to do the Father's will. That's why, now that she is glorified in heaven with her Son, Mary can stretch out her maternal hand to us and lead us, small as we are, to follow her, and say with much more right than the apostle could, "Be imitators of me, as I am of Christ" (1 Cor 11:1).

3. "Unless the grain of wheat dies"

Listening to these things, flesh and blood as we are, we tend to query them in our hearts no matter how much we try not to. Why was all of this necessary? Wasn't Mary already holy, full of faith? Hadn't she been tried enough? Is God really love, as it is written?

The first answer to this is that Jesus went along this path and Mary had to stay close by him to be his first and most perfect disciple. Mary herself would not have exchanged this privilege for anything else in the world.

But there is a more mysterious reason, and we shall let St. Paul help us understand it: "Flesh and blood cannot inherit the kingdom of God, nor does the perishable inherit the imperishable" (1 Cor 15:50). The plan of grace is different from that of nature; what is eternal is different from what takes place in time. It is not possible to pass from one plan to the other painlessly and by straightforward evolution. There's an infinite leap in quality involved. This makes a break necessary, a death, so as to pass from one state to the other; something in the primary order must be disarranged to accede to this different and superior way of being. We have said that Mary's maternity was also a temporal, very human experience that came about in flesh and blood. To become something eternal and spiritual, an event belonging only to the kingdom, it had to pass through a death, as was the case of the sacred humanity of the Son before he was glorified and made a spiritual body.

Is sin involved therefore? It is, as it was for Jesus, in the sense that he came on earth to conquer sin, taking the consequences onto himself, and in this, he associated Mary his mother to him through grace and imitation.

But perhaps the first reason goes beyond sin and really concerns the relation between nature and grace: "The passage to the supernatural order, even for an innocent and healthy nature, could never take place without some kind of death. God's infinite is not a composite infinite or a false infinite that could be reached simply by an extension of the finite! It is not a matter of the finite being simply consenting to having a cubit added to his stature. He must consent to a more total sacrifice."[5]

It is true that the Spirit gives life, but it does so by first putting the flesh to death: "If by the Spirit you put to death the deeds of the body you will live" (Rom 8:13). Grace doesn't gently rest on nature like a lovely crown on the head. Nature must be remolded and spiritualized so as to be resurrected in grace. Jesus used the example of the grain of wheat (see John 12:24). How has the grain of wheat sinned to deserve death in the earth? It hasn't, but only by dying can it bear much fruit. Nature gives an even more striking example in the silkworm, which is a formidable parable for spiritual life. When it has finished its work, the silkworm shrivels, locked in its cocoon, as if it were about to die. First the skin splits on its back; then amidst painful shudders and contractions the worm gets rid of its old skin. With the skin all the rest cracks: the skullcap, jaws, eyes, stomach. In the place of the worm there now appears an almond-shaped creature, round shaped at one end and pointed at the other: this is the chrysalis, the stage between the worm and the moth. In about twenty days the enclosed insect is ready to escape. It makes an opening for itself by which the perfect moth comes forth, still moist and barely able to stand. It rests a little to gather strength, then pierces the cocoon and comes out into the light as a butterfly. What sin has the little silkworm committed to have to go through such a disaster? None at all. But first it crawled along the ground and now it flies, and in this delightful freedom it no longer even recalls its pain.

4. *Mary, Jesus' Disciple*

Let us now turn to what most interests us here. How did Mary react to the way the Son and God himself dealt with her? Let us read again the texts we have recalled, perhaps even with the aid of a magnifying glass. We shall note that never was there the slightest hint of her will being in contrast with God's, of objection or self-justification on Mary's part; there was no attempt ever to get Jesus to change his mind! There was absolute docility. Here we see the unique personal holiness of the Mother of God, the highest marvel of grace. To realize this, all we have to do is make a comparison, with St. Peter, for example. When Jesus informed Peter that in Jerusalem rejection, passion, and death awaited him, Peter rebuked him and said, "God forbid, Lord! This shall never happen to you!" (see Matt 16:22). He was worried about Jesus but also about himself. Mary wasn't worried about herself.

Mary remained in silence. Her answer to everything was her silence. Not a silence of withdrawal and sadness; there is in fact a silence which, in the inner self where God alone hears, is a din made by the old self. Mary's silence was of another quality. This was clear at Cana in Galilee when, instead of being offended, Mary understood through faith and perhaps from the way Jesus looked at her that she could insist, and she said to the servants, "Do whatever he tells you" (John 2:5). (At Cana, Mary received the "gift of science," which, in the series of charisms, seems to indicate the supernatural certainty that God is about to act and will accomplish a certain thing or miracle, which therefore can be announced.) Even after the harsh words Jesus used when they found him in the Temple and which Mary didn't understand, it is written that Mary was silent and "kept all these things in her heart" (Luke 2:51).

The fact that Mary kept silent doesn't signify that everything was easy for her and that she didn't have to overcome struggles, difficulties, and darkness. She was exempt from sin but not from struggle and difficulty in believing. If Jesus had to struggle and sweat blood to get his human will to adhere fully to the Father's will, is it surprising that his mother had to face agony too? One thing, however, is certain: under no circumstance whatsoever, would Mary have wanted to turn back. When certain souls, led by God along similar paths, are asked if they want to pray for it to end and go back to being as they once were, they immediately answer no! No matter how perturbed they are and even at times on the verge of apparent desperation.

Having contemplated Christ's *mother* in the previous meditation, let us now contemplate Christ's *disciple*. Concerning Jesus' words, "Who is my mother? . . . Whoever does the will of God is my brother and sister and mother" (Mark 3:33-35), St. Augustine commented:

> Didn't the Virgin do the Father's will, she who believed in faith and in faith conceived, was chosen for salvation to be born for us among men, and was created by Christ before Christ was created in her womb? The Holy Mary did the Father's will completely; and therefore it is more meritorious for Mary to have been Christ's disciple rather than Christ's mother. It is worth more, it is a greater privilege, to have been a disciple rather than Christ's mother. Mary was happy because before giving birth to a Son, she had carried the Master in her womb. . . . This is why Mary was blessed, she had listened to God's Word and practiced it.
>
> In the flesh Mary is therefore only Christ's mother, but spiritually she is his sister and mother.[6]

A Father of the Reformation gave the same explanation. Referring to the Gospel text "Who is my mother?" he wrote: "Christ didn't deny his mother with these words but showed the hidden meaning of the things she had done. She received God's word and likewise he who listens to his word will receive the Holy Spirit. She conceived as a pure virgin and in the same way, he who keeps God's word, observes it and is nourished on it, will give wonderful fruits.''[7]

Are we therefore to think that Mary's life was one of constant affliction, a dismal life? On the contrary. Judging it in accordance with the lives of the saints, we must say that day by day Mary discovered a new kind of joy, with respect to the maternal joys of Bethlehem or Nazareth, when she pressed Jesus to her breast and he pressed himself to her breast. The joy of not doing her own will. The joy of believing. The joy of giving to God what for him is the most precious thing, just as, also in relation to God, there is greater joy in giving than in receiving. The joy of discovering a God whose ways are inaccessible and whose thoughts are not our thoughts but who, because of this, makes himself known for what he really is: God, the Holy One. "Truly, thou art a God who hidest thyself, O God of Israel, the Savior" (Isa 45:15). You are a hidden and mysterious God! How well Mary must have understood this, and perhaps bowed her head in assent whenever she heard the prophet's words being proclaimed in the synagogue or at home!

A great mystic who had had similar experiences spoke of a special joy at the very limit of human understanding, which she called the "joy of incomprehensibility" *(gaudium incomprehensibilitatis)*. This consists in understanding that one cannot understand, but that a God who could be understood would no longer be God. This incomprehensibility gives rise to joy rather than sadness because it shows that God is even richer and greater than anything you can comprehend and that he is *your* God! Joy such as this is what the saints possess in heaven and what the Blessed Virgin must have experienced at times even in this life.[8]

5. *"If anyone wants to come after me. . ."*

It is time now, as usual, to move from Mary to the Church. The personal application of what we have so far contemplated in Mary's life comes from Jesus himself in the Gospel. St. Mark relates that one day Jesus, having called to him the multitude with his disciples, as if to give greater solemnity to what he was about to affirm, said to them: "If any man would come after me, let him deny himself and take up his cross and follow me. For whoever would save his life will lose it; and whoever loses his life for my sake and the Gospel will save it'' (Mark 8:34-35). I call this maxim the ascetic core of the Gospel. Together with announcing the kingdom, that is to say, the kerygmatic aspect, the Gospel also contains an ascetic aspect, insofar as it is the way to reach moral perfection by following Christ. Well then, what we have just read is the secret and basis of this way.

What do these words tell us? That if I want to follow Christ I must not side with myself or take on my own self-defense or the defense of my nature, or cling to myself in the attempt to make my life secure; on the contrary, I must deny myself and my natural tendencies, renounce myself in an openness to God, until death. It's curious that in the New Testament the same verb "to deny" *(arnéomai)* constantly occurs in two different contexts: when it talks of self-denial and when it talks of denying Christ: "Whoever denies me before men. . ." (Matt 10:33). These two things, according to the Gospel, are closely connected. Actually, one is an alternative to the other: either you deny yourself or you deny Christ. It isn't possible to say yes to one without saying no to the other because both—the flesh and the Spirit—are opposed to each other (see Gal 5:17).

Denial is never therefore an end in itself, nor is it an ideal in itself. The most important thing is the positive aspect: "If anyone wants to come after me;" it is to follow Christ. To say no to oneself is the means; to say yes to Christ is the end. In the Gospel, Peter is the dramatic illustration of this. He unexpectedly and suddenly found himself (alas, Jesus had tried to warn him) in a situation where he had to make an immediate decision between the two possibilities. But faced with the choice, he denied him: "Again he denied it: I do not know this man!" (Matt 26:70; Mark 14:68). In the original text, the same verb "deny" *(arnéomai)* occurs in all these passages. Peter, by not denying himself, denied Christ. By wanting to save his own life he lost it, that is, he lost his real life, his real self, the best of himself, the very reason for his existence. Poor Peter! Immediately after his denial, he realized that he was lost, because now, what was Peter without his Master? Nothing! That's why he went out and cried bitterly (see Luke 22:62).

This saying of Jesus goes to the heart of the matter. It's a question of knowing what we want to build our existence on, whether it's on the self or on Christ; of knowing who we want to live for, whether it's for ourselves or for the Lord. This was a dramatic choice in the lives of the martyrs. One particular day, they found themselves in the situation of either denying themselves or denying Christ. In a different way, every disciple faces the same choice every day and even every moment. Each no said to oneself for love's sake is a yes to Christ.

Christian ascetics is therefore substantially much more than renunciation; it's much more than self-inflicted suffering. It is the way to a fuller life; it is a fortunate exchange. Would we perhaps say that a poor fellow who abandons his dark and damp little hovel where he has spent his life for a magnificent palace full of all sorts of good things where he has been freely invited, was a renouncer? Or wouldn't he perhaps be more of a renouncer by doing the opposite and staying in his shack with his miserable possessions? Well then, our human self is that miserable hovel compared to the possession of Christ, which is the palace. Even the joy we can experience in our life is in proportion to the object of our choice. If we choose ourselves, we would have a very miserable source of nourishment, a dry nursemaid. If we choose Christ, he is the source of eternal and endless joy because he is risen!

It is not necessary to make a great effort to see how life flies, passes, and ends. Why, then, don't we take this step while there is still time? Imagine someone shipwrecked being carried along on a simple raft by the whirlpool of the raging flood of a river. The mouth of the river approaches, from which there will be no escape. At a bend of the river the raft touches ground! This probably won't happen again. It's a lucky chance for the shipwrecked person to jump off without second thoughts. He is safe; he "has set his feet upon the rock." How beautiful and luminous is this ascetic heart of the Gospel, although apparently so austere!

However, in talking about self-denial there is the serious risk of remaining on a theoretical level. We are not interested here in *knowing* everything there is to know about Christian self-denial and its beauty and advantages; it's simply a question of denying oneself. An ancient spiritual master said:

> The will can be broken ten times in a short spell and I'll teach you how. While walking along you see something and your mind says: "Look over there," but you answer your mind: "No, I

shall not look," and you break your will and do not look at it. Then you meet people talking and your mind says: "Join them and tell what you know"; but you don't say anything and break your will. Again your mind suggests: "Go and ask your brother cook what he is preparing," and you don't go and thus break your will.[9]

These are obviously examples taken from monastic life, but they can be adapted to any kind of life. There's an unsuitable program on television and your old self suggests you watch it. After all, you're no longer a child. What harm can it do? You say, no! You've broken your will; you've dominated the flesh and the world; you may go to sleep in peace. You have a strong urge to release your anger on someone; you know exactly what you want to say, and the words are on the tip of your tongue. But you say, no! You've denied yourself. You have the chance of unlawfully gaining money; you say no and you've denied yourself. You believe you have been wronged; you want to shout it to the four winds by locking yourself in silent reproof, but you don't do so. Instead, you break the silence and reopen communication. You've denied yourself and saved charity—and so on.

This is a lovely program, but let me add that it is also extremely difficult. Nature moves all its defense mechanisms before giving in. It wants to save its own life and not lose it. It defends its own space tooth and nail. It tries to keep God outside its boundaries because the closeness of God would mean the end of its tranquillity and independence. It sees its own human limit as a form of protection and tries to relax in little human things, leaving divine things to God. This, according to some medieval theologians, is the very essence of sin and was what caused the downfall of Lucifer and Adam and, I shall add, is what causes the downfall of many proud spirits of our day who scorn Christian denial. God knows this difficulty and therefore appreciates, more than anyone else, our little efforts at self-denial. He even appreciates the simple desire for self-denial, so long as it is sincere.

We should remember at this point that we have a mother who is able to sympathize with our weaknesses, as she herself went through all that we experience except sin. Let us turn to her: Mary, help us not to do our own will; awaken in us renewed joy in giving something to God while we are in this world, instead of always asking God to give to us.

NOTES

1. John Paul II, *Redemptoris mater,* 18 (AAS 79, 1987, p. 382 f.).
2. Ibid., 17.
3. See *Lumen gentium,* 58.
4. St. John of the Cross, *Ascent of Mount Carmel,* III, 2, 10 (*The Complete Works,* ed. by E. Allison Peers, Wheathamstead, 1978, p. 216.
5. H. De Lubac, *The Mystery of the Supernatural,* London, Chapman, 1967, p. 37.
6. St. Augustine, *Sermons,* 72A (Denis 25), 7 (*Miscellanea Agostiniana* I, p. 162); *The Holy Virginity,* 5-6 (PL 40, 399).
7. H. Zwingli, *Regarding Clarity and Certainty of the Word of God,* in *Hauptschriften,* der Prediger I, Zurich, 1940, p. 104.
8. *The Book of the Bl. Angela of Foligno,* Instruction III (ed. Quaracchi, Grottaferrata, 1985, p. 468).
9. Dorotheus of Gaza, *Spiritual Works,* I, 20 (SCh 92, p. 177).

Chapter V

"Beneath the Cross of Jesus Stood Mary His Mother"

Mary, the mother of hope

In contemplating Mary in the mystery of the incarnation we kept in mind the icon *Our Lady of Tenderness*. The icon shows us the Child Jesus in the embrace of his mother. Their outlines merge; they almost form one body. With her left hand Mary supports the child, while her right hand invites us to draw close to him and enter into his world. The child's hands hold his mother as he presses his cheek to hers; his mouth is close to her mouth, offering her the divine breath of Wisdom. Mary shows nothing of the natural and unrestrained pride of a happy mother. She is sober and thoughtful, almost sad, but no one seeing her would doubt that she is full of spiritual joy in her inner self.

We must now change this icon for the one of Mary in the paschal mystery, *The Crucifixion*. What a contrast! Jesus is no longer in his mother's arms but in the arms of a cross; he no longer presses his cheek to hers but to something much different and harder. Mary now hides her empty and useless hands beneath her shawl. There seems to be an overwhelming distance between her and her son. Jesus is suspended between heaven and earth, "outside the camp" (Heb 13:12). There's a whole world of reality and figures between her and her son: to the left there's an angel urging a woman, who is the symbol of the Church, toward the cross of Christ, while to the right another angel is moving another woman, symbolizing the Synagogue, away from the same cross.

A comparison of these two icons shows us at a glance the path of deprivation and detachment that Mary walked. In Psalm 22, uttered by Jesus on the cross ("My God, my God, why have you abandoned me?"), the psalmist says at a certain point: "Yet thou art he who took me from the womb, thou didst keep me safe upon my mother's breast." How impressive it is to think that perhaps

Jesus murmured these words to himself on the cross as the mother on whose breast he had safely rested stood there before him!

Let us now place ourselves beneath the cross. "Let us go forth to him outside the camp, bearing abuse for him" (Heb 13:13). If you are a man, stay by John's side and, like him, silently bow your head in adoration. If you are a woman, stay close to Mary and share her silence and pain, like the women in the icon.

1. *Mary in the Paschal Mystery*

God's word in this meditation comes to us through John, "who bore witness and who knows that he tells the truth" (John 19:35): "Standing by the cross of Jesus were his mother, and his mother's sister, Mary the wife of Clopas, and Mary Magdalen. When Jesus saw his mother and the disciple whom he loved standing near, he said to his mother, "Woman, behold your son!" Then he said to the disciple, "Behold, your mother!" And from that hour the disciple took her to his own home" (John 19:25-27).

We shall now consider only the first narrative part of this text and leave what Jesus said for the next chapter.

I have already said that Mary was present in the New Testament at all three of the events that make up the Christian mystery: the incarnation, the paschal mystery, and Pentecost. However, it would seem that Mary was present at only half of the paschal mystery. In fact, the complete paschal mystery inseparably embraced the death and resurrection of Christ. It was his passage from death to life, from this world to the Father (see John 13:1), which opened the way for us believers so that we too may pass from death to life. It is true that Mary is mentioned where the cross and death of Jesus are concerned, but no mention is made of her at the resurrection. There is no trace in the Gospel of an apparition of the risen Christ to his mother, and we must abide by the Gospel.

Yet it is precisely through the Gospel that we see that Mary personally experienced the whole of the paschal mystery, composed of the death and resurrection, of annihilation and exaltation, and she experienced all this more closely than any other person. It is, in fact, John the evangelist who told us of Mary beneath the cross. Now, what does the cross of Christ and Calvary represent in St. John's Gospel? The well-known answer is that it represents his hour, the hour in which the Son of Man would be glorified; the hour for which he came into this world (see John 12:23-24). He said to the Father, "Father, the hour has come; glorify thy Son" (John 17:1). And referring to his own death, he said, "When you have lifted up the Son of man, then you will know that I am he" (John 8:27). The moment of death was, therefore, the moment in which the full glory of Christ and his divine sovereignty were revealed and he appears as the one who grants the Spirit. In fact, it is written, "For as yet the Spirit had not been given because Jesus was not yet glorified" (John 7:39).

For John, the passage from the old to the new Passover came about on Calvary. The evangelist stressed this by chronologically placing the death of Jesus in the afternoon of 14 Nisan, that is to say, at the moment in which the paschal lambs were immolated in the Temple of Jerusalem, and by quoting a passage from Exodus relative to the paschal lamb (see John 19:37; Exod 12:46). But beyond the external and chronological development of the events, the evangelist grasped, through divine revelation, the full span of God's plan, in which the cross represented the moment of passing from the old to the new covenant, from prophecy to fact. It was the moment of "it is finished" (John 19:30). The resurrection was contemplated as being virtually present and operating in the way Christ died. The reason for it all is clear, and that is the Son's loving obedience to the Father even to death and the Father's promise to glorify the Son.

This is why the episode of the empty tomb and the apparitions of the risen Christ, although narrated in the Fourth Gospel, do not hold the same apologetic meaning as they do in the Synoptic Gospels. In the light of what Jesus said to Thomas, these events are a concession to the apostles' weak faith, "for as yet they did not know the Scripture, that he must rise from the dead" (John 20:9), rather than an intrinsic need to confirm the fact. In fact, Jesus said to Thomas, "Blessed are those who have not seen and yet believe" (John 20:29).

Seen in this light, the fact that the Fourth Gospel says nothing of an apparition of the risen Christ to his mother doesn't seem so relevant or odd. The apostles discovered the resurrection of Christ at the dawn of the third day, but Mary had already discovered it when the resurrection dawned on the cross, when it was really "still dark" (John 20:1).

Concerning what I have just mentioned—that for John the mo-

ment of Calvary already embraced the resurrection of Christ—
there is also historical confirmation. We know that the Churches
of Asia Minor, which John founded and guided, celebrated Easter
on 14 Nisan, that is, on the anniversary of Christ's death and
not on that of the resurrection like the rest of the Church, which
celebrated Easter on a Sunday. And we also know from transmitted texts that in the liturgy celebrated in those Churches on
that day, it was not only the death of Christ that was commemorated but also, and equally, his victory and resurrection.

Therefore, in presenting Mary to us beneath the cross, John
places her at the very center of the paschal mystery. She wasn't
present only at her son's defeat and death but also at his glorification. "We have seen his glory," John exclaimed in the prologue,
referring principally to the glory of the cross. Mary could have
said the same; she, too, saw his glory, a glory so different, so
new with respect to any other humanly imaginable type of glory.
She saw God's glory, which is love.

2. Mary, the "Pure Lamb"

Did Mary then not suffer on Calvary? Was the cross just a
passing moment for her? Could it be that Jesus, who called this
his hour of glory, didn't suffer? Was, perhaps, the atrocity of
his passion diminished? The Fourth Gospel presents a Jesus who
knew what Gethsemane was like (see John 12:27), the crowning
with thorns, the humiliation of being struck, the scourging (see
John 19:1 ff.), Peter's denial, Judas's betrayal, and all the rest.
The glory is set on a different level from that of the bare historical facts; it concerns the meaning of these facts, what God does:
"God has made him both Lord and Christ, this Jesus whom you
crucified" (Acts 2:36). The crucifixion belongs to man and is set
in history; the glorification belongs to God and is set beyond history, in eschatology, and can be seen only through faith.

Mary, too, drank the chalice of the passion right to the bitter
end. We can say of her, as of the ancient daughter of Zion, she
has drunk at the hand of the Lord the cup of his wrath, who has
drunk to the dregs the bowl of staggering (see Isa 51:17). If Mary,
his mother, was there on Calvary beneath the cross of Jesus, she
was certainly in Jerusalem in those days, and if she was in Jerusalem, she certainly witnessed everything and was present at all that
happened. She was present at the *ecce homo;* she saw the flesh

97

of her own flesh being scourged, bleeding, being crowned with thorns; she saw him almost naked before the crowds, trembling, his body jerking in the rigors of death. She heard the banging of the hammers and the insults: "If you are the Son of God . . . ." She saw the soldiers divide his garments and the tunic she herself had probably woven. Christian piety wasn't wrong, therefore, when it also applied the words of the daughter of Zion in her desolation to Mary beneath the cross: "All you who pass by, look and see if there is any sorrow like my sorrow!" (Lam 1:12). If St. Paul could say, "I bear on my body the marks of Jesus" (Gal 6:7), what should Mary be able to say? Mary was the first person in Christianity to bear the stigmata; she bore the invisible stigmata impressed on her heart which, as we know, happened later on to some saints.

The Gospel tells us that "standing by the cross of Jesus were his mother, and his mother's sister, Mary the wife of Clopas, and Mary Magdalene." There was, therefore, a group of four women (as the icon shows). So Mary wasn't alone; she was one of the women. But Mary was present as his mother, and this fact changes everything by placing Mary in a very different situation from that of the others. I have sometimes attended a young person's funeral, and I am thinking now in particular of the funeral of a young boy. Several women followed the hearse. They were all dressed in black and all were crying, so that they all looked alike. But one of them, the mother, was different, and all those present were thinking of her and almost surreptitiously glancing at her! She was a widow, and this boy was her only child. Her eyes were fixed on the coffin, and you could see her lips continually forming her son's name. At the moment of the *Sanctus,* when those present started to say, "Holy, Holy, Holy, Lord God of heaven and earth," she too, probably without even realizing it, started to murmur, "Holy, Holy, Holy . . . ." I thought of Mary beneath the cross. But something much more difficult had been asked of her: to forgive. When she heard her son call out, "Father, forgive them, for they know not what they do" (Luke 23:24), she knew the heavenly Father wanted her to repeat the same words with all her heart: "Father, forgive them, for they know not what they do." And Mary repeated them. She forgave.

There is no mention of Mary bewailing and lamenting beneath the cross, as there is of the women who accompanied Jesus along the way to Calvary (see Luke 23:27). No words of hers have been transmitted to us, as for the finding in the Temple or at Cana in Galilee. Only her silence is transmitted to us. In Luke's Gospel Mary was silent at the moment of the birth of Jesus, and in John's Gospel she was silent at the moment of the death of Jesus. In his First Letter to the Corinthians, St. Paul compared "the word of the cross" *(verbum crucis)* and the "wisdom of the word" *(sapientia verbi),* that is, the language of the cross and the language of human wisdom. The difference lies in the fact that the wisdom of the word, or the world, is expressed through words and fine discourses, whereas the language of the cross is expressed through silence. The language of the cross is silence! Silence keeps the odor of sacrifice for God alone. It prevents suffering being dissipated and seeking for and finding its reward on this earth.

If Mary was tempted, as even Jesus was in the desert, this took place above all beneath the cross. And the temptation was very deep and painful because the reason for it was Jesus himself. She believed in the promises, she believed that Jesus was the Messiah, the Son of God; she knew that if Jesus had appealed to the Father, he would have sent him "more than twelve legions of angels" (Matt 26:53). But she saw that Jesus didn't do this. If he freed himself from the cross, he would also free her from this dreadful sorrow, but he didn't do it. Yet Mary didn't cry out, "Come down from the cross; save yourself and me!" nor did she cry, "My son, you have saved others, why don't you now save yourself too?" even though it isn't difficult to understand that similar thoughts and wishes must have spontaneously come to her mother's heart. She no longer even asked Jesus, "Son, why have you treated us so?" as she did when, having lost him, she later found him in the Temple (Luke 2:48). Mary was silent. "She lovingly consented to the immolation of this Victim which she herself had brought forth," a text of Vatican Council II tells us.[1] She celebrated his Passover with him.

St. Luke's Gospel tells us that Jesus' parents "went to Jerusalem every year at the feast of the Passover." When Jesus was twelve years old he went with them but he stayed behind in Jerusalem and didn't return home (see Luke 2:41 ff.). And now Mary once again accompanied Jesus to Jerusalem, to celebrate his last Passover there. But this time he himself was the Passover Lamb, and he would never again return home, not even after the three days. The bishop of one of the Johannine Churches in Asia Minor, St. Melito of Sardis, thus evoked the event in a homily given on an Easter night between A.D. 160 and 180: "The law has become the Word, the commandment grace, the figure reality, the lamb the Son. . . . This is a speechless lamb. . . . This is he who was born of Mary, the pure lamb; who at night was immolated and rose from the dead."[2]

To this disciple of John's, Mary beneath the cross appeared as the "pure lamb" who stayed close to the immolated Lamb; she appeared as the one who generated the paschal victim and who offered herself together with him. The silent lamb beside the Lamb who didn't open his mouth (see Isa 53:7). The Byzantine liturgy has used this title of Mary's, "the beautiful lamb," taken from a hymn of *Romanus Melodus,* in its Good Friday service.[3]

The idea of Mary being united to her son's sacrifice is soberly and solemnly expressed in a Vatican Council II text: "The Blessed Virgin advanced in her pilgrimage of faith, and loyally persevered in her union with her Son unto the cross. There she stood, in keeping with the divine plan, suffering grievously with her only-begotten Son. There she united herself with a maternal heart to his sacrifice, and lovingly consented to the immolation of this Victim which she herself had brought forth."[4]

Mary didn't, therefore, just stand close to the cross of Jesus in a physical and geographical sense. She was there in a spiritual sense too. She was in union with the cross of Jesus; she was inside the same suffering. She was the first of those who "share Christ's suffering" (Rom 8:17). She suffered in her heart what her son suffered in his body. And how could anyone who has any idea of what it means to be a mother think differently? "Just as Christ cried out: My God, my God why have you forsaken me—so Mary must suffer through something similar on the human level. A sword will pierce through your soul—and reveal the thoughts of your heart, yours also, if you still dare believe, are still humble enough to believe, that you truly are the one chosen among women, the one who has found grace before God!."[5]

Jesus was also man, and at that moment on Calvary he was, in the eyes of all, just a son being executed before his mother. To avoid placing Mary and Jesus, the Savior and the saved, on the same level, a certain type of controversial theology (or a defensive theology where Catholics are concerned) runs the risk of destroying the true meaning of the incarnation, forgetting that Christ was "in every respect tempted as we are, yet without sinning"

(Heb 4:15). It is certainly not sinful for a son dying in such a way and rejected by all to seek comfort in the heart and eyes of his mother, who is well aware of his innocence. This is simply human nature and compassion. And as it is human compassion and not sin, Jesus experienced it as he was dying. The infinite difference between Christ and Mary mustn't make us forget the infinite similarity between them, otherwise it would be like denying that Jesus was truly man, and this would be Docetism.

Jesus no longer said, "O woman, what have you to do with me? My hour has not yet come" (John 2:4). Now that his hour had come, he and his mother had something very important in common, the same suffering. In those last moments in which even the Father mysteriously withdrew from his human gaze, Jesus had only his mother's gaze from which to draw solace and comfort. Would he who in Gethsemane prayed the three disciples to "remain and watch with me" (Matt 26:38) now disdain his mother's presence and comfort?

Standing upright by the cross, Mary's face was more or less on the same level as the face of Jesus hanging forward from the cross. When he said to her, "Woman, behold your son!" Jesus was certainly looking at her, as he didn't even need to use her name. Who could penetrate the mystery of that gaze between the mother and son at such a time? In every human suffering there is an intimate private aspect lived only by the family—by those united by ties of blood. This was also true for Jesus and Mary.

A tremendous suffering of joy passed from one to the other, like water from communicating vessels, and this joy came from the fact that there was no longer any resistance to pain in them. They had no defenses left against suffering, and they freely allowed themselves to be invaded to their very inmost selves. Peace had taken the place of struggle. They had become one with the suffering and the sin of the world. Jesus had become so directly insofar as he was the victim of expiation for all the sins of the world (see 1 John 2:2), and Mary had become so indirectly because of her double union, of the flesh and spirit, with her son.

The last thing Jesus did on the cross when he exclaimed, "Father, into thy hands I commit my spirit!" (Luke 23:46) was to lovingly adore the Father's will before passing into the darkness of death. Mary knew she must follow him even in this, and so she too adored God's inscrutable and holy will before a dreadful solitude came upon her, which remained with her until her death.

3. *Staying Close to the Cross of Jesus*

Following as usual our guiding principle with Mary as the figure and mirror of the Church, its first flowering and model, we must now ask ourselves what the Holy Spirit wanted to say to the Church by deciding that Mary's presence and Jesus' words to her be recorded in Scripture. Mary, as I have said, is a living letter traced by God's own hand, a letter composed of so few words that we can't afford to lose even one of them.

Once again, it is God's own word that implicitly traces the passage from Mary to the Church and tells us what every believer has to do to imitate her: "Standing by the cross of Jesus was his Mother Mary and near her was the disciple whom he loved." The *parenesis* is contained in the *fact*. What took place that day indicates what should take place every day: we should stay near Mary close to the cross of Jesus, just as the disciple he loved did.

Two things are concealed in this sentence. First, we should stay "close to the cross," and second, we should stay close to the cross "of Jesus." Let us examine them separately, beginning with the second, which is the more important.

Staying close to the cross "of Jesus." These words tell us that the first and most important thing to do is not just to stay close to the cross but to stay close to the cross "of Jesus." It is not sufficient to stay close to the cross in sorrow and silence. No! This might even seem heroic, and yet it is not the most important thing. It may not even signify anything. The vital thing is to stay close to the cross "of Jesus." In other words, what counts is not one's own cross but Christ's cross. It is not suffering that counts but believing, thereby making Christ's sufferings our own. The main thing is faith. The greatest thing about Mary beneath the cross was her faith, which was even greater than her suffering. St. Paul said the cross is the power and wisdom of God to us who are being saved (see 1 Cor 1:18, 24), and he said that the gospel is the power of God "to everyone who has faith" (Rom 1:16). It is, therefore, for all those who are being saved or have faith and not for those who suffer, even if, as we shall see, both things are usually linked. This is the source of the strength and fecundity of the Church. The strength of the Church comes from preaching the cross of Jesus, which is the very symbol of folly and weakness in the eyes of the world, thereby rejecting any possibility or desire to face the incredulous and unthinking world with its own means, such as the wisdom of speech, the force of argument, irony, ridicule, sarcasm, and all the other "strong things" of the world (see 1 Cor 1:27). It is necessary to renounce human superiority so that the divine power of Christ's cross can be seen. We must insist on this point because there is still need. The majority of believers have never been helped to grasp this mystery, which is the heart of the New Testament and of the kerygma and which changes one's life.

Staying close to the cross. What is the sign and proof that we really believe in Christ's cross and that the "word of the cross" is not just a word, an abstract principle, a fine piece of theology or ideology, but truly the cross? The sign and proof is this: that you take up your cross and follow Jesus (see Mark 8:34). This sign is to suffer with him (see Phil 3:10; Rom 8:17), be crucified with him (see Gal 2:20), to complete in one's sufferings what is lacking in Christ's afflictions (see Col 1:24). The Christian's whole life must be a living sacrifice like Christ's (see Rom 12:1). It is not only a question of passively accepted suffering but suffering that is also active and looked for: "I pommel my body and subdue it" (1 Cor 9:27).

I insist on this point, as our aim in these meditations is usually to make a synthesis of what has gradually become split in the Church when it should be kept united. Mary is the best symbol of a Church not yet divided or split into denominations or schools of thought, and she can therefore help us to find unity again by first of all making us desire unity.

In fact, there are different ways in the Church of considering the cross and passion of Christ. One of these, characteristic of Protestant theology, is based on faith and appropriation. It is based on the cross of Christ and wants no other boast that is not the cross of Christ. The second, cultivated at least in the past particularly by Catholic theology, insists on suffering together with Christ, on sharing his passion, and as in the case of certain saints, of actually experiencing in themselves the passion of Christ.

It is of vital importance therefore to keep these two different views united. Where the cross is concerned, just as for grace and faith, we are called upon to restore Christian faith to its "wholeness," overcoming the false antitheses that, in certain periods, abuse and deviation led to. True and deep ecumenism begins where these gifts are brought together again and the lost equilibrium

103

restored. God's word teaches us that the important thing is not to choose one or the other of these attitudes but to keep both of them, faith and imitation, united. Naturally, it is not a question of placing God's work and ours on the same level but of accepting the word of Scripture, which says that one—be it faith or works—without the other is a dead thing (see Jas 2:14 ff.).

We might say that the problem really concerns faith. It is faith in the cross of Christ that needs to be put to the test for suffering to be real. St. Peter said that suffering is the crucible of faith, that faith is made genuine by suffering trials, as gold is tested by fire (see 1 Pet 1:6-7). In other words, our cross is not in itself salvation or power or wisdom; in itself it is simply human, or even punishment. It becomes the power and wisdom of God inasmuch as it unites us to the cross of Christ, the will of God himself. "Suffering means becoming particularly sensitive and open to the work of God's saving power, given to man in Christ."[6] Suffering unites us to the cross of Christ not only intellectually but also existentially and physically; it is a sort of channel, a means of access, to the cross of Christ, not parallel with faith but one with it.

Can the desire to suffer with Christ and participate in his sufferings lead to the human boast of good works? Certainly, but the risk of boasting unfortunately exists and is even perhaps more insidious when one wishes to pursue faith in its pure state. We can glory in our faith as in our sufferings, and this is more dangerous, as it is more subtle and difficult to realize. It would be very ingenuous to think otherwise, and it would mean we believe that human boasting hasn't interfered, that there is no sense of superiority, no trace of human wisdom in all that has been said by theologians in the past about "faith only" or the "theology of the cross."

Yet it is not said that embracing the cross and doing penance necessarily give rise to boasting. In these cases it is the cross itself that makes us want to get rid of the feeling of pride. True suffering with Christ kills vainglory at least as much as true faith kills it. There is even the chance of boasting in a good way about one's sufferings, and St. Paul himself gave us an example of this: "I will all the more gladly boast of my weaknesses. . . . For the sake of Christ, then, I am content with weaknesses, insults" (2 Cor 12:9 ff.). For the sake of Christ, not because Christ suffered for me! The same apostle gave such great importance to "our affliction" as to exclaim, "It is preparing for us an eternal weight of glory beyond all comparison" (2 Cor 4:17).

4. *The Cross That Separates and Unites*

If we are going to stay close to the cross of Jesus with Mary, we must constantly increase our knowledge of the mystery of the cross to relive it. In St. Paul's letters there is an apparent contrast concerning the power of the cross of Christ. In one set of letters, especially in the so-called proto-Pauline letters (appertaining to the early period of the apostle's preaching), the cross is, above all, what divides and separates. In fact, it separates what belongs to the spirit from what is of the flesh (see Gal 5:24), what belongs to faith from what is of the law (see Gal 5:11), the old self from the new one (see Rom 6:6), believers from nonbelievers, Christians from Jews and Greeks (see 1 Cor 1:18 ff.), and the Christian himself from the world: "The world has been crucified to me, and I to the world" (Gal 6:14). Between the Christian and the world there is the cross.

In another set of letters, the so-called deutero-Pauline letters (appertaining to the second period of the apostle's preaching or, according to some, to one of his disciples or imitators), the cross is what unites, what breaks down the walls of hostility, reconciles men among themselves and with God. To realize this it is sufficient to read the following text from the Letter to the Ephesians, which belongs to this set:

> But now in Christ Jesus
> you who once were far off
> have been brought near in the blood of Christ.
> For he is our peace,
> who has made us both one,
> and has broken down the dividing wall of hostility,
> by abolishing in his flesh
> the law of commandments and ordinances,
> that he might create in himself one new man in place of two,
> so making peace,
> and might reconcile us both to God in one body
> through the cross,
> thereby bringing the hostility to an end.
> And he came and preached peace to you
> who were far off and peace to those who were near;

for through him we both have access
in one Spirit to the Father (Eph 2:13-18).

Thanks to the cross of Christ those who were far off have been
brought near, the dividing wall has been broken down, all are
united. In ancient Christianity it was from this text that the symbolism of the cosmic cross developed, in which the cross is seen
as a tree keeping the whole universe united: "This tree of heavenly
dimensions rose up from earth to heaven, the foundation of all
things, support of the universe, holder of the whole world, cosmic bond keeping unstable human nature united and securing it
with the invisible nails of the Spirit so that, firmly gripped to the
divinity it can no longer break away. With its top branches touching the sky and its roots firmly set in the earth, it holds in its infinite embrace the many and intermediate spirits of the air."[7]

According to this symbolism, the transversal or horizontal arm
of the cross, reunites all that is divided on earth: the Gentiles and
the Jews, man and woman, the free man and the slave. The vertical beam reunites the whole world, already reconciled in itself,
to God; it unites the earth to heaven, man to God, so that thanks
to the cross, "we both have access in one Spirit to the Father."
(In this way we can see, unfortunately, how distant from the spirit
of the New Testament is the fact that in certain icons of the
crucifixion like the one described earlier, an angel can be seen
in one corner pushing the Church toward the cross while another
angel is moving the Synagogue away from it. In the text from
Ephesians we are told that Christ died to unite Jews and Gentiles
as one people and not to divide them.)

Two different ways, therefore, of conceiving the role of the
cross: one separating, the other uniting. But there is no contradiction, either in St. Paul or in the New Testament. The cross is both
these things together. It distinguishes in order to unite. It separates
from the world to unite to God; it rescues from corruption and
unites all those who accept being crucified with Christ. It over-
comes all differences, revealing their relative and secondary nature
before the new radical difference, which distinguishes the friends
from the "enemies of the cross of Christ" (Phil 3:18).

Therefore we must be wary on this point, too, of the temptation to split the Bible and take what best suits us or our own theological tradition. "Let man not separate what God has joined!"
We must gratefully embrace both the proto-Pauline and deutero-
Pauline views.

106

The cross separates and divides. This is true: it is the tool God uses to prune the shoots of the great vine of the body of Christ so that they may bear fruit. Michelangelo said that sculpture is the art of taking away, and holiness is reached in the same way, by the art of taking away, getting rid of the useless pieces: the desires and inclinations of the flesh, which clothe the new self. One day, strolling in a garden in Florence, the great Florentine sculptor saw a half-covered slab of marble abandoned in a corner. He stopped all of a sudden as if he had seen someone and exclaimed, "There's an angel trapped in that slab and I want to get him out." And he seized the chisel. God, too, sees us as we are, like that piece of rough marble covered in soil, and says, "The image of my Son is hidden in there; there's a beautiful new creature in there and I want to get it out!" And this is what he uses the cross for.

But above all the cross unites. It unites us one to the other. It makes us understanding and caring. Whoever suffers often becomes less egoistic and sees the needs of others; he is no longer impervious to compassion.

However, the cross unites us especially to God. St. Bonaventure illustrated this most impressively in his *Soul's Journey into God,* in which he traced the ascent of the soul to God, which he described in seven degrees. In the first, the soul approaches God through his vestiges visible in the universe; in the second, through his very presence in the universe; in the third, through his similitude imprinted in man's natural powers; in the fourth, through his image restored in man by grace; in the fifth, through the contemplation of the unity of God; in the sixth, through the contemplation of the Trinity of God. The seventh level remains: what could be higher than the Trinity? Where did Bonaventure see the effective union between God and man taking place?

At this point the saint brings the reader back to earth, to Calvary, points to the cross and says: This is the way, the means, the place!

> It's up to the soul to transcend and pass over not only this sense world but even itself. In this passing over, Christ is the way and the door, Christ is the ladder and the vehicle, like the Mercy Seat placed above the ark of God (Exod 25:21), and the mystery hidden from eternity (Eph 1:9). Whosoever turns his face fully to the Mercy Seat and with faith, hope and love, devotion, admiration, exultation, appreciation, praise and joy be-

107

holds him hanging upon the cross, such a one makes the Pasch, that is, the Passover, with Christ. By the staff of the cross he passes over the Red Sea, going from Egypt into the desert, where he will taste the hidden manna.[8]

This way of seeing the cross goes back to remote Christianity. In the hymn to the cosmic cross mentioned earlier, we find written:

This tree is for me eternal salvation: it feeds me and I pasture in it. In its roots I sink my roots, in its branches I spread my arms, in its dew I become inebriated, in its spirit, as in a caressing breeze, I am made fecund. In its shadow I have placed my tent and I have found shade from the summer's heat. In its flowers I blossom, in its fruits I find my delight and I freely gather the fruits destined for me from the beginning. This tree nourishes my hunger, sates my thirst and clothes my nakedness. Its leaves are the spirit of life and not fig leaves. This tree is my safeguard when I fear God. I lean against it when I am about to fall, a reward in battle, a trophy in victory. For me this tree is the narrow path, the narrow way; it is Jacob's ladder and the way of the angels on whose summit the Lord rests.[9]

5. *"He hoped against all hope"*

In spite of all that can be said of it, the power of the cross is not enough in itself. The paschal mystery doesn't consist either in the cross of Christ taken by itself or in the resurrection taken by itself and not even in both taken together, one after the other, juxtaposed and combined. It consists in *passing* from one to the other, from death to life, in passing from death to glory and the kingdom (see Luke 24:26; Acts 14:22). It consists therefore in something dynamic, not static, in a movement or event that, as such, cannot be interrupted without being destroyed.

The difficulties of the intellect to reconcile two opposite concepts can be noticed here. The wedge of dialectics has also touched this last nucleus of the faith, separating and at times opposing the death and resurrection, the theology of the cross and the theology of glory. If in the past Christ's victory in the resurrection was sometimes emphasized to the point of overshadowing the importance of the cross, nowadays the tendency is to go to the opposite extreme, exalting the theology of the cross to the point of suspicion toward the theology of glory, as if this could mitigate

Great Panagia *(all holy) (13th century)*
Tretjakov Gallery, Moscow

Virgin of Tenderness, Vladimir (early 12th century)
Tretjakov Gallery, Moscow

Crucifixion, school of Dionisij (15th century)
Tretjakov Gallery, Moscow

Ascension, school of Rublev (15th century)
Tretjakov Gallery, Moscow

the cross and deviate the Church from its mission. Even Protestant theology—a pioneer in the theology of the cross—reacted to this view. Someone wrote that "the unilateral emphasis on the cross unfortunately precluded protestant theology from comprehending the fullness of the New Testament message."[10]

It is not exact, for example, when quoting Romans 3:25, to say that for St. Paul justification depended on the cross alone because, elsewhere, he clearly related this same justification to the resurrection of Christ (see Rom 4:25) and said that without the resurrection we would still be in our sins (see 1 Cor 15:17). Church, faith, justification, and forgiveness of sins: to the apostle all these depended together on the death and resurrection, on the one paschal mystery. It is a question of embracing all the texts and not just one of them.

It could be thought, at times, that contemplating the death and resurrection together on Calvary, as St. John did, might lessen the harshness of the cross of Jesus, almost as if he went toward his death certain of the resurrection, like someone who knew he had an ace up his sleeve that he could produce at the right moment. This would denote a lack of attention to God's ways as they are revealed in the lives of the saints. Jesus, as man, was conscious of one thing only: that his path was guided by the Father and that the ultimate victory, however things went, would be the Father's and not his enemy's, a victory of love and not of hatred. The Gospels unanimously attest to the fact that Jesus' trust in the Father never wavered to the very end, that he didn't die desperate but obedient. St. Paul said that it was exactly because of this obedience that God highly exalted him (see Phil 2:11). If the essential link between Good Friday and the Easter resurrection is not in Christ's *power,* it is, however, in his *obedience.* In the Acts of the Apostles, Peter applied the words of the psalm to the dying Christ: "My flesh will dwell in hope. For thou wilst not abandon my soul to Hades" (Acts 2:26-27). Also, the well-known psalm that Jesus spoke from the cross ("My God, my God, why hast thou forsaken me?") ends in a cry of hope: "Posterity shall serve him; men shall tell of the Lord to the coming generation."

All of this can be applied to Mary in a secondary way. To say that on Calvary she went through the whole paschal mystery and not through just half of it is to say that she was close to the cross "in hope." That she shared not only death with her Son but also hope in the resurrection. An image of Mary beneath the cross such as the one we get from the *Stabat Mater,* in which Mary is only "sad, afflicted, sorrowful," would not be complete. It wouldn't take into account that it was John who shows her there and that the cross signified glory and victory to him. On Calvary, she was not just the "Mother of sorrows" but also the "Mother of hope," *Mater spei,* as the Church invokes her in one of its hymns.

Scripture tells us: "By faith Abraham, when he was tested, offered up Isaac, and he who had received the promises was ready to offer up his only son, of whom it was said; 'Through Isaac shall your descendants be named.' He considered that God was able to raise men even from the dead; hence he did receive him back, and this was a symbol" (Heb 11:17-19). We may wonder what Isaac was a symbol of. According to an exegetic tradition that goes back to the very beginning of the Church, he was the figure of the passion and resurrection of Christ. And if Isaac was the figure of Christ, Abraham, who was to immolate his son, was the figure, in heaven, of God the Father and, on earth, of Mary the mother.

St. Paul affirmed that in this predicament Abraham "in hope believed against hope" (Rom 4:18). With all the more reason we must say the same about Mary beneath the cross: in hope she believed against hope. To hope against hope means this: "without having any reason whatsoever for hope, in a situation that, humanly speaking, is entirely hopeless and in total contrast with the promise made, one never ceases to hope solely in virtue of the word of hope, uttered at the time by God."[11]

In an inexplicable way, which perhaps she was unable to explain to herself, Mary too, just as Scripture says of Abraham, believed that God was able to raise her son "even from the dead." One must completely ignore how bold hope can be to think that what we say of Mary is excessive. One of the texts of Vatican Council II mentions Mary's hope beneath the cross as a determining factor of her maternal calling. It says that beneath the cross, "in an utterly singular way she cooperated by her obedience, faith, hope, and burning charity in the Savior's work."[12]

6. *Accomplices of the Child Hope*

Now, in line with the second part of the paschal mystery, let us look at the Church and at us ourselves: "Our passage from death to life by faith is fulfilled through hope in the resurrection to come and in the final glory," St. Augustine said. Of the three events commemorated by the Church in the paschal triduum— the crucifixion, burial, and resurrection of the Lord—"we, in our present life, realize the significance of the crucifixion, whereas, through faith, we have hope in what the burial and resurrection signify."[13] The Church, like Mary, lives the resurrection "in hope." For it, too, the cross is an object of experience, whereas the resurrection is an object of hope. Mary, who was our guide to faith in the incarnation, is therefore our guide to hope in the paschal mystery.

Just as Mary was close to her crucified son, so the Church is called to be close to the crucified of today: the poor, the suffering, the humiliated, the insulted. How can the Church stay close to these? In hope, like Mary. It is not enough to pity their sufferings or even to try to alleviate them. This would be too little. Anyone can do this, even those who know nothing of the resurrection. The Church must transmit hope, proclaiming that suffering is not absurd, that it is meaningful, because there will be a resurrection after death. She must give the reason for the hope that she has (see 1 Pet 3:15). More than meditation on his earlier life, it was the light of Easter morning that gradually revealed to the first Christian community the meaning of Christ's disconcerting death. And even today, it is only in the light of Christ's resurrection and in the hope of ours that we can understand the meaning of suffering and death. The cross is better understood by its effects than by its causes, which often remain mysterious and inexplicable to us.

People need hope to live just as they need oxygen to breathe. And so great is this need that you only have to mention the word "hope" to see people straighten and look, so to say, at your hands to see if by any chance you are holding something that could quench their thirst. We say there's life while there's hope, but it's also true that while there's hope there's life. In recent years, a sign of this need was the enthusiasm the theology of hope met with. Secular thought also dealt with hope, admittedly with secularized hope: the so-called Hope-principle. This shows the human capacity to hope for and plan a different earthly future, which is something quite different from what is meant by the theological virtue. This is a free gift, infused grace before being man's work, whose direct object is God and eternal life, not just a utopian earthly future. But at least this serves to prove that the world longs for hope, that it cannot do without it, and that if the great God-given hope collapses a smaller one must be invented to man's measure.

Hope has for a long time been, and still is today, the little sister, the poor relation, of the theological virtues. Faith is often spoken of and charity even more so, but we seldom talk of hope. Actually, in the history of Christianity, there have been those who (as in Quietism) felt the need to set hope aside with the excuse that, promising something in return, it would diminish charity or pure love; others who put it aside thinking it would diminish faith by attenuating its gratuitousness and obscurity. This only denotes that the nature of theological hope hasn't been understood. There is a type of pure hope based on God alone through which we hope for something almost more for God's sake than for ours, so that his faithfulness and goodness are not called into question. There is a "hoping against hope," like Mary's. At this depth, hope is no longer something man can use for his own purposes to alleviate darkness and suffering. "Lost is faith and dead is hope," St. Catherine of Genoa used to say from the depths of the dark night of her faith,[14] whereas in fact we know she just went on believing and hoping in increasing perfection.

There are two ways of really sinning against hope: despairing of salvation and presuming to be saved without merit: desperation and presumption. Here again we see the need to keep the cross and resurrection united. To suffer without the hope of being resurrected is desperation; to hope for resurrection without suffering is presumption.

I have often asked myself why hope is so precious to God that he keeps on asking us to hope in him, and I am gradually learning the answer. To go on hoping, despite the fact that things become ever more difficult and each time the evidence systematically belies what we expected, means believing more in God than in the evidence of facts; it means constantly acknowledging that God is right, giving him each time another possibility. It means giving him credit. I would even say that if, for some absurd reason, God hadn't at first thought of creating Paradise, he would have created it because his children hope in it. What father, discovering his child is sure he is going to receive a certain gift at Christmas that the father hadn't even thought of, wouldn't rush, if he could, to get it for him so as not to disappoint him? A human being may fear and not want too much hope placed in him because he knows his own limits and that, no matter how much he tries, he cannot always live up to what others expect of him. But this is not true of God; God doesn't have such problems. So, far from being put out by the fact that we can place too much hope in him, he wishes this and waits for it: "Hitherto you have asked for nothing," Jesus said (see John 16:24); "whatever you ask in prayer, believe that you receive it (this is hope!) and you will" (see Mark 11:24).

Hope encloses a profound mystery that becomes clear when we compare it to faith. Faith concerns God and his works, which are independent of us. God's existence is an object of faith, as is the fact that Jesus Christ is God and that he died for our sins. Also, the existence of eternal life is an object of faith. Whether we believe these or not won't stop them being true and existing. God exists even if I don't believe he does. Faith, therefore, believes in what already is. But the object of hope doesn't exist if I don't hope in it. I make it exist by hoping. Hope, in fact, concerns things God won't do without our free consent. The object of faith is God's existence. The object of hope is that I shall possess God, that God will be mine, that I shall live forever. However, all of this will never exist if I don't hope for it. God will never be mine. Hope is a constitutive aspect of our salvation. St. Paul's statement, "In this hope we were saved" (Rom 8:24), holds a deeper meaning than might appear at a first glance.

As Péguy our friend and poet said, we must become "accomplices of the child hope."[15] Perhaps there's something you've ardently hoped for, hoped that God would intervene, and nothing happened? The next time you hoped again and nothing happened? Things were just as before despite all your supplications and tears, maybe despite some indications that this time God would listen to you? You go on hoping again and again, you never cease to hope, right to the end. You have become an accomplice of hope. This means you allow God to delude you, deceive you on this earth as often as he wishes. More than that, it means being happy deep down in some remote corner of your heart that God didn't listen to you because, in this way, he has allowed you to show him another proof of your hope, to make yet another act of hope, which is increasingly more difficult for you each time. He has granted you a much greater grace than the one you asked for: the grace to hope in him.

However, we must remember that hope is not just a beautiful and poetic interior disposition, as difficult as you like, but that, when all is said and done, doesn't call for activity or specific tasks and is, therefore, in the end, pointless. On the contrary, to hope means precisely that there is still something we can do, a duty to be done, and that we are not, therefore, at the mercy of a vain or crippling inactivity. To hope in God in difficult situations means acknowledging that if, in spite of everything, a trial continues, the reason is not to be found in God—who is infinite love at all times—but in ourselves. And if the reason is in us, then there is still something we can do, there's still a duty to be done, otherwise it would really be a question of despair. Kierkegaard said:

> As man, in respect to God, always suffers in the position of offender, his motive for joy lies in the fact that there must always be something that can be done, a duty to be fulfilled. In doing this duty he has the hope that things can and will improve when he himself has improved and that is when he works harder, prays more and is more obedient, more humble and more abandoned to God, loves more deeply and is more fervent in spirit. And is this not a reason for joy? Yes, when there is nothing else to do, when not even suffering is left as a task, then there is desperation. As long as there is a duty, as long as there is some project, man is not left without hope. So even if the worst fate that has ever happened to a man happened to me, and I could do absolutely nothing about it, there would still be the joy of duty, the duty of being patient. And if patience beyond limits were required of any man, there is still the joy that there is a duty, the duty of not losing one's patience, even when one is at the end of one's endurance.[16]

Therefore, even when in vain we have done our utmost to change a difficult situation, we still have something great to do that will keep us occupied and keep desperation far from us, and that is to patiently endure to the end. This was the great thing that Mary did as she hoped beneath the cross, and she is now ready to help us do the same.

We can find some real surges and unexpected feelings of hope in the Bible. There is one, for example, in the third lamentation, the song of the soul in the most desolate trial, which can be entirely applied to Mary beneath the cross: "I am the one familiar with affliction. God has led and guided me into darkness, not light. He has walled me in so that I cannot escape. Even when

I shout for help, he shuts out my prayer. I thought: I have forgotten what happiness is, my lasting hope in God is lost." Here we find an unexpected surge of hope, and the situation changes. At a certain point the worshiper says to himself: "Surely God's mercies are not over; so I shall put my hope in him! For the Lord will not reject anyone forever. If he brings grief, he will have pity. Maybe there is hope" (see Lam 3:1-32).

I shall put my hope in him! What glory for God and what comfort for man to be able to say these words each time! "I waited, I waited for God, then he stooped to me," one of the psalmists said, who, thanks to hope, had experienced a resurrection (Ps 40:1). Another psalmist said: "I wait for the Lord, my soul waits and in his word I hope" (Ps 130:5); "O Israel, hope in the Lord, from this time forth and forevermore" (Ps 131:3). The Letter to the Hebrews speaks of hope as an anchor we have in heaven, not on earth: "Let us seize the hope set before us. We have this as a sure and steadfast anchor of the soul, a hope that enters into the inner shrine behind the curtain, where Jesus has gone as a forerunner on our behalf" (Heb 6:18-19).

Let us now once again turn to Mary, who stayed close by the cross hoping against all hope. Let us learn to invoke her often as Mother of hope, and if, at this moment, we are distressed and tempted to discouragement, let us take hope and repeat to ourselves, "Surely God's mercies are not over; so I shall put my hope in him!"

NOTES

1. *Lumen gentium* 58.
2. St. Melito of Sardis, *Paschal Homily,* 7 and 71 (SCh 123, pp. 64, 98).
3. Romanus Melodus, *Hymn,* XXXV, 1 (SCh 128, p. 160).
4. *Lumen gentium* 58.
5. S. Kierkegaard, *Journals,* XI 1 A 45 (ed. cit., entry 364).
6. John Paul II, *Salvifici Doloris,* 23 (AAS 76, 1984, p. 231).
7. *Ancient Paschal Homily,* 51 (SCh 27, pp. 177).
8. St. Bonaventure, *The Soul's Journey into God,* VII, 1-2 (trans. E. Cousins, New York, Paulist Press, 1978, p. 111 f.).
9. *Ancient Paschal Homily* (Ps. Hippolytus), 51 (SCh 27, p. 177).
10. See W. Von Löwenich, *Luther's Theologia crucis,* Munich, 1954, p. 2.
11. H. Schlier, *Der Römerbrief,* Freiburg in Br., 1979, ad loc.
12. *Lumen gentium* 61.

13. St. Augustine, *Letter,* 55, 2, 3; 14, 24 (CSEL 34, 2, p. 171, 195).
14. St. Catherine of Genoa, *Life,* 19 (Turin, 1962, p. 207).
15. Ch. Péguy, *The Porch of the Mystery of the Second Virtue,* in *Oeuvres Poétiques Complètes,* cit., p. 655.
16. S. Kierkegaard, *The Gospel of Sufferings,* IV.

Chapter VI

"Woman, Behold Your Son!"

Mary, the mother of believers

In this chapter we shall reflect on the second part of the text in John's Gospel: "When Jesus saw his mother, and the disciple whom he loved standing near, he said to his mother, 'Woman, behold, your son!' Then he said to the disciple, 'Behold, your mother!' And from that hour the disciple took her to his own home" (John 19:26-27).

We concluded our considerations on Mary in the mystery of the incarnation with a meditation on Mary as God's mother. Now we shall conclude our reflections on Mary in the paschal mystery by contemplating her as Mother of Christians, as our mother.

1. *"Let each one live according to the grace received"*

We must immediately state that we are not dealing with two titles and two truths on the same level. "Mother of God" is a solemnly defined title; it is based on a real maternity. It has a close and even essential connection with the main truth of our faith, that Jesus is both God and man in the same person, and, finally, it is a title received by the Church at large. "Mother of the faithful," or "our mother" indicates a spiritual maternity. It is not so closely connected to the main truths of the faith. We can't say it has been a truth held by all Christians, everywhere and always, but it reflects the doctrine and devotion of some Churches, especially of the Catholic Church.

St. Augustine helps us to immediately grasp the similarities and differences between the two maternities. "Physically, Mary is only the Mother of Jesus, whereas spiritually, in that she does God's will, she is both his sister and mother. She wasn't a Mother in spirit of the Head, who is also the Savior, from whom rather she was born but she certainly is a mother in spirit to us, the members, because by her charity she cooperated within the Church in the birth of the faithful who are members of that same Head."[1]

The difference between the two titles given to Mary, "Mother of God" and "Mother of Christians," indicates that we can, rather, must, acknowledge a certain freedom in the various Christian Churches concerning the second title—really reflecting piety and devotion more than dogma—which as we shall see, although strongly based on the Word of God, does not hold the same meaning for everyone. In this meditation, we should like to aim at bringing to light all the richness, and Christ's gift, enclosed in this title so that we may use it not only to honor Mary by attributing to her yet another title but to edify our faith and grow in the imitation of Christ. We should also like to make this title and what it means to us Catholics comprehensible to our Protestant brethren, who don't accept this and other titles given to Mary that indicate her active participation in the redemption and life of the Church.

It would seem the right moment now to recall what Scripture says of the diverse particular gifts, or charisms, that exist in the body of Christ: "As each has received a gift, employ it for one another, as good stewards of God's varied grace" (1 Pet 4:10). These words are not only applicable to individuals in the Church but also to whole sectors of it and to the various currents of thought and traditions that have developed in it. Seen thus, it means, let each Church live according to the special grace received, humbly putting it at the service of the other Churches like good stewards of a God-given grace too great and rich to be enclosed in one form alone.

A certain way of fostering devotion to Mary is a special charism and grace existing in the Catholic Church and shared in great part by the Eastern Church, which these Churches must foster for other Christians without necessarily expecting them to do the same, just as a certain way of fostering Scripture, the written Word of God, was a special gift given to the Reformation Churches and which now the Catholic Church benefits from.

According to the Word of God mentioned earlier, the two things asked in these cases are first of all, to live according to the grace received, to foster this grace and make it bear fruit; secondly, to put it at the service of others. That is exactly what we intend to do now. Seen in this way, the fact that the title "Mother of believers" is not binding for all doesn't make it any less relevant for us. In a certain sense it makes it even more so. We have the responsibility of preserving this grace for others, too.

2. *"We were all born there"*

Like physical maternity, spiritual maternity takes place in two different acts and moments: conception and birth. Neither on its own is sufficient. Mary experienced both of these moments: she spiritually conceived us and gave us birth. She conceived us, that is, welcomed us, when—perhaps even at the moment of her calling at the annunciation and certainly afterward as Jesus gradually advanced in his mission—she learned that her son wasn't like other sons, a private person, but "the first-born among many brethren" (Rom 8:29), that others were following him, a community was being formed.

Following our method of analogy from below, we could think of certain wonderful mothers of priests who founded religious orders, for example, Don Bosco's mother. At a certain point these mothers found their homes crowded every day with groups of the "little friends" or "poor children" their sons brought home to feed. They quietly organized themselves according to the new needs, preparing food and shelter for those friends, and even doing their washing for them as if they, too, were their children.

However, in Mary's case the problem went deeper. These newly arrived people were called brothers, sisters, and mothers by her son. Of them, he said: "I say to you, as you did it [clothe, feed, visit] to one of the least of these my brethren, you did it to me" (Matt 25:40). During those years, whenever Mary heard or was told what her son went about saying, "Come to me, all who labor and are heavy laden. . ." (Matt 11:28), she knew she couldn't hold back and refuse to welcome as her own all those her son invited without ceasing to be his mother in the spiritual sense.

All of this was, therefore, the time of conception, of a heartfelt yes. Now, beneath the cross, it was the time of travail. Jesus, at this moment, addressed his mother as "Woman." Even if we can't be certain, but knowing that John the evangelist, besides being direct in speech also made use of allusions, symbols, and references, these words make us think of what Jesus said: "A woman in childbirth suffers because her time has come" (John 16:21), and of what Revelation says: "A woman, crying out in the pangs

119

of labor" (Rev 12:1 ff.). Even if this woman was first of all the Church, the community of the new covenant giving birth to the new man and a new world, Mary was nevertheless personally involved as the beginning and the representative of this community of believers. At any rate, the comparison between Mary and the Woman was accepted by the Church very early on—already by St. Irenaeus, a disciple of St. Polycarp, one of John's disciples, when he saw Mary as the new Eve, the new "mother of all the living."

Let us now turn to John's text to see if there is any reference to what we have been saying. The words of Jesus to Mary, "Woman, behold your son," and those to John, "Behold, your mother," hold a direct and real meaning. Jesus entrusted Mary to John and John to Mary. A meaning, this, that we must not disregard, as it contains an important message about the Mother of God's spiritual pilgrimage. Once again, she appears as the woman pilgrim and stranger in this world, as one who allowed herself to be "placed" by God. At the moment of her son's birth, when God's Word had placed her in a situation of total solitude, God told Joseph to take care of her: "Joseph, son of David, do not fear to take Mary your wife" (Matt 1:20). And when Joseph woke from sleep, he took her as his wife. Now, at the moment of her son's death, once again alone in the world, God told John to take care of her, and John "from that hour took her to his home." Mary was truly the uprooted woman, who from beginning to end allowed God to rule her life. Mary, indeed, appears to be "Madonna Poverty."

Yet this is not the full significance of the scene. Modern exegesis, which has made enormous progress in understanding the language and expressions of the Fourth Gospel, is even more convinced of this than the Fathers were. If you simply read the passage straight through, only as his last testamentary disposition, it would appear, it has been said, as a fish out of water or, rather, as clashing with the rest of the context. For John, the moment of death was the moment of the glorification of Jesus, the final fulfillment of Scripture and all things. Immediately preceding the words about Mary, the title "King of Jews" is mentioned, clearly alluding to its prophetic and meaningful significance; mention is made of the tunic without seams (see John 19:23 f.), which appears to recall the high priest's tunic, which was also woven without seams (see Exod 28:31 ff.) and which is the fulfillment of a prophecy. Immediately following those words, we read that Jesus "gave up his spirit," that is, he died but also that he gave out the Holy Spirit. This fact is also indicated by the episode that follows of the water and blood, seen in the light of what John wrote in his first letter: "There are three witnesses, the Spirit, the water, and the blood" (1 John 5:7-8). The pierced side refers to Ezekiel's prophecy on the new temple from whose side water issued (see Ezek 47:1 ff.); in fact, Jesus himself spoke of his body destroyed and raised as being the new temple (see John 2:19 f.).

Therefore, given the context, it would be straining the text if we were to see only a private and personal significance and not, in accordance with traditional exegesis, a more universal and ecclesial significance linked, in some way, to the Woman in Genesis 3:15 and in Revelation 12. The ecclesial significance is that the disciple was not simply representing John but the disciple of Jesus as such, that is, all his disciples. The dying Jesus gave them to Mary as her sons just as Mary was given to them as their mother.

The words of Jesus often describe something already present, they reveal what exists; at other times, instead, they create and bring into existence what they express. The words of the dying Jesus to Mary and John are of the second type. Like when he said, "This is my body," Jesus made the bread his body, and when he said, "Behold, your mother" and "Behold, your son," Jesus made Mary John's mother and John Mary's son. He didn't just proclaim Mary's new maternity, he instituted it. It doesn't, therefore, come from Mary but from God's Word; it is not founded on merit but on grace.

Beneath the cross, Mary therefore appears as the daughter of Zion, who after the death and loss of her sons received a new and more numerous family from God, but by the Spirit and not the flesh. A psalm, which the liturgy applies to Mary, says: "Behold, Philistia and Tyre, with Ethiopia—'This one was born there.' Of Zion it shall be said, 'This one and that one were born in her. . . .' The Lord records as he registers the peoples, 'This one was born there' " (Ps 87:2 ff.). And it is indeed true, we were all born there! It shall be said of Mary, the new Zion, this one and that one were born in her. Of me, of you, and each person, even of those who do not know it yet, it is written in God's register, "This one was born there."

But haven't we been "born anew through the living and abid-

121

ing Word of God" (1 Pet 1:23)? Haven't we been "born of God" (John 1:13), born anew of "water and the Spirit" (John 3:5)? This is all very true, but it doesn't take from the fact that in another sense, subordinate and instrumental, we are also born of Mary's faith and suffering. If St. Paul, as Christ's servant and apostle, could say to his followers, "I became your father in Christ Jesus through the Gospel" (1 Cor 4:15), how much more can Mary say, I became your mother in Christ! Who has more right to use the apostle's words, "My little children, with whom I am again in travail" (Gal 4:19)? She gave us birth anew beneath the cross, because she had already given us birth a first time, in joy and not in suffering, when she gave the world the "living and abiding Word," Christ, in whom we are born again.

God's promises don't refer to abstract things, or to towns or walls. They refer to real people of whom all these things are symbols and images. And if they refer to real persons, who could the words of the psalm just quoted refer more to, or in whom were they more realized, than in Mary, the humble daughter of Zion? She was also, chronologically speaking, the beginning of the remnant (see Rom 11:5) to which the promises were destined.

Therefore, just as we applied to Mary beneath the cross the lamentation of the ruined Zion, which had drunk the chalice of divine wrath, now, trusting in the power and endless richness of God's Word, which goes well beyond exegetical schemes, we apply to her the hymn of Zion rebuilt after exile, as, full of wonder, it gazes upon its new children and exclaims: "Who has borne me these? I was bereaved and barren, but who has brought up these?" (Isa 49:21).

We are dealing with an objective and not a subjective application, as it is not based on whether or not Mary thought of these words at that moment (most likely, she didn't) but on the fact that these words, by God's design, were objectively realized in her. A spiritual reading of Scripture, done with the Church and within the Church, reveals all this to us, and what a deprivation for those who never do this! In fact, they lose the spirit and content themselves with the letter only. Modern interpretation has formulated an interesting principle: to understand a text we cannot disregard the results obtained or the resonance it has had in history *(Wirkungsgeschichte)*. This is even truer of the texts from Holy Scripture; they can only be understood in content and virtuality from the results in history, first in Israel and then in the

Church, and from the life and light they give forth. This is especially true of texts like the one we are studying. This history of realization is what the Church calls tradition.

3. *The Marian Synthesis in Vatican Council II*

The traditional Catholic doctrine on Mary, Mother of Christians, was newly expressed in the constitution on the Church of Vatican Council II, where Mary's role is inserted into the wider theme of the history of salvation and the mystery of Christ. It states that

> the Blessed Virgin was eternally predestined, in conjunction with the incarnation of the divine Word, to be the Mother of God. By decree of divine Providence, she served on earth as the loving mother of the divine Redeemer, an associate of unique nobility, and the Lord's humble handmaid. She conceived, brought forth and nourished Christ. She presented him to the Father in the temple, and was united with him in suffering as he died on the cross. In an utterly singular way she cooperated by her obedience, faith, hope and burning charity in the Savior's work of restoring supernatural life to souls. For this reason she is a mother to us in the order of grace.[2]

The council itself undertook to explain Mary's maternal role by stating: "The maternal duty of Mary toward men in no way obscures or diminishes the unique mediation of Christ, but rather shows its power. For all the saving influences of the Blessed Virgin on men originate, not from some inner necessity, but from the divine pleasure. They flow forth from the superabundance of the merits of Christ, rest on his mediation, depend entirely on it and draw all their power from it. In no way do they impede the immediate union of the faithful with Christ. Rather, they foster their union."[3]

Besides the titles "Mother of God" and "Mother of the faithful," the council also used the terms "model" and "figure" to illustrate Mary's role: "Through the gift and role of divine maternity, Mary is united with her Son, the Redeemer, and with his singular graces and offices. By these, the Blessed Virgin is also singularly united with the Church. As St. Ambrose taught us, the

Mother of God is a model of the Church, in the matter of faith, charity and perfect union with Christ."[4]

In the light of these texts and of what has been said so far, we can now summarize Mary's dual role with Jesus and in the Church. She is the *mother and disciple* of Jesus and she is the *mother and teacher,* or model, or exemplary figure, of the Church. With Paul, and more than Paul, she can truly say, "Be imitators of me as I am of Christ" (1 Cor 11:1). In fact, she is our model and teacher simply because she is the perfect disciple and imitator of Christ.

The novelty of this teaching on Mary is, as we know, its inclusion in the constitution on the Church. As is inevitable in such cases, it was not without suffering and conflict that the council deeply renewed the conventional Mariology of the last centuries. Mary is no longer treated separately, as if her role were intermediary between Christ and the Church. She has been linked again with the Church, just as in the days of the Fathers. As St. Augustine said, Mary is seen as the most noble member of the Church but still a member of it and not outside or above it. "Holy is Mary, blessed is Mary, but the Church is more important than the Virgin Mary. Why is this so? Because Mary is part of the Church, a holy and excellent member, above all others but, nevertheless, a member of the whole body. And if she is a member of the whole body, doubtlessly the body is more important than a member of the body."[5]

However, this did not impede the council from emphasizing the unique relation between Christ and Mary, his mother, which is not shared by the rest of the Church. In fact, the document on her is called "The Role of the Blessed Virgin Mary, Mother of God, in the Mystery of Christ and the Church." Not only, let us note, in the mystery of the Church but in the mystery of Christ too, as the incarnate Word.

Immediately after the council, Paul VI further developed the idea of Mary's maternity for believers and solemnly and explicitly honored her with the title "Mother of the Church": "To the glory of the Virgin and for our solace, We proclaim the most Holy Mary as Mother of the Church, of all God's people, both the faithful and pastors, who invoke her as their most loving Mother. May this most gentle name make the Virgin ever more honored and invoked by all Christians."[6]

4. *Mary, the Mother of the Faithful, in the Light of Ecumenism*

Let us now try to understand the meaning of the titles "Mother of the faithful" and "Mother of the Church" from a biblical point of view, in the hope of rendering this Catholic belief more comprehensible and no longer offensive to our Protestant brethren.

I would first of all like to clarify the basic principle of these reflections. If, as we have seen, Mary is basically linked with the Church, it follows that the biblical texts used to explain her role should be those relative to the human persons constituting the Church and applied to her *a fortiori,* rather than those relative to the divine persons or to Christ and applied to her by way of reduction. For example, for a more correct understanding of the delicate concept of Mary's mediation in the work of salvation, it would, perhaps, be better to start with the creature role, from below, so to say, for example, with Abraham, St. Paul, the apostles, rather than with the divine-human mediation of Christ. In fact, the greatest distance is not the one that exists between Mary and the rest of the Church but that which exists between Mary and the Church on the one hand and Christ and the Trinity on the other hand: between creatures and Creator. It is not possible, or at least it is risky, to build a Christology from below, starting with man rather than with God, as "no one has ascended into heaven but he who descended from heaven" (John 3:13). No one can postulate the dignity of God for Christ if he isn't acknowledged as God right from the beginning. God in fact can become a man if he wants to, but man cannot become God. Instead, it is duly possible to attempt a study of Mariology from below. There was a time when practically all the titles and prerogatives of Mary were established deductively from a dogmatic principle. Now, in the light of the documents of Vatican Council II, we prefer to use the process of induction, starting with the Word of God.

The first of these analogies from below found in the Bible is between Mary and Abraham. We have briefly referred to the comparison between Abraham and Mary several times. Now it is time to give this point greater consideration. It is quite singular that Christ is never called the new Abraham in the New Testament, whereas he is called or implicitly referred to as the new Adam, the new Isaac, the new Jacob, the new Moses, the new Aaron, and so on. It is really Isaac, the son, who is the figure of Christ. Abraham actually foreshadows Mary, not Christ, because he is father through his faith, and he represents faith, something that the New Testament never attributes to Jesus, whereas it does attribute it to Mary when it proclaims her blessed because of her belief (see Luke 1:45).

The comparison between Abraham's faith and Mary's is outlined in the story of the annunciation. When Mary told the angel she was a virgin, which contrasted with the promise, she was given the same answer (even clearer in the Septuagint text) as was given to Abraham when Sarah remarked on her age and barrenness: "With God nothing will be impossible" (Luke 1:37; Gen 18:14).[7]

But this correspondence is even clearer from the facts. In Abraham's life we notice two great acts of faith. First of all, he believed by faith when God promised him a son, even "when he considered his own body which was as good as dead or when he considered the barrenness of Sarah's womb" (Rom 4:19; see Heb 11:11), and secondly, "By faith Abraham, when he was tested, offered up Isaac and he who had received the promises was ready to offer up his only son" (Heb 11:17). Abraham, therefore, believed when God told him he would give him a son and when he told him to immolate his son. In Mary's life, too, there were two great acts of faith. She believed when God told her that she, a virgin, would give birth to a son who would be the heir of all the promises. And secondly, she believed when God asked her to be present at the immolation of the son he had given her. At this point light disappears and the human being really enters into the darkness of faith. God seems to belie himself, to forget his promises. It had been said, "He will be great and called the Son of the Most High," and, instead, he seemed crushed by abuse and blows; it had been said, "He will reign forever over the house of Jacob," and, instead, he was nailed to a cross! Mary must have hoped to the very end—because she, too, walked in faith and hope—that God would intervene, that the situation would change. She hoped after his arrest, when he was in front of Pilate, before the sentence was pronounced, and on Calvary before the first nail was struck; she hoped right up to the moment when, bowing his head, he gave up his spirit. But nothing happened!

Much more was asked of Mary than of Abraham. With Abraham, God stopped at the last moment and saved his son's life; he didn't do this with Mary but went beyond the point of no return, death. Here we can see the difference between the Old and the New Testament: "Abraham draws the knife and he gets Isaac again; it was not carried out in earnest; the highest earnestness was the 'test,' but then once again it became the joy of his life. It is different in the New Testament. The sword did not hang as if on a horsehair over the Virgin Mary's head in order to 'test' her to see if she would keep the obedience of faith in the crucial moment—no, it actually did penetrate her heart, stabbed her heart—but she got a claim upon eternity, which Abraham did not get."[8]

Let us now draw the conclusion to all of this. If Abraham deserved the name "Father" in the Bible for what he had done, (see Luke 16:24), "Father of us all," of all believers (see Rom 4:16), is it really so strange that Mary is called "Mother of us all" and "Mother of all believers"? The title wasn't attributed to Abraham in life. It was given later on, when his people meditated on his faith. Mary, too, was given the title later on by her people, the Church. During her life it was only noted that she believed in the fulfillment of the Lord's words. Abraham's title, "Father of all believers," is part of Scripture and therefore enjoys the benefit of a universal and unquestioned authority. But shouldn't the same title, given by the Church to Mary, at least enjoy the benefit of respect and pious devotion, seeing that it is based on the same Scripture?

However, the comparison between Abraham and Mary has something else to teach us, which doesn't concern only the title but also its content and meaning. Is the title "Mother of the faithful" simply an honorary title, or is it something more? Calvin interpreted in this way the text from Genesis, where God said to Abraham, "By you all the families of the earth shall bless themselves" (Gen 12:3): "Abraham will not only be an example and patron, but a source of blessing."[9] A well-known modern Protestant exegete wrote, in the same way: "The question has been raised (in relation to Gen 12:3) whether the meaning is simply that Abraham is only to become a formula for blessing, that his blessing is to become far and wide proverbial. . . . It is, however, hermeneutically wrong to limit such a programmatic saying, circulating in such exalted style, to only one meaning restrictively. . . . The accepted interpretation must therefore remain. It is like 'a command to history' (B. Jacob). Abraham is assigned the role of mediator of blessing in God's plan, for all the families of the earth."[10]

All of this is an enormous help in understanding what tradition, from St. Irenaeus on, says of Mary: that she is not a mere *example* of blessing and salvation but somehow—depending entirely on grace and God's will—she is also the *cause* (subordinate and instrumental, of course) of salvation: that her maternal role in the Church is not just one of honor or idiom. As St. Irenaeus wrote, "Just as Eve, being disobedient became the cause of death for herself and for the whole human race, so Mary . . . being obedient became the *cause of salvation* for herself and for the whole human race."[11]

My Protestant brethren, the words "All generations shall call me blessed" (Luke 1:48) were not put into Scripture by us Catholics but by the Holy Spirit! Should these words not also be taken as a command given by God to history, like the words uttered to Abraham: "By you all the families of the earth shall bless themselves"? If we attribute the role of mediator to Abraham, how can we possibly not attribute it more rightfully to Mary?

It is impossible to say that a real mediation, like Abraham's, was possible in the Old Testament economy but not in the New Testament, when we have the one unique mediator between God and men, the man Christ Jesus (see 1 Tim 2:5). In fact, even in the new covenant Christ's mediation doesn't exclude created and human mediations instituted by himself, such as the sacramental signs and the personal mediation of the apostles.

These observations are not made in the spirit of *ex ore tuo te iudico* (I judge you on your own words). They are made to demonstrate the indispensable contribution our Protestant brethren can make, with their sense of Scripture, to the edification of a common faith, including what concerns Mary in it. They are not a judgment on coherence or incoherence but rather an invitation to communion and a desire for it. It is, in fact, increasingly more obvious that the Bible will be the basis on which Catholics and Protestants can also find full communion where the Mother of God is concerned.

Actually, if in one respect Mary is part of the Church and has coherently been inserted into the constitution on the Church by Vatican Council II, in another respect she is an important chapter of Scripture and God's Word, and when explaining her, the document on revelation, *Dei Verbum,* must also be kept in mind. St. Gregory the Great said, "God, at times, instructs us through words, and at other times through works."[12] And a text of *Dei Verbum* states that the plan of revelation is realized in two ways, by works and words *(gestis verbisque).*[13] This emphasizes a well-known fact about the Bible: it doesn't contain only words but gestures and symbolic actions too, or even persons that are in themselves prophetic. Mary is one of those prophetic persons and as such is a channel of revelation, not only and not so much because of what she says but because of what she does and is. In her own way Mary, too, is a "visible word," a "word in action," as St. Augustine defined the sacramental signs.[14]

A second analogy from below, following that of Abraham, concerns the apostles. In the Letter to the Ephesians, it is written that the faithful are "built upon the foundation of the apostles and prophets, Christ Jesus himself being the cornerstone" (Eph 2:20). How is it that the apostles and prophets are here called the "foundation" if it is written elsewhere that "no other foundation can anyone lay than that which is laid, which is Jesus Christ" (1 Cor 3:11)? The answer is that there are different ways of being founded on someone, and if we can be founded on the apostles because they were the first to transmit the Word of life to us, much more so can we be founded on Mary and generated by Mary, who transmitted the author himself of the Word, not to any particular Church, as was the case of each of the apostles, but to the whole world.

The God that did not disdain to call man and woman, creatures as they are, to collaborate with him in giving natural life, can well call a creature, Mary, if he so wishes, and in different ways each person, to collaborate with him in giving supernatural life and to be his "instrument of grace." Even then, the creature remains nothing before God; it is all purely and simply a question of grace. Let it not happen that in order to safeguard God's transcendence we should form a petty and narrow-minded unbiblical idea of him, as if he were a jealous God, humanlike, like the god of the Greeks. God's "jealousy" in the Bible doesn't concern his instruments and intermediaries but idols. Would it offend a king to see his subjects kiss even the ground he walks on out of respect and love for him?

It is encouraging to discover that those pioneers who started the Reformation acknowledged Mary's title and prerogative of "Mother" in the meaning that she is our mother and mother of salvation, too. In his sermon at a Christmas Mass, Luther stated: "This is the consolation and overflowing goodness of God, that man, insofar as he believes, can glory in the precious fact that Mary is his true mother, Christ his brother and God his Father. . . . If you believe this, then you really sit in the Virgin's lap as her dear child."[15]

In a sermon in 1524, Zwingli called Mary "the pure virgin Mary, mother of our salvation," and he stated that where she is concerned, he never "thought, let alone taught or publicly affirmed the slightest thing that could be impious, dishonoring, unworthy or bad of her."[16]

How, therefore, did we arrive at the present unpleasant situation with our Protestant brethren on the question of Mary, to the point that certain marginal groups think it is even their duty to belittle Mary and continuously quarrel with Catholics on the question, and, in any case, overlook all that Scripture says of her? Something similar to what happened to the doctrine on the Eucharist happened here, too. What should have been for all Christians the strongest signs and points of unity and in the case of the Eucharist, the sacrament of unity itself, have become the most blatant opportunities for discord and disunity.

I do not presume to know the answers to these questions. I just wish to express what I think could be a way out of this sad situation. This would require, on the part of Catholics, a sincere acknowledgment of the fact that we have often, especially in the last centuries, very definitely contributed to making Mary unacceptable to our Protestant brethren, at times by our exaggerated and inconsiderate way of honoring her and, above all, by not giving this devotion a clear biblical setting in pointing out her subordinate role to the Word of God, to the Holy Spirit, and to Jesus himself. In these last centuries, Mariology has become a constant source of new titles and new devotions, often in controversy with Protestants and, at times, using Mary—our common mother!— as a weapon against them. Vatican Council II opportunely reacted to this tendency by exhorting the faithful "to painstakingly guard against any word or deed which could lead separated brethren or anyone else into error regarding the true doctrine of the Church" and by reminding the faithful that "true devotion consists neither in fruitless and passing emotion, nor in a certain vain credulity."[17]

On the Protestant side, I think we should note the negative influence that not only anti-catholic controversy but rationalism, too, had on their attitude toward Mary. Mary is not just an idea, she is a real person, a woman, and as such it is not easy to reduce her to an abstract principle. She is the icon itself of God's simplicity, and that's why she couldn't but be eliminated from the theological field in an atmosphere dominated by exaggerated rationalism.

After recalling several of Luther's texts on Mary, a Lutheran woman, who founded a community called "the Sisters of Mary," wrote:

> Reading these words of Martin Luther, who revered the mother Mary to the end of his life, observed the festivals of the Virgin Mary and daily sang the Magnificat, we can sense how far the majority of us have drifted away from the proper attitude towards her, which Martin Luther has indicated to us on the basis of Holy Scripture. Rationalism has lost the sense of the sacred. In rationalism man sought to comprehend everything, and that which he could not comprehend he rejected. Because rationalism accepted only that which could be explained rationally, Church festivals in honor of Mary and everything else reminiscent of her were done away with in the Protestant Church. All biblical relationship to the mother Mary was lost, and we are still suffering from this heritage.
>
> When Martin Luther bids us to praise the mother Mary, declaring that she can never be praised enough as the noblest lady and, after Christ, the fairest gem in Christendom, I must confess that for many years I was one of those who had not done so, although Scripture says that henceforth all generations would call Mary blessed (Luke 1:48). I had not taken my place among these generations.[18]

This is not an isolated voice. After the council, theologians from various Protestant denominations—Lutherans, Calvinists, Anglicans, Evangelicals—made similar declarations. One of them, referring to the council documents, stated: "Catholics have gone a first mile in trying to reestablish theological rapport on this issue [on Mary], Protestants have an obligation to go a second mile in opening themselves to an examination with their Catholic brethren of what the New Testament says about the place of Mary in christian faith" (R. McAfee Brown). "Christ," says another Protestant theologian, "is the second Adam, the New Man, and we are incorporated to form part of his total Humanity. Does this mean that we are adopted into a relationship not only with him but with her from whom he took his flesh? If so, then she is not only his mother; she becomes our mother too." "For its own good, evangelical Christianity needs a far more positive relationship with our Lord's Mother and with all the saints than it has normally encouraged'' (J. C. De Satgé). And yet another wrote, ''A re-examination of the meaning of Mary may well form part of this larger *metanoia* which Protestants, at their best, have always sought'' (J. A. Ross Mackenzie).

The most promising fruit of the new atmosphere surrounding Mary is the birth and spreading of The Ecumenical Society of the Blessed Virgin Mary, in which theologians and pastors from various Christian denominations reflect together and confront one another on Mary's role in the history of salvation and the Church.[19]

All of these premises make it possible for us to nourish a hope in our hearts that one day in the not too distant future, Catholics and Protestants will no longer be divided but united by Mary in mutual veneration of her, different perhaps in form and expression but united in acknowledging her as the Mother of God and, in a different sense, the mother of believers. We are approaching the year 2000. Would it be fitting that on the anniversary of the birth of the Child, we should completely forget her who gave him to the world? Would this be Christian or even human? But above all, would the Christ we proclaim really be the Word made flesh, the God who entered into history, who became one of us in all things: in birth, in living, and in dying?

5. *"And from that hour the disciple took her to his own home"*

It would now be fitting to move on from the contemplation of certain titles given to Mary or specific moments in her life to a practical imitation of her: to consider Mary as figure and mirror of the Church. However, in this chapter, where we have seen Mary as our mother, the practical application is rather particular. Obviously it doesn't consist in imitating Mary but in accepting her. We must imitate John by taking Mary into our lives from this moment on. That is all there is to it.

The words ''The disciple took her to himself'' *(eis ta idia)* in the original text can mean two things, which should be kept united: he ''took her to his home'' and took her ''among what was most dear to him.''

We don't think enough of the significance of these few words. They contain information of great importance, which also has a historical basis, as they were given by the person involved. Doubt has been raised on the historical truth of this fact because Acts 1:14 places Mary with the twelve apostles and not singularly with John. However, both facts are compatible. Wasn't John, the disciple Jesus loved, also present in the cenacle among the Twelve? And if he was there, is it surprising that Mary was there too? Mary passed the last years of her life with John. What the Fourth Gospel says of Mary at Cana in Galilee and beneath the cross was written by someone who actually lived in the same house, and it would be impossible not to admit the close relationship, if not the same identity, that existed between the disciple Jesus loved and the author of the Fourth Gospel. The words "and the Word became flesh," were written by someone living under the same roof as Mary, in whose womb this miracle had been fulfilled, or at least by someone who knew her and lived in the same environment with her.

Who can tell what it meant to the disciple Jesus loved to have Mary with him in his home day and night, to eat with her, to have her listen to him when he spoke to his disciples, to celebrate the mystery of the Lord with her? Is it credible that Mary lived within the circle of the disciple Jesus loved without having had the slightest influence on the slow, intense, and thorough work of meditation that went into the compilation of the Fourth Gospel? It seems that in ancient times Origen at least sensed the secret that lies behind this fact, to which scholars and critics of the Fourth Gospel and those researching into its sources usually give no consideration. In fact, Origen wrote:

> John's is the first flowering of the Gospels, and anyone who had not rested his head on the heart of Jesus and had not been given Mary as his mother could not grasp its meaning and depth. Whoever is to become a perfect disciple like John must become such, to be chosen, as it were, like the John who is Jesus. If, in fact, in the opinion of the well-meaning people there is no other son of Mary besides Jesus and yet Jesus said to his Mother: "Behold your son," and not: "Behold, this too is your son," what does this mean if not: "This is Jesus whom you brought forth." In fact, he who is perfect no longer lives but Christ lives in him (see Gal 2:20). And as Christ lives in him, when he is spoken of to Mary, it is said: "Behold your son," meaning Christ.[20]

This text demonstrates that Origen, on the basis of the doctrine of the mystical body and the perfect Christian who is another

Christ, interpreted the words uttered by Jesus dying on the cross as having been addressed not only to John but to every disciple.

We can now ask ourselves what it would actually mean for us to take Mary into our homes. I think this is the right place to mention de Montfort's sober and fruitful spirituality on entrusting ourselves to Mary. It consists in

> doing all one's actions through Mary, with Mary, in Mary and for Mary, so as to enable us to do them with greater perfection through Jesus, with Jesus, in Jesus and for Jesus. . . . We must abandon ourselves to Mary's spirit to be prompted and guided according to her will. We must try to place ourselves, and then remain, in her virginal hands like a tool in the hands of a worker or a lute in the hands of a good lutist. We must lose ourselves completely in her like a stone thrown into the sea. It's possible to do this quite simply and in an instant with a quick inward glance or slight motion of the will or with a few brief words.[21]

But wouldn't this be usurping the place of the Holy Spirit in Christian life, as it is by the Holy Spirit that we are to be led (see Gal 5:18)? Is it not the Holy Spirit that prays and intercedes for us (see Rom 8:26 ff.) so that we become like Christ? Isn't it written that Christians must do everything in the Holy Spirit? It has been admitted that the mistake of attributing, at least tacitly, things that are really the function of the Holy Spirit in Christian life to Mary existed in certain forms of Marian devotion prior to the council, though not in de Montfort himself.[22] This was due to the lack of a clear and active consciousness of the role of the Holy Spirit in the Church. The development of a strong pneumatology does not in the least make it necessary to reject the spirituality of trust in Mary. It just helps to make it clearer. Mary is precisely one of the privileged channels through which the Holy Spirit guides souls and leads them to imitate Christ, and this is because Mary is part of God's Word and is herself a visible word of God. The saying *ad Jesum per Mariam,* (to Jesus through Mary) is acceptable only in the sense that the Holy Spirit leads us to Jesus through Mary. Mary's created mediation between us and Jesus can be seen in all its importance if its subordinate role as a channel of the uncreated mediation of the Holy Spirit is clearly understood.

Once again, we use an analogy from below to understand this. Paul exhorted his followers to do as he did: ''What you have learned and received and heard and seen in me, do" (Phil 4:9). It is clear that Paul had no intention of placing himself in the role of the Holy Spirit; he simply believed that imitating him was complying with the Spirit, as he believed that he also had the Spirit of God (see 1 Cor 7:40). This holds *a fortiori* for Mary and explains what to "do everything with Mary and like Mary" actually means.

An analogy from above on the contrary could be that of divine Wisdom. Both the Latin and the Orthodox Churches see Mary as the "Seat of Wisdom," she who has been molded by God's Wisdom. In this derived sense, Christians can say of Mary what was said of Wisdom in the Old Testament: "Therefore I determined to take her to live with me, knowing that she would give me good counsel and encouragement in cares and grief." ". . . She knows what is pleasing in thy sight and what is right according to thy commandments" (Wis 8:9; 9:9).

In a spiritual sense this is what taking Mary means: to take her as companion and counselor, aware that she knows better than we do God's wishes for us. If we learn to consult Mary and listen to her in all things, she will really become our incomparable teacher in God's ways, guiding our inner selves without the din of words. This is not an abstract possibility but a real fact, experienced today, as in the past, by numerous persons. Here, for example, is a living testimony of this type of experience with Mary: "For some time now I have had the desire to give Mary more space in my life. I like to invite her to re-live in me her love for Jesus and the Trinity, her silence and her prayer. With great trust I offer myself to her as a place where she can come to live again on earth; I offer myself to her as a continuation of her human life here on earth. Therefore, I think I must become a space, a vessel, awaiting God, with my heart and mind fixed on Mary."

Yet this kind of life with Mary is not the only and necessary way to be imposed on everyone. The Holy Spirit himself, who guides some souls along this beautiful path, can guide others through other means, for example, through the Bible, God's written word, read with the Holy Spirit, as in *lectio divina*. We mustn't be absolute even about this practice, no matter how good it is. For some it may last a lifetime. But it can also last only for a period of time to nourish and guide a soul and help it advance, and then another of God's ways takes over the soul's guidance. God doesn't guide all souls in the same way nor does he guide a single soul in the same way from start to end. It often happens that what was a great light for a soul, a restoring spring whenever it was needed, fades and dries at a certain point. Then the soul must be docile and accept this change in nourishment and not expect God to change his plans and his ways.

It is a bad habit, therefore, to judge one's brethren on the basis of their personal Marian devotion and, worse still, on certain forms of it. A parish priest might not happen to talk of the Father or the Holy Spirit for years, or even never do so, and no one notices or is shocked, whereas if he gives two or three sermons without mentioning the Madonna, he is likely to receive complaints accusing him of not loving Mary.

The history of Christian spirituality shows that Mary's maternal action, while being addressed to all believers, has remained quite sober and discreet and almost totally implicit in certain periods or places, as in the spirituality of the Fathers of the Desert and some mystics, including St. John of the Cross. Here, too, we must apply the principle already mentioned concerning ecumenism: "As each has received a gift, employ it for one another, as good stewards of God's varied grace" (1 Pet 4:10).

6. *"Your hope . . ."*

Before concluding our contemplation of Mary in the paschal mystery, close to the cross, I wish to dedicate yet another thought to Mary, model of hope.

A time comes in life when we need Mary's faith and hope. When God no longer seems to listen to our supplications, when he seems to belie himself and his promises, when he lets us experience defeat after defeat and the powers of darkness seem to triumph all around us and all becomes dark within, like the darkness that day "over all the land" (Matt 27:45). When, as one of the psalms says, he seems "to have in anger shut up his compassion" (Ps 77:10). When you are facing this hour, remember Mary's faith, and you, too, cry out as others have done, "Father, I no longer understand you, but I trust in you!"

Perhaps God is asking us right now to sacrifice our "Isaac," like Abraham—the person, the thing, the project, the foundation, the office that is dear to us, that God himself entrusted to us and to which we have dedicated our lives. This is the occasion God is offering us to show him that he is dearer still, more so than his gifts, even than the work we are engaged in for him. God put Mary to the test on Calvary, as he tested his people in the desert to know what was in their hearts (see Deut 8:2). And in Mary's heart he discovered that same yes, amen, she uttered on the day of the annunciation, unshaken and even stronger. May he at such moments find our hearts ready to say yes and amen to him. As Mary stood close by the cross of Jesus, it's as if by her actions she were continually repeating in silence, "Here I am, my God; I am always here for you!" Humanly speaking, there was every reason for Mary to cry out to God, "You have deceived me!" or, as the prophet Jeremiah one day cried out, "O Lord, thou hast deceived me, and I was deceived!" (Jer 20:7), and escape from Calvary. Instead, she didn't run away but remained there, standing, in silence, and she thus became in a very special way a martyr of faith, a supreme testimony of trust in God, after her Son.

God said to Abraham: "Because you have done this, and have not withheld your son, I will indeed bless you and I will multiply your descendants. . . . I will make you the father of a multitude of nations (Gen 17:5; 22:16 f.). Now he says the same thing and even more to Mary: I shall make you mother of a multitude of nations, mother of my Church! In your name all the generations of the earth will be blessed. All generations will call you blessed!

Therefore, like the Israelites who in moments of great trial addressed God saying, "Remember Abraham, our father," we can now say, "Remember Mary, our mother!" And just as the Israelites said to God, "Do not withdraw thy mercy from us, for the sake of Abraham thy beloved" (Dan 3:12), we can say, "Do not withdraw thy mercy from us, for the sake of Mary thy beloved!"

We have already mentioned in the preceding chapter that on Calvary Mary was united to her son in adoring the Father's holy will. Thus, she fulfilled to perfection her calling as figure of the Church. She is still there waiting for us. It has been said of Christ that "he will be in agony even to the end of the world and we must not sleep during that time."[23] And if Christ will truly though incomprehensibly be in agony and on the cross even to the end of the world, where else could Mary be but with him, close by the cross? It is there that she invites and welcomes generous souls so that they may join her in adoring the Father's holy will. Adore even without understanding. It is not a time for sleep. Mary knows that this is absolutely the greatest, the most beautiful and most Godworthy thing we can do, at least once in our lives before we die. This is not something that dispenses us or diverts us from searching for and alleviating the real sufferings of those around us and in the whole world. It should actually make us more aware of those who suffer, because they are united to God's heart. It is precisely because Mary is the "Mother of sorrows" that she is also "Consoler of the afflicted."

The Bible tells us that when Judith, after risking her own life for her people, returned to her city, the people ran together to meet her, and the high priest blessed her and said: "O daughter, you are blessed by the most high God above all women on the earth. . . . Your hope will never depart from the hearts of men" (Jdt 13:18 ff.). Let us address the same words to Mary: You are blessed above all women! Your hope will never depart from the heart and memory of the Church.

Let us now recapitulate Mary's presence in the paschal mystery by applying to her, due distinctions made, the words St. Paul used when summing up Christ's paschal mystery, which he intended to be the pattern of every Christian life:

> Mary, though she was the Mother of God,
> did not count her closeness to God
> as something to hold on to,
> but emptied herself
> calling herself a servant,
> and living in the likeness of all other women.
> She humbled herself and stayed hidden,
> obedient to God, to the death of her Son,
> even death on a cross.
> Therefore God has highly exalted her
> and bestowed on her the name,
> which, after Jesus, is above every name,
> that at the name of Mary
> every head should bow,
> in heaven and on earth and under the earth,
> and every tongue confess
> that Mary is the Mother of the Lord
> to the glory of God the Father. Amen!

NOTES

1. St. Augustine, *The Holy Virginity,* 5-6 (PL 40, 399).
2. *Lumen gentium* 61.
3. Ibid., 60.
4. Ibid., 63.
5. St. Augustine, *Sermons,* 72A (Denis 25), 7 (*Miscellanea Agostiniana* I, p. 163).
6. Paul VI, *Opening Discourse of the 3rd Period of the Vatican Council* (AAS 56, 1964, p. 1016).
7. See M. Thurian, *Mary, Mother of the Lord, Figure of the Church,* London, The Faith Press, 1963, p. 61 f.
8. S. Kierkegaard, *Journals,* X 4 A 572 (ed. cit., II, entry 2222).
9. Calvin, *Le Livre de la Genèse,* Geneva, 1961, p. 195.
10. G. Von Rad, *Genesis: A Commentary,* London, SCM Press, 1972, p. 160.
11. St. Irenaeus, *Against the Heresies,* III, 22, 4 (SCh 211, p. 442).
12. St. Gregory the Great, *Homilies on the Gospels,* XVII, 1 (PL 76, 1139).
13. *Dei Verbum* 2.
14. St. Augustine, *Commentary on the Gospel of John,* 80, 3 (CC 36, p. 529).
15. Luther, *Sermons on the Gospel (Kirchenpostille)* (ed. Weimar 10, 1, p. 73).
16. Zwingli, *Sermon on the Mother of God,* in *Hauptschriften,* der Prediger I, Zurich, 1940, p. 159.
17. *Lumen gentium* 67.
18. Basilea Schlink, *Mary, the Mother of Jesus,* Lakeland, Marshall Pickering, 1986, p. 114 f.
19. See E. R. Carroll, *Understanding the Mother of Jesus,* Wilmington, Michael Glazier, 1979, p. 37-61.
20. Origen, *Commentary on the Gospel of John,* I, 6, 23 (SCh 120, pp. 70-72).
21. St. L. Grignion de Montfort, *True Devotion to Mary,* n. 257-259 (trans. F. W. Faber, Rockfort, Ill., 1985, p. 161 f.).
22. See H. Mühlen, *Una Mystica Persona* (11, 92), Paderborn, 1967.
23. B. Pascal, *The Mystery of Jesus* (= *Pensées* 553 Brunschvicg).

Part Three

Mary, Mirror of the Church at Pentecost

Chapter VII

Persevering in Prayer
with Mary, the Mother of Jesus

With Mary in the cenacle waiting for the Holy Spirit

In the Acts of the Apostles after listing the names of the eleven apostles, Luke continued with these words, so precious to Christians: "All these with one accord devoted themselves to prayer, together with the women and Mary the mother of Jesus, and with his brethren" (Acts 1:14). In this chapter we shall move from Calvary to the cenacle, from the paschal mystery to the mystery of Pentecost.

Pentecost came about at the end of the life of Jesus when the history of salvation had reached its culmination. The reason is obvious. There existed, so to say, two separating walls between us and the Holy Spirit, which prevented him from uniting himself with us: the wall of nature and the wall of sin. The wall of *nature* existed because the Holy Spirit is spirit and we are flesh; he is God and we are men (see Isa 31:3). There's an abyss between the two. The wall of *sin* existed because the distance created by sin was added to that of nature: "Your iniquities have made a separation between you and God" (Isa 59:2). Both these walls had to be knocked down, or the two abysses had to be filled, which is the same thing, so that the Spirit could be poured into us. And this is precisely what happened, thanks to the redeeming work of Christ. By his incarnation he destroyed the separating wall of nature, uniting God and man, the Spirit and the flesh, in himself, thus creating an indestructible bridge between the two realities. By his death and resurrection he destroyed the separating wall of sin. St. John's Gospel tells us: "For as yet the Spirit had not been given, because Jesus was not yet glorified" (John 7:39). It was necessary for Jesus to die for the Counselor to come to us (cf John 16:7). In fact, by dying for sin, Jesus destroyed the second wall; as St. Paul said, "He destroyed the sinful body"

(Rom 6:6). Now nothing remained to prevent the outpouring of the Spirit,[1] which, in fact, would come about at Pentecost.

But if Pentecost came at the end in the historical development of salvation, it comes at the beginning when applied to us. To be more precise, we do not end with the Holy Spirit, we begin with him. In the life of the Church and each one of us, the Holy Spirit doesn't come at the end to crown everything or as a reward for all that we have done and suffered. It's the very opposite. We wouldn't be able to do anything, not even to say "Jesus is Lord!" (1 Cor 12:3) in a fruitful sense if we didn't have the Holy Spirit. Our spiritual life begins with baptism, which is our Pentecost.

This alone is enough to make us realize how this third step in our spiritual journey in Mary's wake is not just a sort of appendix, something extra with respect to the great mysteries of the incarnation and Easter, but necessary for these great mysteries to become efficacious in our lives. It is thanks to the Holy Spirit that we can imitate Mary in the incarnation by conceiving and giving birth to Christ and becoming, spiritually, his mother. It is also thanks to the Holy Spirit that we can imitate Mary in the paschal mystery, staying, like her, beneath the cross in faith and hope.

1. *Mary During Pentecost and After*

If we consider how rarely Mary is mentioned in the New Testament, it is surprising to discover her again, after Calvary, in the cenacle at Pentecost. Thus, Mary was present at all the three stages that form the Christian mystery and the Church, that is, as we have seen, the incarnation, the paschal mystery and Pentecost.

We must, first of all, get rid of a false impression. In the cenacle, too, Mary is mentioned together with other women, just as she was on Calvary. To all appearances, she was present just like any one of these, neither more nor less. But here too, the title "Mother of Jesus," which immediately comes after her name, puts her on a much higher level than the women and even the apostles themselves. What does the fact that Mary was present as the mother of Jesus signify? That the Holy Spirit, who was about to come, was "the Spirit of her Son"! There was an objective and indestructible bond between her and the Holy Spirit: the same Jesus that together they both gave birth to. In the Creed we say that Jesus became incarnate "by the power of the Holy Spirit from the Virgin Mary." Mary was not, therefore, in the cenacle simply as one of the women.

Beneath the cross Mary appeared as the mother of the Church; now, in the cenacle, she appeared as the godmother of the Church—a strong and sage godmother. In order to become a godmother, a person must first have been baptized. This was the case of Mary: she was baptized by the Spirit and now assisted the Church at its baptism by the Spirit. When an adult is being baptized, the godmother helps with the preparations, and this was what Mary did with the apostles and does with us.

Before we take leave of Mary on this earth, let us try to cast a glance at her life after Pentecost. At this point all our written sources of information become silent. Historically speaking, we only know that she lived in John's house. Nevertheless, we possess a special source of information by induction, that is, by going back from the experience of the saints to her experience. The Vatican II constitution on divine revelation tells us that there is a growth in the understanding of the realities and the words of Scripture through "the contemplation and study made by believers and through the intimate understanding of spiritual things they experience."[1] It grows, that is, not only through the study of the Word but also through the fruits and fulfillments that the same Word has produced in the Church. We cannot learn anything about Mary's exterior life from the experience of the saints, but we can learn something about her interior life, since there are also certain laws and constant factors in the field of holiness just as in art and science. This has nothing in common with knowledge deduced from private revelations on the Madonna's life, both before and after Easter.

First of all, let us note a negative argument, which tells us something very important about Mary. From the letters of the apostles and especially from the greetings they end with, we know many of the men and women, their names, and what they did, of the first Christian community. We know Lydia, Aquila, and Priscilla. Once, a certain Mary is even referred to, but she was not the Lord's mother. Of Mary, the mother of Jesus, there is no mention. She has sunk into the deepest silence. Mary, I like to say, was the first cloistered woman in the Church. Her life is now "hid with Christ in God" (Col 3:3). Mary opened the way to the second calling in the Church, the hidden vocation of prayer, side by side with the apostolic and active vocation. When the apostles received the Holy Spirit, they immediately went into the squares preaching; then they departed to found and guide Churches; they held trials and even called a council. Of Mary there is no mention; ideally she stayed in the cenacle with the women in prayer thereby showing that activity, even if done for the kingdom, is not everything in the Church and that it cannot do without those who pray and support it. Mary is the prototype of the praying Church.

This is what is represented in the icon of Mary at the ascension of Jesus into heaven, which we are going to use in these last chapters. The icon doesn't just fix the moment of the ascension but, through it, shows Mary's real charism and place in the Church, which started with the death of Jesus. In fact, St. Paul is also present in the icon (to the right, looking at the Virgin), and he certainly wasn't present at the ascension of Christ. Mary is standing upright with her arms open in an attitude of prayer, isolated from the rest of the scene, from the figures of the two angels in white, who almost form a wall around her. She is in the center, like the mainmast assuring the boat of balance and stability. The apostles surround her. They all move either a hand or a foot, representing the active Church going on her mission, talking, doing. Mary is still, beneath Jesus, in the exact spot from which he ascended, almost as if she were keeping his memory and the expectation of him alive.

We can understand this charism by going back to Mary through the experience of the saints. St. Thérèse of the Child Jesus described how she discovered her vocation in the Church. Listening to St. Paul listing the various charisms, she burned with the desire to practice all of them. She wanted to be an apostle, a priest, a virgin, a martyr. But how could she reconcile these desires? They had become a real martyrdom for her, until one day she made a discovery: the body of Christ has a heart that gives life to all the members and without which everything would cease to move. At the peak of happiness she exclaimed: "I have found my vocation and my vocation is love!. . .To be nothing else than love, deep down in the heart of Mother Church: that's to be everything at once."[2] What did Thérèse discover that day? She discovered Mary's vocation. To be, in the Church, the heart that loves, the heart that no one sees but that moves everything.

After Pentecost, therefore, Mary's life was woven with prayer.

The author of the first biography on St. Francis of Assisi said that toward the end of his life he was no longer a man who prayed but "a man made prayer."[3] What should we now say of the Mother of God? She was a woman made prayer.

We don't know what Mary's prayer was like, but again we can sense something of it from the knowledge of spiritual things we find in the lives of the saints. The saints, and especially the mystics, have described what happens in a soul when it has gone through the dark night of faith and has been completely transformed in Christ. The soul becomes a flame of love. According to St. Augustine, life becomes "just one holy desire."[4] St. John of the Cross wrote a little poem called "The Canticle of the Soul Consumed with the Desire to See God." Each verse of this canticle ends with the same refrain: "I die because I do not die."[5] At this point, separation from God is much more painful and difficult for the soul to bear than separation from the body. That is why it says "I die because I do not die." An ancient Syrian mystic, expressing the same sentiments as St. John of the Cross, said, "I am not fainting for the banquet but because I desire the Spouse."[6] He meant that the soul doesn't yearn for heaven to receive its reward but simply out of pure love for God.

Such is the longing and need at this point to be reunited with God and to possess him totally that, as these saints said, it becomes a true martyrdom to go on living on this earth. The soul no longer understands why God wants to keep it distant from him, in exile, as if he had completely forgotten it, while knowing it cannot go on living without him. It has been written of a Mexican woman, a mother and later a widow, whose canonization process is going on at the moment and whose mystical life, some say, is comparable to that of St. Teresa of Avila, that "through divine inspiration, a new form of Marian devotion could be seen growing in her in the last twenty years of her life: she imitated the solitude and isolation of the Mother of God towards the end of her life, at the moment when her life of love reached its highest peak."[7] This solitude, or as she called it, *soledad,* of Mary, signifies both solitude and isolation at the same time, silent martyrdom in pure faith, in the apparent absence of God and his Son in heaven.

All of this gives us a new glimmer of light on Mary's life after Easter. What must Mary have experienced when in certain circumstances, like all other believers, she recited Psalm 42: "My soul thirsts for God, for the living God, when shall I come and behold the face of God?'' (Ps 42:2). When shall I come, when? Jesus said that where our treasure is, there would our hearts be also (see Matt 6:21), and where else could Mary's treasure be but where Jesus was? If this is humanly true for many mothers who are alone, having lost a child in its tender years, we can imagine what it must have been like for Mary. If Paul, who was a great friend of Jesus, but a friend and not his mother, could say, ''My desire is to depart and be with Christ'' (Phil 1:23), what must Mary have felt? And what must she have experienced when she happened to recite the Pilgrim Psalms, which say: ''My flesh faints for thee,'' and ''My soul longs, yea, faints for the courts of the Lord'' (Ps 63:2; 84:3)? After the ecstasy in Ostia, where together with her son Augustine she had foretasted something of eternal life, St. Monica went about repeating, ''What am I doing here any longer?'' and a few days later she died.[8] ''What I am doing here?'' These words were surely familiar to the mother of Jesus, too. The Protestant philosopher Kierkegaard wrote, ''Let the Church experts go on disputing about the assumption of the Madonna into heaven; it doesn't seem incomprehensible to me, seeing that she was no longer of this world.''[9]

We have mentioned that Mary, at Pentecost and after, is the prototype of praying souls. Do we know anything about the nature of her prayer? St. Augustine rightly explained that the essence of prayer is a desire for God that springs from faith, hope, and charity:

> Your desire is your prayer; if your desire is continuous, then your prayer is continuous, because the Apostle didn't say, in vain: *pray constantly* (1 Thess 5:17). Do we constantly pray on our knees, prostrate our bodies or raise our hands to obey the order *to pray constantly?* If that's what prayer means to us, then I think we cannot do it constantly. But there's an interior prayer that goes on ceaselessly and that is desire. If you desire that Sabbath day, never cease to pray, whatever you are doing. If you wish not to interrupt your prayer, never cease to desire. Your ceaseless desire will be your ceaseless prayer.[10]

Mary knew what ceaseless prayer was because ceaseless was her desire for God and the eternal ''Sabbath,'' where we can rest in the heavenly Jerusalem.

In the time following Pentecost, too, Mary's life must have conserved the basic characteristic that, as we have already mentioned, is true of all God's great works: a great exterior simplicity together with the magnificence and splendor of the interior reality. It has been written that exteriorly, Mary must have looked like "a little old lady, with more and more wrinkles and gentleness as time passed." Besides being a virgin and mother, Mary was also a widow, sanctifying with her life this state too, which is the state of so many women.

What Mary was like in her inward self is a secret God kept for himself. An ancient author described the unfolding of the interior life of a person who has reached the fullness of union with God, which may help us to sense something of what was in Mary's mind and heart at that time:

> At times they are sunk in sadness and tears for mankind and praying ceaselessly for all men, they dissolve into tears because of the ardent love they nourish for mankind. At other times, instead, they are inflamed by the Holy Spirit to great joy and love, and, if it were possible, they would hold everyone, good and bad, without distinction, in their hearts. And yet, at other times, their humility makes them feel they are beneath all others. . . . Often, the soul rests in a mystic silence, in tranquillity and peace and relishes all spiritual delights and perfect harmony. It receives special gifts of intelligence, ineffable wisdom and an inscrutable knowledge of the Spirit. And grace instructs them on things that language cannot explain nor words express. At other times they behave like any normal person.[11]

What the Blessed Angela of Foligno wrote of herself can help us grasp a little of what took place between God and Mary toward the end of her pilgrimage on this earth:

> Even if I can feel joy and sorrow for what takes place outside me, depending on the moment and place, and within limits, yet, within me, my soul is a cell into which neither joy nor sorrow, delight in any virtue nor pleasure in any definable thing, enters. In it dwells the one and only God, outside which there is no good. . . . I see myself alone with God, all pure, all holy, all truth, all uprightness, all assurance, all heavenly in him. And when I am in this state I recall nothing else. Sometimes, when I am like this, God says to me: "Daughter of divine wisdom, temple of the Beloved, joy of the Beloved and daughter of peace, the whole Trinity rests in you, the whole of truth, so that you are holding me and I am holding you."[12]

149

These are the first flashes of eternal life that prelude the vision of God face to face. And certainly Mary experienced them more intensely than any of these saints.

2. *Pray to Obtain the Holy Spirit*

Let us now, once again, go on to consider Mary as the figure and mirror of the Church. What does Mary teach us by her presence in the cenacle at the moment of Pentecost and, after Pentecost, by her prayerful presence in the Christian community? Wishing to be as faithful as possible to what the Acts of the Apostles tell us, I think we can safely group Mary's teachings, on this occasion, into three points: the first point is that before undertaking anything at all and setting out into the world, the Church needs to receive the Holy Spirit; the second point is that prayer, above all, is the way to prepare for the coming of the Holy Spirit; the third is that this prayer must be of one accord and persevering.

First of all, therefore, the need the Church has of the Holy Spirit. When the apostles asked Jesus if the time had come to restore the kingdom, Jesus answered, "You shall receive power when the Holy Spirit has come upon you; and you shall be my witnesses" (Acts 1:6-8). Jesus was therefore advising them not to leave Jerusalem but to wait until the promise was fulfilled and they were "baptized in the Holy Spirit" (Acts 1:4-5). Luke's Gospel also ends with this recommendation: "Stay in the city, until you are clothed with power from on high" (Luke 24:49).

The disciples still had a mistaken idea of the kingdom and its coming. With these words Jesus explained the kingdom and how it would come. They would receive the Holy Spirit; with this Spirit they would become witnesses of Jesus, they would announce his Gospel, people would be converted, and this would be the kingdom that was to come. The rest of the text shows that this was precisely what happened. The disciples waited; the Holy Spirit came; they were clothed with power from on high; they began to preach to the crowds with courage; three thousand people felt their hearts being touched, and the first Christian community was born. This is clearly a sort of law, a paradigm placed at the beginning of the narration of the history of the Church to show to the Church of all ages how the kingdom comes, what its law is, and what the requirements or dynamics of its development are. This holds for us today, too. No one can go out preaching without having first been in the cenacle to be clothed with power from on high. All the work of the Church either gets its power and meaning from the Holy Spirit or it lacks power and Christian meaning. In truth, it has been said that

> without the Holy Spirit: God is far away, Christ stays in the past, the Gospel is a dead letter, the Church is simply an organization, authority a matter of domination, mission a matter of propaganda, liturgy no more than an evocation, christian living a slave morality. But with the Holy Spirit: the cosmos is resurrected and groans with the birth-pangs of the Kingdom, the risen Christ is there, the Gospel is the power of life, the Church shows forth the life of the Trinity, authority is a liberating service, mission is a Pentecost, the liturgy is both memorial and anticipation, human action is deified.[13]

The second point is, as I have said, that prayer opens the way to the gift of the Holy Spirit. In fact, how did the disciples prepare for the coming of the Holy Spirit? Was it by prayer or by discussing the nature of the Holy Spirit or in other ways? I must add a detail on this point. After telling us about the small group that devoted itself to prayer (see Acts 1:14), the Acts of the Apostles talks about the election of Judas' successor (see Acts 1:15-26), and the account of Pentecost (see Acts 2:1 ff.) comes immediately after this. It would seem, therefore, that the Holy Spirit didn't come upon the apostles while they were gathered in prayer but while they were discussing and deliberating. However, a study of the text shows us that the episode described in Acts 1:15-26 has been inserted at this point but probably took place at another time and in another place. (The text mentions that 120 people were present on that occasion; it would have been difficult for such a number to get into the upper room, which was mentioned earlier.) The coming of the Holy Spirit was clearly connected with the fervent prayer of the restricted group, described earlier.[14]

We have, therefore, a repetition of what happened at the baptism of Jesus: "When Jesus also had been baptized and was praying, the heaven was opened and the Holy Spirit descended upon him" (Luke 3:21-11). We could say that it was the prayer of Jesus that rent the heaven and brought down the Holy Spirit upon him.

The same thing happens now for the Church: while she was praying, "a sound came from heaven like the rush of a mighty wind . . . and they were all filled with the Holy Spirit" (Acts 2:2-4).

The constancy with which the coming of the Holy Spirit is related to prayer in the Acts of the Apostles is really striking. The determining role of baptism is clearly mentioned (see Acts 2:38), but the role of prayer is even more emphasized. Saul was praying when the Lord sent him Ananias so that he might regain his sight and be filled with the Holy Spirit (see Acts 9:9-11). After Peter and John had been arrested and released and the community "had prayed, the place in which they were gathered together was shaken; and they were all filled with the Holy Spirit" (Acts 4:31). When the apostles heard that Samaria had received the Word of God, they sent to them Peter and John, who "came down and prayed for them that they might receive the Holy Spirit" (Acts 8:15). When on the same occasion Simon tried to obtain the Holy Spirit by offering them money, the apostles reacted indignantly (see Acts 8:18 ff.). The Holy Spirit cannot be bought, he can only be implored in prayer. It is the only weapon we possess, but, as Jesus assured us, it is an infallible weapon.

In fact, Jesus himself bound the gift of the Spirit to prayer when he said, "If you then, who are evil, know how to give good gifts to your children, how much more will the heavenly Father give the Holy Spirit to those who ask him!" (Luke 11:13). Not only did he bind it to *our* prayer, but also to *his* own, saying, "I will pray the Father, and he will give you another Counselor" (John 14:16). The prayer of the apostles gathered in the cenacle with Mary is the first great *epiclesis,* the beginning of the "Come, Holy Spirit," which echoes in the Church for all time and which the liturgy sings before every important function.

We might make a first objection here. If the Holy Spirit is a gift, rather, the gift of God in absolute, how is it that we have to pray to obtain it? What kind of gift is it if it is not freely given? Both points are true: it is a gift, and God normally gives it only to those who ask. God doesn't force his gifts on us; he offers them. Prayer is precisely the expression of the person's acceptance and desire. It is an expression of freedom opening out to grace.

A second objection might be that in the New Testament we can find verses that seem to state the opposite, that is to say, that we must have the Holy Spirit in order to pray. St. Paul said, in fact, that the Holy Spirit helps us in our weakness, praying in us and teaching us how to pray (see Rom 8:26 f.); that without the Holy Spirit we would not even be able to say that Jesus is Lord (see 1 Cor 12:3), which is the simplest of prayers. How is it, then, that God gives the Holy Spirit to those who ask? Does the Holy Spirit or prayer come first? Once again, both these points are true. The same circular movement and interpenetration exists between prayer and the Holy Spirit as between grace and freedom. We need the Holy Spirit to pray, and we need to pray to receive the Holy Spirit. We have the gift of grace at the beginning, but then we must pray to keep this gift and let it grow in us.

There isn't just one Pentecost. The same Acts of the Apostles tell us so. At the beginning Mary and the apostles devoted themselves to prayer (see Acts 1:14), and the Holy Spirit came (see Acts 2:1 ff.). At this point we might think that everything had been done. The Church had all it needed to continue alone until the parousia. Instead, shortly after when faced with a grave difficulty, the Church had to pray again and obtain a new releasing of the Holy Spirit to be able to go on preaching the word of God with boldness (see Acts 4:23-31). The Church left the cenacle but had to go back there periodically to be repeatedly "clothed with power from on high."

This must not remain historical and general knowledge. It must speak to us personally. Do you want to receive the Holy Spirit? Do you also feel weak and wish to be clothed with power from on high? Do you feel lukewarm and wish to be warmed? Discontented with your past life and wish to be renewed? Then you must pray and pray and pray again! Do not let the gentle cry *Veni Sancte Spiritus,* Come Holy Spirit, die on your lips! "Spirit of the living God fall afresh on me, melt me, mold me, fill me, use me." If a person or a group of persons kneel to pray with faith, resolved not to get up from their knees until they have been clothed with power from on high and baptized in the Spirit, that person or group will not stand up without having received what they were asking and much more.

3. *Persevering in Prayer*

Let us now come to the third and most relevant point. How must we pray in order to obtain the Holy Spirit? How did Mary and the apostles pray? It was "persevering and with one accord."

"In accord" *(homothymadon)* literally means "done with one heart" (concordant) and "with one soul" (unanimous). Jesus said that if you are going before God to offer your gift, you must first be reconciled to your brother (see Matt 5:23). St. Paul exhorts Christians to live in harmony with one another that "together you may glorify God with one voice" (Rom 15:5-6).

The Holy Spirit is communion; he is the very bond of unity both in the Trinity and in the Church. Whoever breaks the unity cannot receive it. St. Augustine said, "The Holy Spirit is to the Church what the soul is to the body."[15] Now if a member of the body, the hand for example, claimed its independence from the rest of the body and no longer wanted to be part of the body, would the soul leave the body to go with the hand? Would it let the rest die to make the hand live? Or wouldn't it be the hand that would end up without life? It would become a withered hand, like the hand of the man in the Gospel (see Matt 12:10). The same is true on the spiritual level. From this we see the definite importance of unity, concord, and reconciliation among those who desire and are preparing to receive the Holy Spirit. As St. Paul said, we must be "eager to maintain the unity of the Spirit in the bond of peace" (Eph 4:3).

A few weeks earlier, the apostles were with Jesus in the same cenacle to celebrate the Passover, and they were still disputing about which of them was to be regarded as the greatest (see Luke 22:24). Now, instead, we learn from St. Luke that they were in accord, that they formed one heart. Perhaps the presence of the mother of Jesus among them helped to create this new atmosphere of unity and peace. As they all prayed with one heart, no one prayed just for himself, but each one prayed for all; prayer reached God from the whole body. This is the miracle of charity, which multiplies the power of prayer. St. Augustine was right, therefore, to end his preaching on Pentecost saying, "If, therefore, you wish to receive the Holy Spirit, keep charity, love charity and desire unity."[16]

Let us now move on to consider the third aspect of Mary's and the apostles' prayer: persevering prayer. The original Greek term used to denote this characteristic of Christian prayer *(proskarterountes)* indicates doing something with regular application and constancy. We could translate it as "tenaciously clinging" to prayer. This is an important word, as it is one that recurs frequently every time prayer is spoken of in the New Testament. We find it again in Acts where the first baptized Christians are mentioned as being "devoted to the apostles' teaching and to the breaking of bread and prayers" (Acts 2:42). St. Paul, too, tells us to be constant in prayer (see Rom 12:12; Col 4:2). A verse of the Letter to the Ephesians says: "Pray at all times in the Spirit, with all prayer and supplication. To that end keep alert with all perseverance" (Eph 6:18). In all these cases we find in the original text the same word we have explained.

This teaching goes back to Jesus himself. He told the parable of the troublesome woman to teach us that we "ought always to pray and not lose heart" (Luke 18:1). The Canaanite woman illustrates this type of prayer that never loses heart and that, in the end, obtains what is desired. She asked that her daughter be cured, and Jesus "did not answer her a word." She insisted, and Jesus answered that he was only sent to the lost sheep of the house of Israel. She then came and knelt before him, and Jesus said it was not fair to take the children's bread and throw it to the dogs. Surely this was enough to discourage anyone. But the Canaanite woman didn't give up and said: "Yes, but even the dogs. . . ," and Jesus, happy, exclaimed: "O woman, great is your faith! Be it done for you as you desire" (Matt 15:21 ff.).

To pray at length and perseveringly doesn't mean using many words, heaping up empty phrases like the Gentiles did (see Matt 6:7). It means asking often, never ceasing to ask, never ceasing to hope, never giving up. It means never taking rest and giving God no rest either: "You who put the Lord in remembrance, take no rest, and give him no rest, until he establishes Jerusalem" (Isa 62:6-7).

Why must prayer be persevering, and why doesn't God answer at once? Doesn't he himself promise in the Bible to hear us at once, as soon as we pray, and even before we have finished our prayer? God tells us: "Before they call I will answer, while they are yet speaking I will hear" (Isa 65:24). Jesus confirmed this: "And will not God vindicate his elect, who cry to him day and night? Will he delay long over them? I tell you, he will vindicate them speedily" (Luke 18:7).

Doesn't experience crushingly belie these words? No, not really. God promised to hear our prayers always and at once, and he does precisely this. It's up to us to open our eyes. It is very true that he keeps his word; in delaying his help, he is already helping us. Actually, the delay is in itself help. If he were to listen too quickly to the *will* of the petitioner, he might not be helping him toward perfect *well-being*. We must distinguish between the will of the petitioner and his need, which is his salvation. God always hears at once, according to the salvation of the petitioner (which is also, or should be, the innermost will of the petitioner) and not always according to the will of the petitioner, as this might not always be the best thing.[17] We often repeat with the Psalms: "Hear me, O God, hear me. . . . Incline your ear, Lord," and God never seems to answer us. But, mind, he has heard you! If you go on praying, it's because he has heard you, otherwise you wouldn't pray.

God has promised to give those that pray good things, the Holy Spirit. He has promised to grant us anything we ask "according to his will" (1 John 5:14). He doesn't give us what is not according to his will or what is not good for us and which would, therefore, be harmful to us. But isn't this hearing us and taking our life and prayer to heart? If a son asks his father for bread, will he give him a serpent? No! (see Matt 7:7). But if the son asks his father for a serpent without probably knowing what a serpent is, would the father give him a serpent, even if the child cries and yells and unjustly accuses him of not loving him? No! He would suffer the unjust accusation rather than give the child what would be dangerous for him.

Therefore, God hears even when he doesn't seem to hear. His delay in granting even what is good is, in itself, hearing and granting. In fact, by making us wait he makes our faith increase and helps us to ask for something better. At the beginning, we usually ask God for little things, for the little needs of this life. We are not aware of what really counts. When we are not heard at once, little by little our real needs emerge, the need to have God, faith, patience, charity, humility, more than material things. And so in the end when God has opened our hearts, he can fill them in a measure worthy of himself. Let us take the Canaanite woman, for example. If Jesus had heard her at once, at her first petition, what would the result have been? Her daughter would have been freed of the demon, but then things would have gone on as before, and the mother and daughter would have ended their days like all others. Instead, by delaying his answer Jesus allowed her faith and humility to grow and grow until she forced him to exclaim with joy, "O woman, great is your faith!" (Matt 15:28). She went back home not only to find her daughter cured but herself transformed. She had become a believer in Christ, one of the first pagan believers, as she was Syrian-Phoenician. And this would remain for eternity. This is what happens when we are not answered immediately, so long as we continue to pray.

When we are praying for the good gift in absolute, what God himself wants to give us above all things—the Holy Spirit—we must guard against being misled. We can even manage to make the Holy Spirit become a bad gift instead of a good one. This happens when we see the Holy Spirit, more or less consciously, as a powerful help from on high, a breath of life that comes to pleasantly revive our prayer and fervor, to facilitate our ministry and make it easy to carry our cross. You have probably prayed for years like this for your Pentecost, and a breath of air hasn't seemed to stir. Nothing of what you expected has happened. But the Holy Spirit is not given to strengthen our egoism. Look more carefully around you. Perhaps the Holy Spirit you've been asking for *yourself* has been given to you by God, but for *others*. Perhaps the prayer of those around you has been enriched through you, and yours has gone on as before, with great difficulty; the hearts of others have been pierced, they have repented and in tears converted, and you are still asking the same grace. Leave God free; make it a point of honor to leave God his freedom. This is the way he has chosen to give you his Holy Spirit, and it is the best way. Who knows whether some apostle or other on the day of Pentecost, seeing all the crowd beating their breasts in remorse, pierced by the Word of God and asking, "What shall we do, brethren?" did not experience envy and distress at the thought that he himself had never cried for having crucified Jesus of Nazareth? St. Paul, who in his preaching was accompanied by the revelation of the Spirit and his power, besought the Lord three times to free him from the thorn in the flesh, but he wasn't answered, and he had to resign himself to living with it so that the power of God be made manifest (see 2 Cor 12:8 f.).

At times, especially if the person's spiritual life is serious and profound, something strange occurs through perseverance in prayer, which we should be aware of so as not to miss a precious occasion. The roles are reversed. It is God that prays, and you are prayed to. You have started praying to ask something of God, and while you are praying you gradually realize that it is God who is stretching out his hand to you, asking something of you. You wanted to ask him to free you from the thorn in your flesh, a particular cross, a particular trial, to free you from a particular office, a situation, the closeness of a certain person. And what happens? God asks you to accept precisely that cross, that situation, that office, that person.

There is a poem by Tagore that might help to explain this. The speaker relating his experience is a beggar. This is what he more or less says:

> I had gone a-begging from door to door in the village path, when the golden chariot appeared in the distance like a gorgeous dream and I wondered who was this King of all kings! My hopes rose high and methought my evil days were at an end, and I stood waiting for alms to be given unasked and for wealth scattered on all sides in the dust. The chariot stopped where I stood. Thy glance fell on me and thou camest down with a smile. I felt the luck of my life had come at last. Then of a sudden thou didst hold out thy right hand and say, "What has thou to give to me?" Ah, what a kingly jest was it to open thy palm to a beggar to beg! I was confused and stood undecided, and then from my wallet I slowly took out the least little grain of corn and gave it to thee. But how great my surprise when at the day's end I emptied my bag on the floor to find a least little grain of gold among the poor heap! I bitterly wept and wished that I had had the heart to give thee my all.[18]

Let it not happen to us, too, at the end of life to cry over not having given God what he asked of us. "What a kingly jest it was to open your palm to a beggar to beg!" Yes, what a divine jest on God's part: he becomes a beggar to allow us to offer him something.

The sublime case of this inversion of the parts is Jesus. In Gethsemane Jesus prayed the Father to take the chalice from him. The Father asked Jesus to drink, to ransom all the other children. Jesus replied, "Not my will but thine be done," and he offered his yes to the Father. He offered not just one drop of his blood but all of it. And in the evening, when the chalice was completely drained, Jesus found the Father, who constituted him Lord, also as man, who gave him a name above all names and glorified him. We cannot say what he received in exchange for his yes, his "grain of pomegranate."

4. *Ceaseless Prayer*

After the apostles, Mary, and the others had received the Holy Spirit, Acts tell us they "devoted themselves to the prayers" (Acts 2:42). However, something had changed. The object and quality of the prayer had changed. Now they did nothing else but tell "the mighty works of God" (Acts 2:11). They even partook of food "with glad and generous hearts, praising God" (Acts 2:46 f.). Their prayer had become a prayer of praise. It was no longer just petition. What had first come about in Mary was now coming about in the Church. When Mary had received the Holy Spirit at the annunciation, she started to magnify the Lord and rejoice in God and proclaim the great things he had done for her (see Luke 1:46 f.). The coming of the Holy Spirit doesn't put an end to ceaseless prayer. It actually enriches it and widens its horizons. It raises prayer to the highest and most Godworthy form of praise, adoration, the proclaiming of God's greatness and holiness.

The New Testament doesn't talk of perseverance only when we are asking for something but also, and even more so, when we are praising, thanking, and blessing God. Again, in the Letter to the Ephesians we find these verses: "Do not get drunk with wine, for that is debauchery, but be filled with the Spirit, addressing one another in psalms and hymns and spiritual songs, singing and making melody to the Lord with all your heart, always and for everything giving thanks in the name of our Lord Jesus Christ to God the Father" (Eph 5:18-20). We could say that the real reason we are urged to invoke and await the Holy Spirit is, once we have been filled with him, to adore God "in Spirit and truth," to bless him and glorify him before all men. The Holy Spirit enabled the apostles to pray in other tongues even before preaching (see Acts 2:4 ff.). The same thing happened when the Holy Spirit came upon Cornelius and his household: "They heard them speaking in tongues and extolling God" (Acts 10:46).

It was with this prayer in the Spirit in mind, made up of invocations and, even more so, of praise, that St. Paul formulated the principle of ceaseless prayer, destined to have an enormous resonance in the history of Christian spirituality: "Rejoice always, pray constantly, give thanks in all circumstances" (1 Thess 5:16-18). An echo of what Jesus said, that we should "always pray and not lose heart" (Luke 18:1). A principle that helps us to overcome a certain ritualistic and legalistic concept, which confines prayer to specific times and places, to render it a basic attitude and a constant pole of attraction, a spontaneous action, almost like the body breathing. How many times must we forgive? Jesus answered: "Always!" (see Matt 18:22). How many times must we pray? Jesus answered: "Always!" To ask how many times a day must we pray to God would be like asking how many times a day must we love God. Prayer, like love, doesn't tolerate calculation in numbers. You can love with various degrees of awareness but not at more or less regular intervals.

The sublime idea of constant prayer was realized in different forms in the East and West. Eastern spirituality practiced it with the so-called Jesus Prayer, which has been described as follows:

> The ceaseless Jesus Prayer is a continuous, uninterrupted call on the holy name of Jesus Christ with the lips, mind, and heart; and in the awareness of his abiding presence it is a plea for his blessing in all undertakings, in all places, at all times, even in sleep. The words of the Prayer are: "Lord Jesus Christ, have mercy on me!" Anyone who becomes accustomed to this Prayer will experience great comfort as well as the need to say it continuously. He will become accustomed to it to such a degree that he will not be able to do without it and eventually the Prayer will of itself flow in him.[19]

In its highest form this prayer gradually dispels all thoughts and leaves the mind free for prayer alone. It comes through soberness, vigilance, and abstinence from anything that doesn't lead to God, and its fruit is pureness of heart. Even while they were still living in this world, it has kept hosts of souls united to God and in deep quiet *(hesychia)*. The *Philocalia,* a basic work on Russian Orthodox spirituality, was written to help cultivate this type of prayer.

By its very nature, this kind of continuous prayer is associated with monastic life, even if not altogether exclusively. In the West, St. Augustine proposed a more flexible kind of continuous prayer so that everyone could take advantage of it, not only those who explicitly professed the monastic life. As we have already recalled when talking of Mary's prayer, St. Augustine said that the essence of prayer is desire. If the desire for God is continuous, then prayer is continuous, too. If desire is lacking we may shout all we wish, but it's as if we were mute as far as God is concerned. So the secret desire for God, which means remembering him, being constantly intent toward the kingdom, and longing for God, can be alive in us even when we are obliged to do other things: "It is not bad or futile to pray at length when we have time, when our responsibility to other good and necessary deeds is not hindered, although we should pray through desire even when we are doing those deeds. In fact, to pray at length is not the same, as many believe, as praying with many words. Talking at length is one thing, an intimate and lasting desire is another thing. . . . To pray a lot means to kindle a continuous and devout movement of the heart towards the one we are invoking."[20]

The author of *The Cloud of Unknowing,* following this line of thought, said:

> Therefore, be attentive to this wonderful work of grace in your spirit. When it is genuine it is simply a spontaneous desire springing suddenly toward God like a spark from a fire. It is amazing how many loving desires arise from the spirit of a person who is accustomed to this work. And yet, perhaps only one of these will be completely free from attachment to some created thing. Or again, no sooner has a man turned toward God in love when through human frailty he finds himself distracted by the remembrance of some created thing or some daily care. But no matter. No harm is done; for such a person quickly returns to deep recollection.[21]

The desire is simply a pure impulse toward God. It is pure or naked because it desires nothing but God; it is an impulse or a soaring because through it the will is elevated toward God. Just as the waves of the sea never cease to roll high and low toward the shore, so the spirit never ceases to urge the mind and the impulse of the heart toward God. The body, too, participates, repeating over and over one simple word such as "God" or "Jesus" or *Abba,* Father. This helps to still the mind while allowing it to be active to the minimum indispensable to keep it fixed. You don't need to see or hear anything at this point. Actually, this prayer usually takes place between two clouds: a cloud of forgetting beneath you, between you and every created thing, and the cloud of darkness and faith—the cloud of unknowing—above you, between you and God.

We could call this prayer "karstic prayer." The karstic rivers sometimes flow above the soil and at other times below it. When they find a certain type of compact soil, they flow above it; then, if they meet a different, porous type of soil, they go below it and continue to flow underground until they emerge again. This is what this constant prayer is like. At times, when we are free to pray, our prayer surfaces and becomes a conscious prayer of praise, adoration. At other times, when our activities absorb us, prayer sinks to the bottom of our hearts and continues to flow hidden there, like an invisible movement of love toward God, ready to be aroused again as soon as we can do so. In this way it can go on even when we are asleep, as the spouse in the canticle tells us: "I slept but my heart was awake" (Song 5:2). I have met factory workers who had the grace of this prayer for long periods. With God's grace, it is not incompatible with any profession or work. One of these workers used to wake up in the night under the impression that his spirit was praying, as it just seemed to continue something already started. He wanted to get back to sleep, thinking of work the following morning, but he was unable to interrupt such a sweet experience. And on getting up in the morning, he used to feel fresh and rested, as if he had slept the whole night long.

It would be a serious mistake to cultivate the so-called ceaseless prayer and neglect to devote precise and set times to prayer. Jesus passed the nights in prayer, but we know that he also went up to the synagogue or Temple to pray together with the others. Three times a day—at sunrise, in the evening during the vespertine sacrifice, and at sunset—he joined all devout Israelites in turning toward the Temple and reciting the ritual prayers. St. Augustine wrote: "Let us pray, therefore, with ceaseless desire springing from faith, hope and charity. But at fixed times and on given occasions let us pray to God with words, so that these signs may be an incentive to us and make us realize how much we have progressed in our desire and urge us on to make it grow in us."[22]

5. When Prayer Becomes an Effort and a Struggle

We must guard against putting prayer into a scheme, or against thinking that once we have discovered a certain type of prayer, we can go on using it for the rest of our lives. Prayer is like life and is therefore subject to good and bad seasons. However, one particular season, winter, arrives sooner or later for everyone. So let us not delude ourselves. There comes a time when prayer, like nature in winter, becomes bleak and bare and is apparently dead.

162

Then prayer is a struggle, a hardship, an agony. It is no longer water pouring from the heavens or flowing smoothly along the surface or under the soil. As St. Teresa of Avila would say, it is like water that has to be drawn up with effort in a bucket from the bottom of a well, and a good deal of it spills over on the way."[23]

There are two different types of struggle in prayer. One is the *struggle against distractions.* Even the saints experienced this. St. Teresa of Avila herself confessed: "Sometimes I find I can't even form in a fitting way a thought about God or of any good, or practice prayer, even though I'm in solitude; but I feel that I know him. I understand that it is the intellect and imagination that does me harm here, for the will is all right, it seems to me and disposed toward every good. But this intellect is so wild that it doesn't seem to be anything else than a frantic madman no one can tie down: nor am I master of it long enough to keep it calm for the space of a Creed."[24]

To start praying in such an arid state is like setting out on the open sea in a boat that lets the water in through fissures. You spend all your time emptying the boat, otherwise it will sink. You have no time to relax and enjoy the sky. And you get back to shore without having even glimpsed the peaceful blue sky and the vastness of the sea you had set out to contemplate. Neither have you caught any fish. All you've managed to do is empty the boat. Likewise, we start praying to enjoy God, to contemplate his wonders, to listen to him, to discover new things about him and us, but the mind is dissipated and full of distractions, and prayer becomes an exhausting battle against vain thoughts and there is no escape; we must struggle on.

In the struggle against distractions we must arm ourselves with patience and courage and not fall into the error of believing that there is no point in praying. We must humbly adjust to the situation. Say short prayers, and try to tell God quickly what you are anxious to tell him. It will only take you a few seconds to say: Jesus, I love you! Lord, I believe and hope in you. I'm sorry for my sins. Forgive me. Thank you for the gift of the Holy Spirit. Thank you for being there listening to me! and yet, you've said all the essential things and God has heard you. We should try to find again the beauty of ejaculations, which literally mean short prayers "hurled like darts" *(iacula)*. Others, instead, find it useful in these circumstances to slowly repeat the words of a prayer that has a particular meaning for them. St. Thérèse of the Child Jesus said, "Sometimes, when the darkness of my spirit is so deep that I am incapable of a thought that would unite me to God, I very slowly recite the Our Father and then the Angelus; then these prayers enrapture me and nourish my spirit much more than if I'd recited them quickly a hundred times."[25]

Each one has his own method, which will never be completely perfect and victorious, simply because this is the moment of defeat, the moment in which we become aware of our basic impotence to pray and acknowledge that if sometimes we have been able to pray with fervor, that was God's work. There's a verse in Psalm 31 that perfectly describes what happens in this prayer:

> I had said in my alarm,
> "I am driven far from thy sight."
> But thou didst hear my supplications
> when I cried to thee for help.

When we feel nothing, we think that God feels nothing either and doesn't hear us, that we have been driven from his sight, rejected, whereas he is listening to us attentively and is more pleased with us than ever.

As I have said, it is important not to give up and gradually substitute prayer with work when we don't get very far in praying. When God is absent, his place should at least be kept for him and not be given to an idol, for example, the idol of work. To prevent this from happening it is wise to take a pause from work every now and then to raise the mind to God, or at least to dedicate a little time to him. This prayer is precious to God, even if to us it means "eating the bread of anxious toil" (Ps 127:2).

In the lives of the Fathers of the Desert, we read this anecdote about Anthony, the father of hermits:

> One day, while he was sitting in the desert, the holy Father Anthony became a prey to discouragement and dark thoughts. And he said to God: "O Lord! I want to save my soul but my thoughts hinder me. What can I do in my trouble?" Then, leaning forward a little, he saw another monk, like himself, sitting there working. At a certain point the monk stopped working, stood up and prayed, and then sat down again and went on plaiting cord. After a little while he got up to pray again. It was an angel of the Lord, sent to correct and encourage Anthony. He heard the angel saying: "You do likewise and you

164

will be saved." When he heard these words he felt very happy and took heart. He did as the angel advised him and he was saved."[26]

Perhaps, at this precise moment, that angel is telling me as I am writing this and you as you are reading it what he one day said to Anthony: "You do likewise and you will be saved!" None of this is useless. Does the Lord, perhaps, need our fervor or our ecstasies? Is he, perhaps, consoled by them? He needs and loves our submission, humility, steadfastness, and it is prayer that makes these virtues possible, especially when it is an exhausting struggle.

There is another kind of struggle in prayer, *the struggle with God,* which is much more delicate and difficult than the struggle with the mind. This takes place when God asks something of you that your nature is not ready to give him and when God's way of acting is incomprehensible and bewildering to you. Job experienced this struggle. Perhaps Mary experienced it, too, at some moment in her life, like when she was beneath the cross. But, above all, Jesus experienced it in Gethsemane. It is written: "Being in an agony, he prayed more earnestly" (Luke 22:44). In anguish, Jesus didn't cease to pray, he prayed "more earnestly." He became the most sublime example of persevering prayer. We can ask ourselves why Jesus struggled. It wasn't to bend God's will to his but to bend his own human will to God's. We find a similar case in the Bible that shows us the difference between Jesus and every other worshiper, the case of Jacob struggling with God (see Gen 32:23-33). This struggle took place at night, across the river Jabbok, like the struggle of Jesus, which also took place at night beyond the river Cedron. Why did Jacob wrestle with the angel in his prayer? "I will not let you go unless you bless me," he said, meaning, unless you do what I ask. And again he said, "What is your name?" He was convinced that if he could learn the name he would be able to prevail on his brother who was pursuing him by using the power that is inherent in knowing the name of God. But God blessed him without telling him his name.

Jacob prayed to bend God to his own will; Jesus prayed to bend himself to God's will. Who are we like when we pray in anguish? More often than not, if we think of it, we are like Jacob, the man of the Old Testament, and not Jesus. We strive to make God change his mind and not to change ourselves and accept God's will. We strive more to make him remove our cross than to be able to carry it with him. The results of both prayers are also different. God didn't give Jacob his name, which is the symbol of his power, but he gave Jesus the name that is above every name and with it all power (see Phil 2:11).

6. *Forced Prayer*

When you cannot pray and you are struggling, then you must have recourse to a special type of prayer: forced prayer. As the Blessed Angela of Foligno said: "It is a very good thing and very pleasing to God that you pray with the fervor of divine grace, that you keep watch and feel the burden of each good load; but it is more pleasing and acceptable to God that you do not pray less or keep watch less or do fewer good deeds when you can no longer count on fervor. Do all of this without fervor, just as you did when you had fervor. . . . You do your part, my child, and God will do his. Forced prayer is very pleasing to God."[27] Jesus prayed this kind of prayer in Gethsemane. He fell on his face and prayed, came to his disciples, went away and prayed again and his sweat became like great drops of blood (see Matt 26:36 ff.; Luke 22:44). The Letter to the Hebrews is referring to this moment when it says that Jesus, in the days of his flesh, "offered up prayers and supplications with loud cries and tears" (Heb 5:7).

This type of prayer can be better done with the body than with the mind. The will often commands the mind, but the mind doesn't obey it, whereas when it commands the body, the body obeys. There is a secret alliance between the will and the body, and this must be used to bring the mind to reason. Often, when the will cannot command the mind to have or not have certain thoughts, it can command the body: it can command the knees to bend, the hands to join, the mouth to open and utter certain words, for example, "Glory be to the Father, the Son, and the Holy Spirit."

We must not disdain bodily prayer, which is the only thing left to us at times. It holds a secret. When your spirit cries out in rebellion or is in a tumult of hostility toward your brethren, simply kneel before the tabernacle or a crucifix. You have made all the enemies of Christ that were in your mind a footstool at his feet! Get up now, you have won. There's a beautiful saying by Isaac the Syrian: "When our hearts are dead and we cannot utter the

166

smallest prayer or supplication, may he find us perpetually prostrate on the ground when he comes to us.''

Just physically remaining in church or in the place you have chosen to pray, just staying in prayer, is, then, the only way left to us to be persevering in prayer. God knows we could find a thousand more useful things to do that would be more gratifying to us, but we remain there and give him all the time destined for him in our schedules or in our proposals. This for God is an act of filial love. An old monk told a disciple who was so distracted that he couldn't pray, ''Let your thoughts go where they will, but don't let your body leave your cell!''[28]

This advice is useful for us when we find ourselves so badly distracted that it is beyond our control: let our thoughts go where they will, but let our bodies remain in prayer! And if you can do nothing else, get your poor body to kneel, raise your eyes to heaven, and say to God, ''Lord, my body is praying to you!'' This effort, so useless in appearance, in fact gives us the Holy Spirit.

In these situations, we must remember that we have a mother, our teacher of prayer. Some years ago I spent some time in a small, solitary convent. A little girl often came to kneel beside someone who was praying, she would join her little hands and look up at who was beside her and firmly say, ''Come on, make me pray!'' We can imitate that little child by placing ourselves, in spirit, close to Mary and saying to her, ''Make me pray!''

This long reflection on prayer has been, in its own way, a form of perseverance in prayer while we are waiting for the Holy Spirit to come. A very practical and simple way of persevering in prayer with Mary the mother of Jesus is to recite the Rosary, through which we can live again all the mysteries and transform the whole Bible and the whole history of redemption into prayer. Let us ask Mary to be our strong and loving godmother to prepare us for the releasing of the Spirit and for Pentecost. Would that, through her intercession the promise Jesus made be ours too: ''Before many days you shall be baptized with the Holy Spirit'' (Acts 1:5).

NOTES

1. *Dei Verbum* 8.
2. St. Thérèse of Lisieux, *Autobiographical Manuscripts* B, f.3 (trans. R. Knox, cit., p. 186).

3. Thomas of Celano, *Second Life of St. Francis,* 95 (*Writings,* cit., p. 441).[1]
4. St. Augustine, *Commentary on the First Letter of John,* 4, 6 (PL 35, 2008).
5. St. John of the Cross, *Poems* V (trans. E. A. Peers, cit., p. 427).
6. St. Gregory of Narek, *Prayers,* 12 (SCh 78, p. 103).
7. M.-M. Philipon, *Conchita: A Mother's Spiritual Diary,* New York, Alba House, 1978, p. 172 f.
8. St. Augustine, *Confessions,* IX, 10 f.
9. S. Kierkegaard, *Journal of a Seducer.*
10. St. Augustine, *On the Psalms,* 37, 14 (CC 38, p. 392).
11. *Homily Attributed to St. Macharius the Egyptian,* 18, 7 f. (PG 34, 649).
12. *The Book of the Bl. Angela of Foligno,* cit., pp. 388–390.
13. Ignatius of Latakia, *The Uppsala Report,* 1968, Geneva, WCC, p. 298.
14. See C. Schneider, *Die Apostelgeschichte,* I, Freiburg in Br., 1980, ad loc.
15. St. Augustine, *Sermons,* 267, 4 (PL 38, 1231).
16. Ibid.
17. See St. Augustine, *Commentary on the First Letter of John,* 6, 6–8 (PL 35, 2023).
18. Tagore, *Gitanjali,* 50.
19. *Tales of a Russian Pilgrim* I (trans. H. Bacovcin, *The Way of a Pilgrim,* New York, Image Books, 1978, p. 18).
20. St. Augustine, *Letter,* 130, 10, 19–20 (CSEL 44, p. 62 f.).
21. *The Cloud of Unknowing,* ch. 4, ed. cit. p. 52.
22. St. Augustine, *Letter,* 130, 9, 8 (CSEL 44, p. 60 f.).
23. St. Teresa of Avila, *Life* XI, 9 (*The Collected Works,* I, Washington, 1976, p. 81).
24. Ibid., XXX, 16 (ed. cit., p. 201).
25. St. Thérèse of Lisieux, *Autobiographical Manuscripts,* C, f. 25 (trans. R. Knox, cit., p. 229).
26. *Apophtegmata Patrum,* Antony 1 (PG 65, 76).
27. *The Book of the Bl. Angela of Foligno,* cit., p. 567 f.
28. *Apophtegmata Patrum,* Manuscript Coislin, n. 205 (ed. Nau, Revue de l'Orient Chretien, 13, 1908, p. 279).

Chapter VIII

"The Holy Spirit Will Come Upon You"

Mary, the first pentecostal and charismatic in the Church

1. The Awakening of the Spirit

If we can talk of a special grace in the Church today, it is, I believe, connected with the person of the Holy Spirit. Among other things, this century will be remembered in the history of the Church as the century of the rediscovery of the role of the Holy Spirit. Not only because the role of the Holy Spirit has been rediscovered in postconciliar Catholic theology and liturgy but even more so because of the experience the Church has had of a releasing of the Holy Spirit "on all flesh," which has given rise to various charismatic and pentecostal movements in almost every Christian denomination. For many Christians Joel's prophecy is no longer just a lovely quotation in Peter's sermon at Pentecost but a reality to be relished. They can bear witness to the fact that "in the last days God poured out his Spirit on all flesh: on sons and daughters, on young men and old men, on menservants and maid servants" (see Joel 3:1 ff.; Acts 2:17-18).

In spite of all the difficulties the breath of Pentecost is powerfully circulating in the Church again, and this is the basis of the great hope for Christian unity. At the time of Pentecost, the great separation, the great schism, was between Jews and Gentiles. We know what suffering this caused in the early Church. In what way did the Holy Spirit guide the Church to embrace pagans in Christ's faith? He called Peter, the head of the Church, to the house of Cornelius, a pagan centurion (he needed the most qualified witness possible), and while Peter was still explaining why it was unlawful for a Jew to visit a pagan, the Holy Spirit came upon all those present just as on the apostles at the beginning. All Peter had to do was draw a conclusion: "If then God gave the same gift to them as he gave to us. . . who was I that I could withstand God?" (Acts 11:17).

Something similar is happening in the Church today. There are other schisms, other divisions, but now they are among Christians. God sends his Spirit, often in the same identical forms, upon Christians of different denominations, so that we may draw the same conclusion that Peter did: Who are we to reject those brothers or consider them outside the real body of Christ if God gives them the same Spirit he gives us? How can they, too, not belong in some way to the *body* of Christ if they are animated by the *Spirit* of Christ?

One of the fields in which the Holy Spirit is healing the wounds and laying the ground for unity precisely concerns the Mother of God, and I would like this book to be my small contribution in this respect. The rekindling of interest in the Holy Spirit has also been contagious where Mariology is concerned in postconciliar Catholic thought. In a certain sense there has been an inverse movement: from the Church to Mary and not from Mary to the Church. The Church, becoming aware again of her spiritual dimension, of being stirred and animated by the Holy Spirit, spontaneously seeks also in this to find her model in Mary, who through the Holy Spirit conceived her Head and Savior.

The relation "Mary–Holy Spirit" is quite a new aspect in both Latin and Oriental theology. All that can be gleaned in the writings of the Fathers and medieval authors, including St. Bernard's works, does not go beyond the little biblical information we have, that is, that Mary conceived "through the Holy Spirit," with a few occasional comments generally devoted to throwing light on the person of the Holy Spirit much more than on Mary. Now, instead, we are witnessing diverse systematic attempts to give a theological background to the relationship between Mary and the Holy Spirit and to express this in theological terms. On this point too, as on all other points, I wish to keep to the Word of God, to the information Scripture gives us. This doesn't allow us to say much. It forces us to be sober, but in compensation, we shall be on safer ground, more acceptable to all Christians, whereas great theological synthesis must necessarily give more room to hypotheses and principles bound to one particular approach or another and are therefore less universally valid.

I think that one fact contributes to a new approach to the relationship between Mary and the Holy Spirit: the greater knowledge we have, with respect to the past, of the development of biblical revelation about the Holy Spirit, that is to say, our more advanced knowledge of biblical pneumatology. We must thank modern biblical studies for this and, in particular, the new science of Biblical Theology, a science unknown to the Fathers. When reading Scripture the Fathers followed the analytic method used in their time. This consisted in explaining each book, text by text, and each text, word for word. They lacked a historical approach, which makes it possible to see the development of a theme throughout the whole Bible and to note the differences as well as the similarities that exist in the Bible between one epoch and another, between one environment and another, between one writer and another. They had a sense of the unity of the Bible rather than of its variety. We could say that they liked to see the whole in the fragment, that is, the entire Bible reflected in each text they were explaining with no contrast whatsoever. Instead, we like to see the fragment in the whole, that is, a text within its context, a biblical verse in the light of its literary genre and setting.

I am going to take a simple approach to the theme of Mary and the Holy Spirit, which I shall now try to illustrate. All the explicit references to Mary and the Holy Spirit in the New Testament come from St. Luke and St. Matthew. Therefore, let us especially look at St. Luke's concept of the Holy Spirit, at what, according to him, happens when the Holy Spirit comes upon a person or the Church and thereby discover what, according to him, the Holy Spirit worked in Mary. In this way we shall try to exploit the few and spare references to Mary and the Holy Spirit, not on the basis of a systematic and speculative amplification necessarily open to subjective elements but on the basis of an internal amplification of the Bible that is homogeneous and objective because it takes place within the same actual framework and the language of the same author. It's like interpreting a text within a "context," that is to say, like examining a piece of material when you know what "textile" it comes from. We shall see how Mary reflects in miniature the work of the Holy Spirit in the Church.

2. *Mary and the Holy Spirit in St. Luke's Gospel*

The same evangelist, Luke, who at the beginning of his Gospel presented Mary receiving the Holy Spirit to conceive Jesus, at the beginning of his book on Acts presented Mary being "filled with the Holy Spirit," with the apostles. Some factors lead us to think that a strict parallelism exists between the descent of the Holy Spirit on Mary at the annunciation and on the Church at Pentecost, whether or not the evangelist wanted to make this parallelism or whether it was due to an objective similarity between the two events.

Mary was promised the Holy Spirit as the "power of the Most High" that would come upon her (see Luke 1:35); the apostles were similarly promised the "power" that would come upon them "from on high" (see Luke 24:49; Acts 2:8). Once she had received the Holy Spirit, Mary started to proclaim *(megalynei)* in an inspired tongue the great things *(megala)* the Lord had done for her (see Luke 1:46-49); similarly, the apostles, having received the Holy Spirit, started proclaiming in diverse tongues the mighty works *(megaleia)* of God (see Acts 2:11). Vatican Council II also related the two events when it stated that in the cenacle "we see Mary prayerfully imploring the gift of the Spirit, who had already overshadowed her in the annunciation."[1]

All of this, however, is only of relative importance with respect to the clear statement in the Gospel addressed to Mary: "The holy Spirit will come upon you, and the power of the Most High will overshadow you" (Luke 1:35). Besides this precise statement, St. Luke's Gospel reveals another important fact. All those to whom Mary was sent after the Holy Spirit had come upon her were, in their turn, touched, or inspired, by the Holy Spirit (see Luke 1:41; 2:27). It was certainly the presence of Jesus that radiated the Spirit, but Jesus was in Mary and acted through her. She was like the ark or the temple of the Spirit, as the image of the clouds "overshadowing" her suggests. In fact, this recalls the pillar of fire that in the Old Testament was a sign of God's presence or of his coming down into the camp (see Exod 13:22; 19:16). Matthew confirmed this basic information on Mary and the Holy Spirit when he said that "Mary was found to be with child of the Holy Spirit" (Matt 1:18) and that which was conceived in her was "of the Holy Spirit" (Matt 1:20).

The Church took this revealed information and very quickly placed it at the center of its Creed. Right from the end of the second century, the words according to which Jesus "was born of the Holy Spirit and the Virgin Mary," have been attested in the so-called Apostles' Creed. The ecumenical Council of Constantinople in 381, which defined the divinity of the Holy Spirit, inserted this article into the Nicene Creed, saying of Christ that he became incarnate "by the power of the Holy Spirit, from the Virgin Mary."

It is, therefore, an article of faith accepted by all Christians, both of the East and the West, both Catholic and Protestant. It is a safe basis, and this is no small thing. Mary appears to be bound to the Holy Spirit by an objective, personal, and indestructible bond: the very person of Jesus whom they brought forth together, even if their roles were absolutely different. To separate Mary and the Holy Spirit, it would be necessary to separate Christ himself, in whom their diverse roles have been realized and objectivized for all time. Whether or not we want to call Mary the spouse of the Holy Spirit as St. Francis of Assisi and others after him did, it remains that Jesus united Mary and the Holy Spirit more than any child unites his father and mother, because if a child by simply existing proclaims that his parents were united for an instant according to the flesh, this son Jesus proclaimed that the Holy Spirit and Mary were united according to the Spirit and therefore, indestructibly. Also in the heavenly Jerusalem, the risen Jesus remains he who became incarnate "by the power of the Holy Spirit, from the Virgin Mary." In the Eucharist, too, we receive him who became incarnate "by the power of the Holy Spirit, from the Virgin Mary."

Let us now try to understand who the Holy Spirit is and what he does, according to Luke and the Synoptics in general. On this point we can make use of the greater knowledge we possess today of the Holy Spirit, which I mentioned earlier. Luke and Matthew mark the point of arrival of a certain line of thought on the Holy Spirit that comes from the Old Testament. It shows the Holy Spirit as "the power of God which makes possible speech and action of which human resources are not capable."[2]

To understand what is peculiar in this vision we must mention another important line of thought concerning the revelation of the Holy Spirit, which reached its fulfillment in John and Paul and which consists in seeing the Holy Spirit as a sanctifying power that takes possession of a person, changing his heart and making him a new creature. In the first case, the Holy Spirit is effused into a person to enable him to do something beyond his own power. The power received extends beyond the person receiving it—a prophet, a head, a person inspired, and so on—and through him it spreads to the whole community or to history. To himself and to God he can still be what he was, not in the least changed by the passing of the Spirit. The second case is different: the action of the Holy Spirit is directed on the person receiving it, it stays in him, dwells in him, and brings about a new state and a new life. Obviously, it is not a question of contradiction within the Bible but of the two ways, both equally genuine and salvific, the Spirit has of manifesting himself. These must be kept united by the reader of Scripture and not separated or seen in opposition (as sometimes happens, unfortunately). Once again, it is a question of rediscovering the "whole," and in this case the whole is the Holy Spirit in his totality, including both charisms and charity.

The concept of the Holy Spirit as God's power, which enables man to do actions beyond human strength, emerges every time the Spirit is mentioned in the Synoptics. The Holy Spirit came upon Jesus at his baptism, and then we see Jesus overcoming Satan when he was tempted, casting out demons, announcing the kingdom, teaching with authority, and doing wonderful things (see Matt 12:28). The uniqueness of Jesus is seen in the fact that he was the definite bearer of the Spirit, he constantly acted in the Spirit, and he was "full" of the Holy Spirit (see Luke 4:1, 14, 18), not like the prophets and inspired persons before him who only every now and then acted in the Spirit.

As I have said, this was the prevailing line of thought in the Old Testament. In the Old Testament the Spirit *(ruah)* was often seen as a divine creating power that came on one person, filling him with wisdom and artistic ability (see Exod 31:3; 35:31); it came on another and he was infused with the prophetic charism (see Mic 3:8); it came on yet another and he received extraordinary powers in governing (see Isa 11:2) or of discernment in judging (see Dan 13:45-46).

St. Luke gave two quotations, one in his Gospel and the other in Acts, which clearly illustrate that his concept of the Spirit was on the same line as that of the Old Testament. One is from Isaiah 61:1: "The Spirit of the Lord God is upon me . . . ." It tells us that Jesus, insofar as he was man and Messiah, was full of the charismatic power of the Spirit, who enabled him to bring good tidings to the afflicted, to restore sight to the blind, to proclaim liberty to the captives, and the opening of the prison to those who were bound. The other quotation is from Joel 3. With it,

Luke affirmed the same point, but this time with regards to the Church. Luke said that the Holy Spirit would prepare the Church for her prophetic mission, pouring out every type of charism: dreams, visions, and, above all, prophecies (see Acts 2:17-18).

Nevertheless, there is a trait that distinguishes the charismatic and prophetic action of the Spirit in the Church with respect to the Old Testament. In the Old Testament the Spirit had been the privilege of a few, and even these were privileged only on certain occasions related to their particular offices. Now, it was given to each and every member of the new community, and it was given permanently. What Moses had said has been fulfilled: "Would that all the people of the Lord were prophets! Would that the Lord might bestow his Spirit on them all!" (Num 11:29). This desire was now a reality: all were prophets among God's people.

3. *Mary, the First Charismatic in the Church*

What does all of this teach us about the relation between Mary and the Holy Spirit? That, after Jesus, Mary was the greatest charismatic in the history of salvation. Not in the sense that she received the biggest number of charisms. On the contrary, she seems very poor in charisms to the external eye. What miracle did Mary perform? Of the apostles it is said that even their shadows healed the sick (see Acts 5:15). Where Mary is concerned, we know of no miracles while she lived, not of any marvelous or sensational actions. She was the greatest charismatic because in her the Holy Spirit realized the greatest of his wonderful actions, which consisted in giving to Mary not words of wisdom, not governing powers, not visions, not prophecies, but the very life of the Messiah!

In fact, when we read in St. Luke's Gospel, "The Holy Spirit will come upon you, and the power of the most high will overshadow you," we now know that the term "Holy Spirit" means "the power of the most high," the divine creating power that forms the life of this peerless child. In this text as in Matthew 1:20 "the belief in God's unique and creative intervention is linked with the concept of the creative power of the divine Spirit to which the Old Testament already bears witness."[3] St. Ambrose correctly interpreted Luke 1:35 when he wrote: "Mary conceived by the power of the Holy Spirit. . . . We cannot then doubt that the Spirit, the author of the Incarnation of the Lord, is 'creator.'. . . What is produced is fruit of the substance or power producing it. . . . How, therefore, did Mary conceive by the Holy Spirit? Not by the substance because that would mean the Holy Spirit became flesh. If, then, Mary conceived by the grace and work of the Spirit, who can deny that the Spirit is creator?"[4] St. Ambrose was certainly identifying the Holy Spirit in Luke 1:35 with the person of the Holy Spirit, the third person of the Trinity, which was to be the common belief of the whole Church in the light of the development of the theme of the Holy Spirit in John and Paul, even if St. Augustine precisely stated that it was only by appropriation that the incarnation of the Word, like inspiration in Scripture, was attributed to the Spirit, as it was in itself the work of the whole Trinity.[5]

To help us grasp the singularity of the relation between Mary and the Holy Spirit, we can start with the different and superior relation that this event created between Mary and the Holy Spirit with respect to all the prophets. To the prophets, up to John the Baptist, God's Word "comes" *(factum est verbum Domini super. . .)* (see Luke 3:2), meaning that the Word became an active reality in them. In Mary, thanks to the intervention of the Holy Spirit, the Word didn't just come for a moment, he dwelt in her; he didn't become just an active reality, he became flesh. We no longer hear *factum est Verbum Domini,* but *Verbum caro factum est* (John 1:14). Again, the prophet is he who "eats" the scroll containing God's Word and "fills his stomach with it" (see Jer 15:16; Ezek 3:1 f.; Rev 10:8 f.). But what is all of this compared to what took place in Mary? Her womb was really filled with the Word and not only in a metaphorical sense.

The Fathers sometimes attributed the title "prophetess" to Mary,[6] especially in relation to the *Magnificat,* or because they wrongly applied Isaiah 8:3 to her.[7] Strictly speaking, Mary does not form part of the rank of prophets. A prophet speaks in God's name; Mary didn't "speak" in God's name. She almost always kept silent. If she was a prophet, she was so in a new and sublime way: in the sense that she silently "offered" God's only Word, she brought it forth.

If what the Holy Spirit worked in Mary was not a simple case of prophetic inspiration, it can and must nevertheless be consid-

176

ered a charism, the absolutely greatest charism ever given to a human being, superior even to the hagiographers themselves, who were inspired or moved by the Spirit to speak on God's behalf (see 2 Pet 1:21). In fact, what is a charism and how can it be defined? St. Paul defined it thus: "The manifestation of the Spirit for the common good" (1 Cor 2:7). Now then, what manifestation of the Spirit was more singular than Mary's was? What manifestation of the Spirit was more for "the common good" than Mary's divine maternity? It is painful to think that among the Christian denominations most hostile to Mary are certain Pentecostal groups. This is not even natural, and only our past heritage of misunderstanding can explain it.

Theology also explains a charism as a grace *gratis data,*[8] unlike the other type of action of the Holy Spirit already mentioned—that which creates a new heart and charity—which is a grace *gratum faciens,* that is, it makes us acceptable to God. Now, as we saw at the beginning, the divine maternity was grace, absolute gratuity, due only to God's free and sovereign choice.

Luke, therefore, in placing Mary in such an intimate relation with the Spirit, presented her, in accordance with his general view of the Holy Spirit, as the most sublime example of a Spirit-filled person and as the place of the manifestation of God's creative power. All this, however, must not induce us to see the relation between Mary and the Holy Spirit as only objective and functional, not touching the most inward depth of the person, the feelings and emotions. Mary wasn't just a "place" in which God acted. God doesn't treat people as places but as persons, as collaborators and interlocutors. The prophet Amos said: "Surely the Lord God does nothing, without revealing his secret to his servants the prophets" (Amos 3:7). What, then, should we say of Mary?

Luke was well aware of the "sober intoxication" provoked by God's Spirit. He pointed out that one day Jesus "was filled with joy by the Holy Spirit" (Luke 10:21). He said that when the apostles had received the Spirit they began to speak in other tongues and were so excited that some thought they were filled with new wine (see Acts 2:13). And he said that when the Holy Spirit had come upon her, Mary hastened to Elizabeth and said the *Magnificat,* through which she expressed all her joy. St. Bonaventure who was familiar with the effects of the Holy Spirit's action described Mary as she was at that moment:

The Holy Spirit came upon her like a divine fire, inflaming her soul and sanctifying her flesh in perfect purity. But the power of the Most High overshadowed her so that she could endure such fire. By the action of that power, instantly Christ's body was formed, his soul created and, at once both were united to the divinity in the person of the Son, so that the same person was God and man, with the properties of each nature maintained. Oh, if you could feel in some way the quality and intensity of that fire sent from heaven, the refreshing coolness that accompanied it, the consolation it imparted; if you could realize the great exaltation of the Virgin Mother, the ennobling of the human race, the condescension of the divine majesty; if you could hear the Virgin singing with joy; if you could go with your lady into the mountainous region; if you could see the sweet embrace of the Virgin and the woman who had been sterile and hear the greeting in which the tiny servant recognized his Lord, the herald his judge and the voice his Word, then I am sure you would sing in sweet tones with the Blessed Virgin that sacred hymn: "My soul magnifies the Lord. . ." and with the tiny prophet you would exalt, rejoice and adore the marvellous virginal conception."[9]

Luther, too, attributed the Virgin's canticle to the extraordinary intervention of the Holy Spirit. She really experienced and felt the Spirit. The Spirit fulfilled one of its most important privileges in her, which was the unfolding of the meaning of the Word, to reveal the deep intelligence of God's ways. In fact, Luther wrote:

To understand this sacred hymn of praise well, we must remember that the blessed Virgin Mary speaks through personal experience as she was illuminated and taught by the Holy Spirit; for no one can rightly understand God and God's Word if not directly through the Holy Spirit. But to be given such a gift means to experience the Spirit, to feel him; the Holy Spirit teaches through experience, his own school as it were, outside which we learn nothing but words and gossip. Therefore, the Holy Virgin, having experienced in herself that God worked great things in her, and in spite of her humility, poverty and the contempt of others, the Holy Spirit taught her the rich art and wisdom of knowing that God is the Lord who delights in raising what is humble and putting down the mighty."[10]

4. *Mary, the Figure of a Spiritual and Charismatic Church*

On very few points is the passage from Mary to the Church as clear and natural as it is in this case. We shall stress two possible ways of applying what we have said about the relation between Mary and the Holy Spirit: one, of a sacramental order concerning the Church as a whole as the "universal sacrament of salvation," and the other, more personal, concerning the charismatic dimension of the Church and each baptized Christian.

The Vatican Council II text on Mary states: "For, believing and obeying, Mary brought forth on earth the Father's Son. This she did, knowing not man but overshadowed by the Holy Spirit. . . . The Church, moreover, contemplating Mary's mysterious sanctity, imitating her charity, and faithfully fulfilling the Father's will, becomes herself a mother by accepting God's word in faith. For by her preaching and by baptism she brings forth to a new and immortal life children who are conceived by the Holy Spirit and born of God."[11]

This text reflects the ecclesial meaning of an article of the Creed: "By the power of the Holy Spirit he became incarnate from the Virgin Mary." In fact, in defining the birth of Christ as a spiritual birth ("by the power of the Holy Spirit"), and virginal ("from the Virgin Mary"), the article of the Creed already seemed to the Fathers of the Church to be the basis and model of the sacramental birth of Christ, by the power of the Holy Spirit, of the Virgin Church. Didymus of Alexandria wrote that the baptismal font, which here means the Church herself, "becomes the mother of all believers by the power of the Holy Spirit, while remaining Virgin."[12] And St. Ambrose wrote: "The Holy Church, immaculate where coitus is concerned and fertile where birth is concerned, is virgin through chastity and mother through issue. She gives us birth in a virginal way, made pregnant not by man but by the Holy Spirit."[13]

St. Augustine constantly related the article of the Creed concerning the birth of Jesus by the Holy Spirit and the Virgin Mary to the article concerning "the Holy Church." In relation to the first he wrote: "Born by the power of the Holy Spirit and from the Virgin Mary: that's how he came, and to whom he came: from the Virgin Mary in whom the Holy Spirit, and not a human husband, acted; he made the chaste one fecund, conserving her intact." Going on then, in the same sermon, to the article on the

179

Holy Church, he said: "The Holy Church is virgin and gives birth. She imitates Mary who delivered the Lord. Could it perhaps be that the Holy Mary wasn't a virgin and yet she delivered and remained a virgin? It's the same with the Church: she gives birth and is virgin. And if you think about it, she gives birth to Christ himself, as it is the members of Christ that are baptized. . . . If, therefore, the Church gives birth to Christ's members, that means she is very similar to Mary."[14]

In Catholic theology up to recent times, biblical doctrine on the "creator" Spirit, given to carry out certain supernatural works, existed almost only in this sacramental application and in the exercise of the magisterium, that is to say, in its institutionalized forms. The Spirit comes in the Eucharist and changes the bread and wine; the Holy Spirit is conferred on certain people at ordination, giving them power to do supernatural works, such as forgiving sins, or assisting the magisterium in interpreting the revelation.

However, this approach neglected the action of the Holy Spirit we have seen at work in Mary. She can, therefore, be an example to us in helping us to appreciate the free and unpredictable action of God's Spirit, who intervenes in the form of gifts being lavished outside the instituted channels. This is always done for the common good and service. This is what Vatican Council II was referring to in its well-known text on charisms:

> It is not only through the sacraments and Church ministries that the Holy Spirit sanctifies and leads the people of God and enriches it with virtues. Allotting his gifts "to everyone according as he will" (1 Cor 12:11), he distributes special graces among the faithful of every rank. By these gifts he makes them fit and ready to undertake the various tasks or offices advantageous for the renewal and upbuilding of the Church, according to the words of the Apostle: "The manifestation of the Spirit is given to everyone for profit" (1 Cor 12:7). These charismatic gifts, whether they be the most outstanding or the most simple and widely diffused are to be received with thanksgiving and consolation for they are exceedingly suitable and useful for the needs of the Church.[15]

In his infinite wisdom God established two ways for the sanctification of the Church, like two different directions where the same Spirit blows. There is, so to say, the Spirit that comes from on high and who works through the pope, the bishops, the priests, and who intervenes in the teaching of the Church, in the hierarchy, in those in authority, and especially in the sacraments. There is, then, the opposite direction, from the bottom, as it were, where the Holy Spirit blows from the basis or single cells of the body that form the Church. This is the wind that blows where it wills (see John 3:8); it is the Spirit who apportions his gifts individually, as he wills (see 1 Cor 12:11). The entire Church, a living organism, irrigated and animated by the Holy Spirit, is these two channels taken as a whole, or the result of the two directions of grace. The sacraments are the gifts given to all for the profit of the individuals; the charisms are the gifts given to the individuals for the profit of all. The sacraments are gifts given to the Church as a whole for the sanctification of the individual members; charisms are gifts given individually for the sanctification of the Church as a whole.

It is easy to understand, then, what a loss it would be for the Church if, at a certain point, it was thought that one or the other of these two channels could be done without, either the charisms or the sacraments. Unfortunately, something similar did happen in the Church, at least on a practical level if not in principle. Since Vatican Council II, everyone admits that in the past there has been a certain curtailment of the sanctifying powers of the Church at the expense, precisely, of the charisms. Everything went through the so-called vertical channels alone, made up of the hierarchy or entrusted to the hierarchy. Through these, Christians received God's Word, the sacraments and prophecy considered as being the charism inherent in the magisterium of the Church to teach the truth infallibly.

The balance and copresence of sacraments and charisms ensures, among other things, a good balance between repetition and invention, between continuity and innovation, for the Church. A Christian life, let us say, that consisted only in the sacraments and ministerial functions would soon become repetitive and pure habit. But a Christian life deprived of these things, and which consisted only in charismatic spontaneity and innovation, would inevitably end in confusion and the arbitrary use of the will.

The synthesis of the two perspectives allows the Church to enjoy, once again, the whole. Invention keeps repetition alive, and repetition assures the soundness of invention. In other words, the charisms renew the institution and the institution preserves the charisms, both pertaining to the same Spirit. In this sense Christian life finds a kind of model in the Holy Mass, which is made up of unchangeable parts, like the Eucharistic Prayer, and changeable parts, like the readings, the prayers, the homily, alternating repetition with innovation.

The sense of charisms seen as God's direct intervention to break through stagnant situations and put his people back on the right path would seem to be reflected in these words of Isaiah: "Because these people draw near with their mouth and honor me with their lips . . . and their fear of me is a commandment of men learned by rote; therefore, behold, I will again do marvelous things with the people" (Isa 29:13-14). God intervenes explosively, especially through the prophets, to renew a tradition and a cult that have become simple routine and formalism, and knowledge that has gradually become a layout and codification of human knowledge and book notions. In fact, this was what the great new event, the coming of the Messiah, worked in history, and Jesus himself compared it to new wine. Mary, because of her divine maternity by the Holy Spirit, found herself at the center of God's greatest innovation, and she was the tool he used. She was the first "wineskin" who kept Jesus the new wine par excellence, in herself for all of us (see Mark 2:11).

5. *"When you give, give with simplicity"*

The exercise of charisms is not exempt from danger and difficulty. Just as man can make bad use of the natural gifts of intelligence, the will, the capacity to love, and even use them against God, so he can make bad use of the supernatural gifts, which are charisms. It is precisely on this point that Mary, the first and greatest charismatic, comes to our aid with her example.

More than any other person, St. Paul was aware of the dangers involved in the use of charisms due to human frailty. At a certain point, having listed the various charisms, he described the interior disposition necessary to practice them: "When you give, you should give generously from the heart; if you are put in charge, you must be conscientious; if you do works of mercy, let it be because you enjoy doing them" (Rom 12:8). The inner disposition recommended to those who give is simplicity *(aplotes)*, which can also mean "largeness of heart" and is therefore sometimes translated as "generosity."

182

Let us look at this first disposition necessary to us all: simplicity. "He who gives" is usually one who shares part of his property or earnings and therefore gives alms and cares for the poor. The apostle says he must do it with simplicity and without second thoughts but with a pure heart because he, too, has received. Jesus made this clear when he said: "You received without pay, give without pay" (Matt 10:8). "Without pay" doesn't refer simply to money but to all forms of recompense: neither gratitude nor glory, not wanting to appear as a benefactor or count what one has given.

In Mary we see this disposition implemented to its fullest. Her charism has been precisely "to give." She gave the Messiah to the world and she did it with simplicity, without second thoughts, looking for no recompense. When considering Mary during Jesus' public life and in the paschal mystery, we saw how she deprived herself of her maternal rights over Jesus, and she did this to give him to others. There was a time when she alone didn't have free access to Jesus her son. She even had to turn to others for help to speak to him.

But let us reflect on the interior disposition that Paul called simplicity. From the few references in the Gospels and the *Magnificat,* Mary emerges as simplicity in person. She wasn't exalted by the gift showered on her causing her to become what every other Israelite woman would have desired to be, the Messiah's mother. Not only did she not exact honors and acknowledgment for this, she never even made the slightest reference to such a privilege. Her closest reference to it highlighted only what God had done and not she herself: "He who is mighty has done great things for me." The Gospels relate meetings and conversations in which Mary took part—at the visitation, Christmas, the presentation in the Temple—but she never showed the slightest sign of self-gratification. What discretion and humility even at Cana!

How did Mary's heart bear the tension created by the thought, You are the mother of Jesus, the Messiah's mother? Lucifer couldn't deal with the temptation of being the most luminous of creatures; he was full of self-complacency and fell. Mary remained humble, through God's grace certainly, but God's grace wasn't in her in vain. Her simplicity forced these words of praise from Luther:

> The Mother of God shows such a pure spirit because in the midst of the abundance of good things, she didn't become attached

183

to them nor look for her own interests. She conserves her spirit pure in the love and praise of God's goodness alone, ready, if it were God's will, to be deprived of everything and be left with a poor naked and needy spirit. It is much more difficult to be moderate in wealth, great honors and power than in poverty, ignominy and weakness, as wealth, honor and power are strongly attracted to evil. Therefore Mary's marvelously pure Spirit must be celebrated all the more because although such a great honor was endowed upon her, she did not let herself be tempted but, as if unseeing, she remained on the right path and gripped on to the divine goodness alone. . . . She didn't seek her own interests so that she could really and truthfully sing: "My spirit rejoices in God my Savior."[16]

I have called Mary the first "pentecostal" and "charismatic" in the Church; we should call her the first "evangelical" as well!

I am often amazed and embarrassed by the thought of Mary's simplicity and soberness when I am sent to announce God's Word somewhere. If at times I feel in my heart that I have a strong message to announce, words that I think might illuminate and console hearts, what a struggle it becomes to remain sober and detached, to leave the Word free to act, and how often I fail! Mary gave the entire Word to the entire world, the Word made flesh, and she remained so humble, so apart! In this the Mother of God is truly a sublime model for the charismatics of the Church. Her silence is so eloquent!

Simplicity-humility is what helps those with charisms to keep the right attitude of freedom and submission before the Church and the hierarchy. Mary had Jesus with her, but she didn't feel dispensed from doing what the Law of Moses ordered. After Pentecost, in the Church where she lived with the Apostle John, perhaps at Ephesus, it wasn't Mary that governed or presided over the group but John. We have no knowledge of ordinances emanated or suggested by Mary, whereas numerous sources refer to John's authority. Once her charism of giving Christ birth and accompanying him steadfastly to the cross had ended, Mary dissolved in the Church like salt in water.

Another important lesson from Mary's example concerns the place of a charism in the spiritual life of the person possessing it. St. Augustine not only affirmed that "being Christ's disciple was more meritorious for Mary than being Christ's mother," but he even said that "the maternal relationship would have meant nothing to Mary if she hadn't carried Christ in a more blessed way in her heart than in her flesh.''[17] This is a close reminder of what St. Paul said about the relation between charisms and charity: "And if I have prophetic powers. . . but have not love, I gain nothing" (1 Cor 13:2).

If this principle is true about Mary's maternal charism, what can we say about our own small charisms of prophecy, teaching, governing, assisting, prayer animation? Jesus warned us that it is possible to end up in Gehenna even after using the charisms, like prophecy, casting out demons, and doing mighty works (see Matt 7:21-23).

I have highlighted Mary's charism of maternity. But the Gospel tells us that in her, this charism was singularly united to the charism of virginity. She received both these things from the same Spirit as one charism. Thus she is close to both mothers and virgins, and neither of these ways of life in the Church lacks the honor of having in Mary its beginning and model.

Let us conclude by contemplating Mary as virgin and mother or, as our friend and poet said, as a carnal and pure creature, that is, totally at the service of life and all pureness, who offered her womb to God but also her heart and faith:

> There is something missing in all creatures. . . .
> Those that are carnal
> are in want of pureness.
> This we know.
> But those that are pure
> are in want of being carnal.
> But in her nothing is lacking. . . .
> Because being carnal, she is pure.
> But being pure, she is also carnal.
> And it is for this she is not only a unique woman
> among all women.
> She is a unique creature among all creatures.
> She comes literally first after God. After the Creator.
> She is next.[18]

NOTES

1. *Lumen gentium* 59.
2. E. Schweizer, *Pneuma*, in *Theological Dictionary of the New Testament,* VI, Grand Rapids, 1968, p. 402.

3. Ibid., 404.
4. St. Ambrose, *On the Holy Spirit,* II, 38–42 (CSEL 79, p. 101).
5. See St. Augustine, *Sermons,* 213, 7 (PL 38, 1063).
6. St. Irenaeus, *Against the Heresies,* III, 10, 2 (SCh 211, p. 118).
7. See Eusebius of Cesarea, *Eclogae Propheticae,* 4, 5 (PG 22, 1205).
8. St. Thomas Aquinas, *Theological Summa,* I-IIae, q.111, a.1 ff.
9. St. Bonaventure, *The Tree of Life,* 1, 3 (trans. E. Cousins, cit., p. 127 f.
10. Luther, *The Magnificat,* Introduction (ed. Weimar 7, p. 546).
11. *Lumen gentium* 63–64.
12. Didymus of Alexandria, *On the Trinity,* II, 13 (PG 39, 692).
13. St. Ambrose, *Commentary on the Gospel of Luke,* II, 7 (CSEL 32, 4, p. 45).
14. St. Augustine, *Sermons,* 213, 3 and 7 (PL 38, 1961, 1064).
15. *Lumen gentium* 12.
16. Luther, *The Magnificat* (ed. Weimar 7, p. 558).
17. St. Augustine, *Sermons,* 72A (Denis 25), 7 (*Miscellanea Agostiniana* I, p. 162); *The Holy Virginity,* 3 (PL 40, 398).
18. Ch. Péguy, *The Porch,* in *Oeuvres Poétiques,* cit., p. 57 ff.

Chapter IX

"He Bowed His Head and Gave Up His Spirit

Mary in the Johannine Pentecost

The New Testament recounts not one Pentecost but two. There is the Lucan Pentecost described in the Acts of the Apostles and the Johannine Pentecost described in John 20:22, when Jesus breathed on them and said to them, "Receive the Holy Spirit." Both Pentecosts took place in the same cenacle but at different times. The Johannine Pentecost took place on the evening of Easter Day, not fifty days later. In this ninth step of our pilgrimage in Mary's wake, let us try to discover her presence in this Pentecost and see what she has to teach the Church.

1. *The Johannine Pentecost*

The existence of a second Pentecost in the New Testament was a well-known fact to the Fathers of the Church. "My brothers," St. Augustine said, "someone might ask me: 'Why did Christ give the Holy Spirit twice?' Not once, but twice did the Lord freely and generously manifest his gift of the Holy Spirit to the apostles. In fact just after he had risen from the dead, he breathed on them and said to them: 'Receive the Holy Spirit.' And wasn't it the same Spirit he breathed on them then that he later sent them from heaven?"[1]

St. Augustine gave a symbolic explanation of this fact: the Holy Spirit was given twice perhaps to remind us that the precepts of charity are two, love of God and love of one's neighbor. Other Fathers gave different explanations. For example, the gift of the Spirit referred to by John was a partial gift, less intense, restricted in content and in the numbers receiving him with respect to the more complete and universal gift bestowed fifty days later.[2] An-

187

other explanation was that of the first fruits of the Spirit: "The Savior breathed and manifested the gift of the Spirit to the Apostles, as the first fruits of a renewed nature. . . . It was to be clear that he is the one who gives the Spirit. . . . Thus they were allowed participation in the Holy Spirit at the moment he breathed on them and said: 'Receive the Holy Spirit.' Christ, in fact, couldn't deceive them and say: 'Receive,' without giving anything. On the other hand, in the days of the Holy Pentecost God gave clearer expression to grace and more powerfully manifested the Spirit already abiding in them."[3]

The greatest difficulty the Fathers faced in explaining the Johannine Pentecost came from the words in John 7:39. How could Jesus, they wondered, give the Spirit before he ascended into heaven, if it is said that the Spirit couldn't be given until Jesus was glorified? To them the glorification of Jesus took place essentially when he returned to the Father.

The progress made in biblical studies permits us today to give a more simple answer to the problem of the existence of a double Pentecost. The two Pentecosts correspond to two different ways of understanding and presenting the gift of the Spirit. They do not exclude but integrate one another, though it is better to deal with them separately. Luke and John described, from two different angles and two different theological approaches, the same fundamental event in the history of salvation and that is the outpouring of the Holy Spirit as a consequence of Christ's death and resurrection. This outpouring was manifested at different times and in different ways. Luke, who saw the Spirit essentially as a gift made to the Church for her mission, emphasized what took place fifty days after Easter, the day on which the Jews celebrated Pentecost. This happening must have had a particular resonance and importance at the beginning of the Church's mission. John, who saw the Spirit essentially as the Easter gift of Jesus to his disciples, emphasized the first manifestations of the new presence of the Spirit, which came about on Easter day itself. After all, Luke didn't mean that the coming of the Spirit related in Acts 2 was the only manifestation of the Spirit, because later, in Acts, he referred to other comings of the Spirit that are quite similar to the first (see Acts 4:31; 10:44 ff.).

Luke interpreted the gift of the Spirit promised for the "last days" in the light of Joel's prophecy and Genesis 11:1-9, that is to say, as the definite effusion of the prophetic Spirit and the restoration of the one language that had been confused in Babel. John interpreted it in the light of Genesis 2:7 (God breathing the breath of life into Adam) and Ezekiel 37:9 (the breath of the Spirit giving life to the dry bones); he interpreted it, that is to say, as the beginning of a new life and a new creation.

Right at the beginning of John's Gospel a promise was made: that there would be a baptism in the Holy Spirit (see John 1:33). This promise was confirmed and clarified in the discourse on the living water made to the woman of Samaria (see John 4:14). Later on, it was closely linked to Jesus' glorification (see John 7:39), which, we know, to John didn't simply mean the ascension of Jesus into heaven after his resurrection but also his exaltation on the cross, that is to say, his glorious death. It's unthinkable that John could end his Gospel without showing the fulfillment of this promise or even by referring its fulfillment to a later book—the Acts of the Apostles—which he probably didn't even know.

Therefore, there is a Pentecost, an account of the coming of the Holy Spirit, in John's Gospel too, just as for Easter, we have a clear confirmation of this in history and the Church liturgy. We know that in the first centuries of the Church there were two fundamental ways of understanding Pentecost. According to one of these, which was later to prevail and become universally accepted, Pentecost was the feast of the descent of the Holy Spirit, which took place on the *fiftieth day* after Easter. According to the other and older way, Pentecost was the feast of the *fifty days* following Easter, and it commemorated the spiritual presence, or "according to the Spirit," of Jesus among his disciples. Starting with the resurrection, this presence was seen as the blossoming of a new life and an anticipation of eternal life. To Tertullian, for example, Pentecost was "a time in which the resurrection of the Lord was confirmed numerous times to the disciples, the grace of the Holy Spirit was inaugurated and hope in the return of the Lord was manifested."[4] In the same sense St. Athanasius said, "After Easter comes the feast of Pentecost which we shall welcome, one feast after the other, to celebrate the Spirit already with us in Christ Jesus."[5]

In this ancient concept, Pentecost began with the end of the paschal vigil, and it was like one long feast day, like one continuous Sunday. In the Johannine concept the gift of the Spirit inaugurated Pentecost, while in the Lucan view it concluded it.

2. *"At once there came out blood and water"*

From ancient times, therefore, the Church has been conscious of a double Pentecost, or of a double way of presenting the eschatological effusion of the Spirit. Modern exegesis goes even further. Not only has it acknowledged a Johannine Pentecost but it sees its inauguration on Calvary at the very moment of Christ's death, which is the beginning of his glorification. We can say that this is an accepted fact today, even if not all exegetes give it due consideration.

When John the evangelist said that Jesus "gave up his spirit" (John 19:30), he was talking of two things (quite a common process for John), one natural and historical and the other mystical: he died, and he gave up his Spirit. John saw the blood and water from Jesus' pierced side as the fulfillment of the promise of the rivers of living water that would flow out of his heart and as a sign of the Spirit that those who believed in him were to receive (see John 7:37). The dove at Jesus' baptism (see John 1:32) has now become the water in the baptism of the Church: a visible sign of the invisible presence of the Spirit. The evangelist himself gave us confirmation when, undoubtedly referring to this, he spoke of the three witnesses to Jesus: "the Spirit, the water and the blood" (1 John 5:8). The water and the blood are the sacramental symbols through which the Spirit would act in the Church or, simply, the symbol of the effusion that had taken place upon the Church. This symbolic reading from John 19 has been accepted in an ecumenical version of the Bible."[6]

The first "fountain" effusion of the Spirit by the dying Christ, as seen by John, was not ignored by the ancient Fathers, who spoke of it in connection with the nuptial theme of the birth of the Church, the new Eve coming from Christ's side, the new Adam sleeping the sleep of death. A paschal homily of the end of the second century or the beginning of the third stated: "Wishing to destroy the works of the woman (Eve) and oppose her, the bearer of death who had come from Adam's side, he now opens his sacred side from which flow his sacred blood and water, initiations into the spiritual and mystical nuptials, signs of our adoption and regeneration. 'He will baptize you with the Holy Spirit and with fire' (Matt 3:11): the water indicated Baptism in the Spirit, the blood baptism in fire."[7] The unknown writer saw a cosmic allusion in this effusion of the Spirit in Luke 23:46: "The whole universe was on the point of chaos and being scattered in consternation because of the passion, if the wonderful Jesus hadn't given up his divine Spirit exclaiming: 'Father into thy hands I commit my Spirit!' (Luke 23:46). And at the moment that everything shook and was rent with fear, the divine Spirit was given up and the universe became stable again as if reanimated, vivified and consolidated.'"[8] The Spirit Jesus gave up on the cross was seen as corresponding to God's Spirit hovering over the face of the waters (see Gen 1:2), and so Christ's death was seen as the new creation.

Now we have come to what most interests us: who was there beneath the cross to receive the breath and first fruits of the Spirit? Mary was there, with the other women and John. They were the "believers in him" assisting the fulfillment of the promise and receiving the Spirit. We mustn't strain this point or exploit it for simplistic or triumphalistic purposes, as if we'd found the winning ticket, but neither can we fail to accept a fact that, in all likelihood, the evangelist himself meant to communicate to the Church.

Let us go back now to contemplating the icon of the crucifixion we studied for the paschal mystery. The various events and episodes recalled by John in connection with the paschal mystery are closely linked to one another; they all form part of the fulfillment and final realization of the Scripture. When Jesus had given Mary into John's care and John into Mary's, he, the evangelist related, knew that all was now finished (see John 19:28). The fulfillment of all his mission was the birth of the Church, represented by Mary in the guise of mother and by John in the guise of all believers. "The scene described in John 19:25-27 could be called the birth of the Church in the person of Mary and the beloved disciple. . . . The act through which Jesus fulfilled his mission was to show that his mother was the 'Woman,' the eschatological Daughter of Zion spoken of by the prophets and who is therefore the figure of the Church. . . . On the cross Jesus manifested his supreme love when, in the person of his Mother and beloved disciple, he constituted the new people of God and gave them the gift of the Spirit.'"[9]

Behind all these meaningful signs and symbols there is a concrete fact, the historicity of which cannot be doubted, that is, the mixture of blood and water that came from Christ's side after it had been pierced by the soldier. As we are dealing with a fact

191

that really took place, I believe it is reasonable to think—even if this deduction doesn't have the same value as the preceding ones—that it was his mother who moved to dry with her hand or the hem of her dress the little flow coming from the body of her dead son. I cannot think of a mother who, when at last able to move close to her dead son, would not do this or passively let others do it. If this was the case, then we can say that Mary gathered also the tangible sign of the first fruits of the Spirit. She was the first to be "baptized in the Spirit" beneath the cross as the representative of the whole Church.

3. *The Spirit That Gives Life*

Obviously the evangelist was less worried about bringing to light what at the moment concerned the immediate receivers of the gift, Mary, John, the women, than what concerned the giver of the gift, Jesus, and the gift itself, the Holy Spirit. For him, that was the moment in which God's gift was finally given to the world, the promise fulfilled, the alabaster jar broken, and the house filled with the fragrance of the ointment (see John 12:3; Matt 26:6). Taking precautionary measures to give this text only an indirect Marian significance, we can, nevertheless, accept what it offers us on the relation between Mary and the Holy Spirit.

We have only one way, the one we used for the Lucan Pentecost, of examining the bond between Mary and the Holy Spirit in the Johannine Pentecost without becoming arbitrary: to try to discover who the Holy Spirit is and what he does in St. John's Gospel and then apply our findings to Mary. In John as in Paul, the line of development of the revelation of the Holy Spirit referred to in the preceding chapter is brought to fulfillment. The Holy Spirit is seen not so much as the divine power that comes on some people in particular circumstances, enabling them to do extraordinary things, as the *principle,* or even as the divine *person* who makes the heart of man his abode, transforming him interiorly into a new man. More than being a question of the Spirit, worker of wonders, it's a question of the sanctifying Spirit.

In the Old Testament we find this new and profound view of the Holy Spirit in Ezekiel when he spoke of a new covenant: "I will sprinkle clean water upon you and you shall be clean from all your uncleannesses, and from all your idols I will cleanse you. A new heart I will give you, and a new spirit I will put within you; and I will take out of your flesh the heart of stone and give you a heart of flesh. And I will put my spirit within you, and cause you to walk in my statutes and be careful to observe my ordinances" (Ezek 36:25-27). The Spirit, here again associated with water, appears as the principle of interior renewal, finally enabling man to observe God's law and, like a living spring, germinating a new life.

John reexamined these themes of the living spring. To him the Spirit was fundamentally the principle of a new birth or a birth from God (see John 1:12-13; 3:5), a new life that is precisely the life of the Spirit: "It is the Spirit," he said, "that gives life" (John 6:63).

In place of being born of the Spirit, St. Paul referred to the Spirit who makes us children of God (see Rom 8:15-16: Gal 4:6). The viewpoint is fundamentally the same. Paul also spoke of "the Spirit of life in Jesus Christ" (Rom 8:2), who creates the new man who walks by the Spirit (see Gal 5:16). The Apostle Paul also drew a synthesis between the two viewpoints on the Spirit: the Spirit that gives charisms and the Spirit that effuses love into the heart. All these, he said, are inspired by one and the same Spirit, but the second is better than the first, as charity lives forever and is better than the charisms that will disappear (see 1 Cor 12:13).

According to John, this was the Spirit that Jesus gave to the disciples from the cross and on the evening of Easter Day. The Spirit that was the very life of Jesus, "the Spirit of truth" who would declare Jesus (see John 16:13), who assures us he abides in us and we in him (see 1 John 4:13), the Spirit who would be in the disciples (see John 14:17). This was the Spirit whose first fruits were given to Mary close to the cross of Christ.

4. *Mary, God's Friend*

Didn't Mary already possess this sanctifying Spirit, which, in the final analysis, is identical to grace itself? Certainly she possessed it, being "full of grace" through divine privilege. Yet Mary's presence beneath the cross was a visible testimony to where the Spirit and grace she had been sanctified in came from; it came from Christ's redemption; it was "Christ's grace" and "Christ's Spirit."

St. Augustine wrote: "Without the Holy Spirit we can neither love Christ nor keep his commandments; the less we have the Spirit the less we can do this, whereas the more abundantly we possess the Spirit the more we can do so. It is not therefore without reason that the Holy Spirit was promised not only to those without him but also to those that already have him: to those without him that they might possess him and to those that have him that they might possess him in greater measure."[10] It is possible therefore to possess the Spirit in a more or less greater measure. If it was said even of Jesus as man that he "grew in grace" (see Luke 2:52), what can we say about others, including Mary? She was full of grace at the annunciation, according to the possibilities and need of the moment; she was full of grace in a relative sense, not absolute.

Scripture informs us that God gives the Holy Spirit "to those who obey him" (Acts 5:32). Mary's great act of obedience beneath the cross dilated her heart and enabled her to accept the Holy Spirit to an even greater degree. New and successive effusions of the Holy Spirit in a person's life correspond to new dilations of the soul through which it becomes more capable of accepting and possessing God. For Mary too, the greatest dilations, or lacerations, of the cross corresponded to a greater degree of grace, that is to say, faith, hope, and above all, charity.

The council constitution states that Mary was "fashioned by the Holy Spirit into a new creature."[11] A reference, this, not only to her conception, as if the Holy Spirit's action ended there, but to her whole life and especially to her participation in the paschal mystery. In the light of what John and Paul related about the action of the Holy Spirit on believers, it was at this point that Mary was finally fashioned by the Spirit into a new creature, capable of loving God with all her strength. "She was united with Her Son in suffering as he died on the cross. In an utterly singular way she cooperated by her obedience, faith, hope and burning charity in the Savior's work."[12]

It is time to mention Mary's "burning charity." We have contemplated Mary's faith at the incarnation, her hope at the paschal mystery, and now, her charity at Pentecost. St. Paul saw love as the sublime fruit of the coming of the Holy Spirit: "God's love has been poured into our hearts through the Holy Spirit" (Rom 5:5). St. Augustine called this "the love by which God causes us to love him and our neighbor."[13] It is the love by which God makes us his friends *(dilectores sui).*

The Marian litanies contain numerous titles, even too many,

but we must add yet another one: Mary, God's friend! The Old Testament knew God's antonomastic friend: Abraham. "Abraham, my friend," God called him (Isa 41:8). The people of Israel, who knew this, made use of it to obtain pardon: "Do not withdraw thy mercy from us, for the sake of Abraham thy beloved" (Dan 3:12). Now in the New Testament God has a new friend, Mary. The liturgy applied these words of the Canticle of Canticles to Mary: "Behold you are beautiful my love, behold you are beautiful" (Song 4:1). Indeed, the Church didn't sin against God's Word when she attributed this joyous exclamation of God's to Mary, seeing that God himself exclaimed at the beginning that what he had created was good (see Gen 1:31). And certainly, after Christ's humanity, Mary was his most beautiful work, his masterpiece of grace. We can take advantage of the friendship between God and Mary as Christian people have done in infinite ways throughout the centuries.

As I have said, the work par excellence of the Holy Spirit is to make men friends of God. He takes out the heart of stone and gives a heart of flesh, a heart willing to do his will, because it loves God. Of Wisdom it is written that "in every generation she passes into holy souls and makes them friends of God and prophets" (Wis 7:27). Not only prophets but also friends of God; not only charismatics but holy and beloved of God; not only men who speak in God's name and do signs and wonders by the power of the Spirit, but men with hearts of sons and not slaves, who love God and freely exclaim: *Abba,* Father!

St. Irenaeus said that the Holy Spirit tunes *(aptat)* us into God.[14] The image recalls both the carpenter smoothing the boards to make them fit perfectly and the musician who accords and matches one voice to another and the single voices within the choir. In other words, he tunes our thoughts to those of God, our will to God's will, our feelings to Christ's. It is the principle of our communion with God.[15]

St. Basil, another great pioneer in studying the action of the Holy Spirit in the Church, enumerated the various actions of the Holy Spirit. Creation, he said, didn't take place without him; on him depends the organization of the Church; miracles and wonders come from him. At the center of all these creative actions of the charismatic type that just pass through the person, he placed a special and different one that concerns the person and his relation to God: the Holy Spirit "creates intimacy with God."[16]

It is easier to sense than to define the meaning of "intimacy" *(oi-keiosis)* because it is a state of mind, a sensation more than an idea or a thing, even if it is real. Intimacy destroys the fear of God and fills the heart with the desire to please him and make him happy, a much better means than fear to keep us away from sin. Intimacy is what allows a married couple to be at ease and open with one another.

The word "intimacy" comes from *intus,* which means "within." God is intimate with us because he promised to be with us and dwell within *(intus)* us (see John 14:17). Actually, he is "deeper within me than my innermost being."[17] The Spirit, too, helps us to be intimate with God, that is to say, present to the Present, and not to remain dissipated outside while he is within us.

St. Basil said that souls who have the Holy Spirit diffuse grace around them, like "those limpid and transparent bodies which when struck by the sun's rays become radiant themselves and illuminate others."[18] Mary was the first and the greatest of those persons the ancient Fathers used to call *pneumatophoroi,* that is to say, "Spirit-bearing" or "Spirit-filled." This is not something we have deduced *a priori* from some abstract principle or other. We have obtained it *a posteriori* from what we have seen, heard, and touched throughout the history of the Church. Luther himself said of her, "No other image of woman fills man with such pure thoughts as this virgin."[19] Mary is God's transparency. In her and in her life God shines through.

5. *Love the Lord Your God*

The passage from Mary to the Church will be very brief this time, as we've said almost all there is to say. Actually, it wouldn't even be necessary to trace a line between Mary and the Church because, as John told us, she was beneath the cross to receive the first fruits of the Spirit as the beginning and image of the Church. I shall recall just a few points in which Mary's example and her relation to the sanctifying Spirit appear instructive at this moment in history.

In the Johannine Pentecost Mary reminds us that being baptized and having received grace and the Holy Spirit doesn't hinder us from praying for a new releasing of the Spirit. That there must be at least two Pentecosts in our lives too. That one of these

Pentecosts usually takes place beneath the cross, like Mary's, in submission and love. St. Augustine told us that Jesus alone, insofar as he received the fullness of the Spirit, doesn't need to receive him again, whereas we need to receive him several times to have him ever more abundantly. This is not because the Spirit limits what he gives but because we are limited in receiving him. Even Jesus, who possessed the fullness of the Spirit on the strength of his union with the Word, received him again in the Jordan to be able to carry out his role as Messiah. In fact, we need a corresponding grace and the Holy Spirit anew for each new mission God assigns to us. Mary, too, who was full of grace from her conception, received the Holy Spirit several times: at the annunciation, beneath the cross, in the cenacle.

There is yet another teaching I wish to emphasize in contemplating Mary in the Johannine Pentecost. She reminds us of the first and greatest commandment: "You shall love the Lord your God with all your soul, and with all your strength and with all your mind; and your neighbor as yourself" (Luke 10:27). She reminds us that charity alone "will have no end" (1 Cor 13:8). Everything else will end: virtues, charisms, faith, hope. Love alone will never pass. She reminds us that man is worth his love of God and his neighbor and nothing more.

Mary, as I have already said, is not the figure and model of the Church in the human term of models who stand still to be photographed or painted and the more still they stand the better they are. Mary is an active model, helping us to imitate her. She is like an Alpine guide who has gotten over a difficult pass and waits for those following to go ahead and, if they cannot manage, goes back to give them a hand. She gives us a hand, especially in this final "pass" of leaving our self-love behind to enter into God's love. She teaches us the great art of loving God. It is not for nothing that the Church invokes her with the biblical expression of "the mother of good love" (see Sir 24:24, Vulgate).

The Bible invites us to love God with two different loves, although coming from the same Spirit: filial love and nuptial love. *Filial love* is made up of obedience. It consists in keeping the commandments of God, just as Jesus loved his Father and kept his commandments (see John 15:10). You desire to love God but you don't know how? You are not able to feel the slightest attraction or love for him? It's quite simple: set yourself to keeping his commandments and in particular to what is being given to you now through his Word, and be certain that you are loving him! The prophet Ezekiel said the Holy Spirit is given to us to cause us to walk in God's statutes and observe his ordinances (see Ezek 36:27).

Nuptial love is a choice. You don't choose your mother or father, but you do choose your spouse. To love God with a nuptial love means to choose God and choose him again each time as your God and your all, renouncing even yourself, if necessary, to possess him. "To love is to labor to detach and strip itself for God's sake of all that is not God."[20]

Our pilgrimage with Mary has now reached the point that will never end, charity, the point where our present life looks into eternal life, and we shall stop here. She who has so far been the "way" for us to reach the Lord is now the "gate" through which we shall enter heaven: *Ianua coeli,* "Gate of heaven," as she is called in Christian devotion.

Passing from charisms to charity, St. Paul wrote, "I will show you a still more excellent way" (1 Cor 12:31). There is a precise sense in which these words can be applied to Mary: I will show you a still more excellent way, Mary! We know well that Jesus alone is the true way; Mary is simply "the best way" to go to Christ or, better, through whom the Holy Spirit leads us to Christ. The best way because she is the most accessible, the closest to our state, as she, like us, walked in faith, hope, and charity. Mary is part of the great way that is the Word of God. She is a word in action or, better, a word in flesh and bone.

It's exactly because Mary is part of God's Word that we can apply Isaiah's prophecy to her, as if God were telling us of her, "This is the way, walk in it" (Isa 30:21). St. Bernard said that Mary is the "royal way" through which God came to us and through which we can now go to him.[21] In ancient times the royal way was a particularly well-kept way, exceptionally straight and wide, along which the king or emperor passed when he visited the city.

An artist can form his circle of followers not only by inviting them to read his works and ideas on art, for example, on paintings, but also by showing them his paintings and especially his masterpiece. This is how the Holy Spirit forms us through Mary in Christ's following, even if Mary is part of God's written word, too. An artist would not feel offended at seeing students enchanted round his masterpiece, gazing at it and trying to imitate it instead of reading his works on art. Why then should we think that the contemplation of Mary takes something from Christ or the Holy Spirit? Of course, contemplation and veneration must be done in a spirit and with an awareness that was so strong in her: that she was just a tool in God's hands.

NOTES

1. St. Augustine, *Sermons,* 265, 8, 9 (PL 38, 1222); *On the Gospel of John,* 74, 2 (CC 36, p. 513).
2. See St. Cyril of Jerusalem, *Catechesis,* XVII, 12 and 14 (PG 33, 984 f.).
3. St. Cyril of Alexandria, *Commentary on the Gospel of John,* XII, 1 (PG 74, 716 f.).
4. Tertullian, *On Baptism,* 19, 2 (CC 1, p. 293).
5. St. Athanasius, *Festal Letters,* 14, 6 (PG 26, 1422).
6. See *Traduction Oecumenique de la Bible,* Paris, 1985, ad loc.
7. *Ancient Paschal Homily,* 53 (SCh 27, p. 181).
8. Ibid., 55 (SCh 27, p. 183).
9. I. de la Potterie, *Le Symbolisme du sang et de l'eau en Jean,* 19, 34, in *"Didaskalia"* 14, 1984, p. 217 f.
10. St. Augustine, *On the Gospel of John,* 74, 2 (CC 36, p. 514).
11. *Lumen gentium* 56.
12. Ibid., 61.
13. St. Augustine, *The Spirit and the Letter,* 32, 56 (PL 44, 237).
14. St. Irenaeus, *Against the Heresies,* III, 17, 2 (SCh 211, p. 332).
15. See St. Irenaeus, *Against the Heresies,* V, 1, 1 (SCh 153, p. 20).
16. St. Basil, *On the Holy Spirit,* 19, 49 (PG 32, 157).
17. St. Augustine, *Confessions,* III, 6.
18. St. Basil, *On the Holy Spirit,* 9, 23 (PG 32, 109).
19. Luther, *Sermons on the Gospels (Kirchenpostille)* (ed. Weimar 10, 1, p. 68).
20. St. John of the Cross, *Ascent of Mount Carmel,* II, 5, 7 (trans. by E. A. Peers, cit., p. 78).
21. St. Bernard, *Advent Homilies,* I (ed. Cister. IV, Rome, 1966, p. 174).

"My Spirit Rejoices in God"

Mary in glory, a pledge of hope for the Church

"Come, I will show you the Bride, the wife of the Lamb" (Rev 21:9)—so said the angel in Revelation to John as he carried him away in the Spirit to show him "the holy city Jerusalem coming down out of heaven from God, having the glory of God." If this holy city is not made up of just walls and towers but of saved persons, if it is not abstract but real, then Mary, whom John presented to us in his Gospel as the "Woman," the daughter of Zion, is part of it. Just as Mary beneath the cross was the symbol and almost the personification of the pilgrim Church, now, in heaven, she is the first flowering of the glorified Church, the most precious jewel of this holy city. The holy city, the heavenly Jerusalem, St. Augustine would say, is greater, more important, than she is because it is "the whole," whereas, instead, she is a member, even if the noblest![1]

Now, at the end of our spiritual journey in Mary's wake, I dare to use the angel's words for those of you who have made this pilgrimage with me: "Come, I will show you the Bride, the wife of the Lamb!" How can I show her to you? Because I've been there or can go there perhaps? No, I shall show her to you as she is shown to me and all of us by faith: through the words of Scripture and, in addition, through the most credible testimonies of those who, like Paul, were enraptured and heard things that cannot be repeated. We have now reached the shore where time ends and eternity begins. From this point on we must walk on the waters. The old "shoes" of science and human experience no longer serve and must be left on the seashore. Faith alone can walk on these waters.

Having contemplated Mary on earth as the sign of what the Church *should be,* let us now contemplate her as the sign of what she *will be. Lumen gentium* states: "In the bodily and spiritual glory which she possesses in heaven, the Mother of Jesus continues in this present world as the image and first flowering of the Church as she is to be perfected in the world to come. Likewise, Mary shines forth on earth, until the day of the Lord shall come, a sign of certain hope and comfort for the pilgrim People of God.''[2] According to Catholic doctrine, which is based on a tradition shared by the Orthodox Church (even if not dogmatically defined by this), Mary entered into glory not only in spirit but as a whole integral person, body and soul, as the first flowering, after Christ, of the coming resurrection. Dante has St. Bernard say in heaven:

> Here unto us thou art a noonday torch
> of charity, and below there among mortals,
> thou art the living fountain-head of hope.[3]

Mary is the clearest example and demonstration of the truth of these words from Scripture: "Provided we suffer with him, we will also be glorified with him" (see Rom 8:17). No one suffered like Mary with Jesus, and therefore no one is as glorified as she is with Jesus.

What is Mary's glory? There's a glory we can see with our own eyes. What other human creature has been more loved, invoked in joy and sorrow, what name has been more on man's lips? Isn't this glory? After Christ, to whom have men raised more prayers, more hymns, more cathedrals? Which face has been more depicted in art? "All generations will call me blessed," Mary had said of herself, or rather, the Holy Spirit had said of her. And twenty centuries have proved that this was a real prophecy. It wouldn't have been possible for a poor unknown young girl to say these things of herself or for others to have said them of her without God's intervention.

This makes us reflect about whether it is right to be hasty in deciding that the *Magnificat* already existed as a psalm and was only attributed to Mary. Who but Mary could have said these words? If it is true that they were said by someone else of himself, it is certain that they were not fulfilled in him but in Mary, thereby proving that the *Magnificat* is Mary's even if she didn't compose it. Whoever wrote it did so *for her*. It was of her the Holy Spirit was talking. What was said in Isaiah about the Servant of the Lord also holds for this canticle about the handmaid of the Lord; whoever wrote it was not speaking about himself but about someone else (see Acts 8:34). With right do we use the *Magnificat* to better comprehend Mary's spirit and her story, just as we use Isaiah 53 to better comprehend Christ's passion, even more so because it is the Bible itself that openly attributes it to Mary.

All generations will call you blessed, O Mother of God, and this generation too, thereby obeying God's "command to history" in your regard. Even this book is a small sign through which our generation—which is benefiting from the wonderful gift of the council—desires to proclaim you blessed. You, Mary, will cease to be "blessed among women" when Jesus ceases to be "the fruit of your womb." One day, God said to our friend and teacher Angela of Foligno, "I desire you to do good to the benefit even of those who think of you or simply hear you mentioned,"[4] and eight centuries later, I myself can bear witness that God kept his promise. But first, God did this and much more for Mary: he blesses even those who hear her name mentioned.

Great, therefore, is Mary's glory on earth. But this isn't all Mary's glory and reward for what she suffered with Christ. We are still fettered by a concept of glory belonging to ancient paganism. This is a concept where glory *(doxa)* essentially concerns the sphere of knowledge, of information or opinion. Glory is "clear knowledge accompanied by praise." But Mary is in God's glory, not man's. Man's glory on earth and in the Church is just a pale reflection of God's glory. And what is God's glory, the *kabod,* referred to in the Bible? It doesn't only concern the sphere of knowledge but also that of being. God's glory is God himself, insofar as his being is light, beauty and splendor and, above all, love. Glory is so real that it filled the tabernacle and passed by Moses (see Exod 33:22; 40:34); it could be seen and beheld on Christ's face (see John 1:14; 2 Cor 4:6). Glory is the splendor of God's power, a pure emanation of the glory of the Almighty (see Heb 1:3; Wis 7:25 ff.). Mary's true glory consists in her participation in God's glory, in being clothed in it and sunk in it, that is to say, in being "filled with all the fullness of God" (Eph 3:19). More than this we cannot think or say.

And Mary's role in this glory? She fulfills the calling for which every human creature and the whole Church was created: she is, in heaven, the pure "praise of his glory" (see Eph 1:14). Mary praises and glorifies God: "Praise your God, O Zion" (Ps 147:12). Now Mary is the Zion glorifying God. The praise of God is the creature's conscious admiration of the fact that God is, and that he is glorious. Mary is God's glory insofar as she glories in God her Creator and God glories in her his creature. If, in the Old Testament, God gloried in Job and said to Satan, "Have you considered my servant Job, that there is none like him" (Job 1:8), what shall he say of Mary?

We contemplate Mary in glory because she is the image and pledge of what the Church will be one day. Mary praises God and in this praise rejoices, delights, and exults. Now her spirit really does rejoice in God. Yet what we can say about Mary's joy is nothing, for it is written: "What no eye has seen, nor ear heard, not the heart of man conceived, that God has prepared for those who love him" (see 1 Cor 2:9). Mary entered the joy of her Master (see Matt 25:21) and the joy of the Master entered her.

I have said that Mary praises and in praising rejoices: "I praise God," says St. Augustine, "and in praising him I rejoice in his praise. Let love and praise be free, which means to love and praise God for himself and not for something else."[5] Now, the prophetic words that Mary echoed in the *Magnificat* have come true. She can say:

> I will greatly rejoice in the Lord,
> My soul shall exult in my God;
> for he has clothed me with the garments of salvation.
> He has covered me with the robe of righteousness,
> as a bridegroom decks himself with a garland,
> and as a bride adorns herself with her jewels (Isa 61:10).

No human creature could bear up to so much glory and beatitude if she weren't enabled to do so by God's power. There have been saints who experienced something of heavenly beatitude and were forced to exclaim, "Enough my God!" My heart can contain no more of this joy. The joy of the consummation of love between the creature and God! It is only through the saints' experience that we can get the slightest idea about this state, so far from our own experience. Once, on the feast day of the presentation of Jesus in the Temple, the Blessed Angela had a vision. She saw what happens when, on entering into eternity, we are presented to God, when the veils are removed and the mysterious revelation of God to his creatures, of the creature to God, and the creature to himself takes place: "Then my soul manifested itself to God with the greatest joy ever experienced, with new and greater delight and in such an unusual miracle, the like of which I had never before experienced. At that moment I encountered God and understood and experienced in myself how God manifests himself to his creatures and the unusual manifestation and presentation of the soul to God. The delight in this differed from anything ever experienced before. I heard such beautiful words which I don't wish you to write down.''[6] In a similar experience, St. Paul, too, heard things that could not be told (see 2 Cor 12:4). Judging from similar revelations experienced by the saints, it must concern the words with which God expresses his pleasure in his creature and reveals how precious and beautiful she is in words that could induce the profane to think the soul wasn't experiencing God but the Tempter.

What place do we have in Mary's heart and thoughts? Has she perhaps forgotten us in her glory? Like Esther, once she had been received into the king's palace, Mary doesn't forget her troubled people but intercedes for them until the enemy who wants to destroy them is gotten rid of. Who more than Mary could say with St. Thérèse of the Child Jesus: "I feel that my mission is about to begin; my mission of making souls love the good God as I love him, to teach my little way to souls. If my desires receive fulfillment, I shall spend my heaven on earth even until the end of time. Yes, I will spend my heaven doing good upon earth."[7] In this too, Thérèse of the Child Jesus discovered Mary's vocation and unknowingly made it her own. She passes her heaven doing good on earth, and we are all witnesses of this.

Mary intercedes. The risen Christ, it is written, intercedes for us (see Rom 8:34). Jesus intercedes for us with the Father, Mary intercedes for us with the Son. The Holy Father, John Paul II, said that "Mary's mediation is intercession."[8] She is a mediatrix in the sense that she intercedes. Also, this title of Mary's, which causes so many reservations, can be made comprehensible to our Protestant brethren through analogies from below contained in Scripture. In the Bible, Jeremiah, already centuries dead, is shown interceding for his people in the Second Book of Maccabees (15:14), which, although not considered inspired by all Christians, nevertheless gives testimony to a belief that existed in the Bible from the Old Testament. Moses and Samuel were presented by Jeremiah as great intercessors (see Jer 15:1). The people asked God to remember Abraham and David and all their hardships (see Ps 132:1). Is it strange, then, that the Church attributed the power of intercession to God's mother? In the Old Testament God lamented at not having found in the land intercessors, that he should not destroy the people (see Isa 59:16; Ezek 22:30). Could the same be true perhaps of his saints in heaven?

Belief in the Mother of God's unique power of intercession is based on the truth of the communion of saints, which is an article of the common Creed. And this communion certainly doesn't exclude the saints already in heaven.

Mary's power of intercession in heaven is different from what she used at Cana when she said, "They have no more wine" (John 2:3). An important transformation has taken place in between. Jesus was God's son also while he was on earth but "according to the flesh," that is to say, his divinity was hidden under a state of humility, suffering, and mortality. At his resurrection he became the "Son of God in power" (Rom 1:3-4). Something similar happened to Mary. She was God's mother on earth, but her life was a hidden one of self-denial. Once she had been associated with her son's glorification, she became "God's mother in power." Now God can fully acknowledge what he had done for her. The power of God's mother is not autonomous and parallel to that of God or Christ; it is the power of intercession.

Can Mary also "command" God, as popular devotion sometimes says? Isn't this a blasphemous thought? St. Catherine of Genoa, a saint highly esteemed and accepted also in Protestant circles for her extraordinary sense of God's transcendence and her refusal to make easy use of indulgences and such things, said she would sometimes start praying to ask God for something but she would hear her Beloved's voice saying, "Command me, because love can command."[9] In a certain true and acceptable sense, but which we mustn't strain, Mary commands God when asking. Her power of intercession is founded on her love for God. If God has promised to do what we ask of him "according to his will" (1 John 5:14), all the more so does he do what Mary asks, because she asks only for what is according to God's will. When a soul desires all that God does, God does all that the soul desires.

We are not discussing abstract deductions. Mary's power of intercession is seen *a posteriori* by history and not *a priori* by some principle or other. From *being,* it is licit to go back to *could be.* It is a recognized truth that Mary obtains graces and help for the pilgrim Church. How many graces have been received by people who well know from clear signs that they come through Mary! If the term "mediatrix" creates a problem, let it be called by another name or no name at all, but let us believe the reality and the "cloud of testimonies," so as not to offend who brought all of this about.

Mary's role in relation to God's pilgrim people can be compared to that of the pillar of fire, which gave the pilgrim people light in the desert that they might travel by day and by night (see Exod 13:21 ff.; Deut 9:16). Perhaps it is in the consideration of this image that Mary is honored in some places with the title "Madonna of light."

Mary's role can also be illustrated by the image of the moon. Light doesn't come from the moon itself but from the light it receives from the sun and which it reflects on the earth. Mary's light doesn't come from her but from Christ. In this sense, too, she is a mirror, because she reflects the light of Christ on the Church. The moon illuminates at night when the sun has set and before the next sunrise; Mary, too, often illuminates those who are in the night of faith and being tested, or those living in the darkness of sin, if they invoke her. When the sun rises in the morning, the moon withdraws and certainly doesn't try to compete with the sun; when Christ comes into a soul, Mary withdraws and says, like John the Baptist: "This joy of mine is now full. He must increase, but I must decrease" (John 3:29 ff.).

The Fathers loved to apply the symbolism sun-moon to the relation Christ-Church,[10] but even in this we can see to what extent Mary and the Church are realities recalling each other, one being the figure of the other.

Mary is all of this and does all of this for us. What should we do for her? The prophet Isaiah gave us the answer. All we have to do is substitute the name "Jerusalem" with Mary's, the daughter of Zion, in his text, and it becomes a wonderful invitation to all of us to rejoice with Mary:

> Rejoice with Jerusalem, and be glad for her,
> all you who love her.
> Rejoice with her in joy,
> all you who mourn over her;
> that you may suck and be satisfied with her consoling breasts;
> that you may drink deeply with delight
> from the abundance of her glory.
> For thus says the Lord:
> "Behold I will extend prosperity to her like a river
> and the wealth of the nations like an overflowing stream;

and you shall suck, you shall be carried upon her hip
and dandled upon her knees'' (Isa 66:10-12).

There is something else we can do besides rejoicing and being
glad for Mary. We can thank the Trinity with her for what it did
for her. A psalmist said, ''Magnify the Lord with me, let us exalt
his name together'' (Ps 34:4). Mary says the same to us. Perhaps
there is no greater joy we can give her than making her canticle
of praise and thanksgiving to God resound on earth through the
centuries.

And then, of course, imitation. If we love, we imitate. Love
has no better fruit than imitation. Our spiritual journey was undertaken to imitate her, to seriously make her our guide on our
pilgrimage toward our complete transformation in Christ and toward holiness. Now that we have reached the end and as we contemplate her assumption into heaven in body and soul, we recall
another, different assumption into heaven, that of Elijah. Before
seeing his master disappear in the chariot of fire, the young disciple Elisha asked, ''Let me inherit a double share of your spirit''
(2 Kgs 2:9). We dare to ask even more of Mary our mother and
mistress: O Mother, may we inherit all your spirit! May your faith,
hope, and charity be ours. May your love for God be ours! ''May
each one of us have Mary's spirit to magnify the Lord with, may
her spirit be in each one of us to rejoice in God.''[11]

In this book we have spoken of Mary and ''mirrored'' ourselves
in her, referring everything to God, seeing her only as God's instrument glorifying God and not herself. However, before we conclude it would be ungrateful and small-minded of us not to offer
this humble instrument and ''stainless mirror'' our heartfelt
thanks as we think of how hard and full of thorns her pilgrimage
was and of her great love for us. Let us do this with the words
of one of the many who found God again through her:

> Because you are there forever, simply because
> you are Mary, simply because you exist,
> Mother of Jesus Christ, we thank you![12]

NOTES

1. St. Augustine, *Sermons,* 72A (Denis 25), 7 (*Miscellanea Agostiniana*
   I, p. 163).

2. *Lumen gentium* 68.
3. Dante Alighieri, *Paradiso,* XXXIII, 10, 12.
4. *The Book of the Bl. Angela of Foligno,* ed. cit., p. 256.
5. St. Augustine, *On the Psalms,* 53, 10 (CC 38, p. 653 f.).
6. *The Book of the Bl. Angela of Foligno,* ed. cit., p. 394.
7. St. Thérèse of Lisieux, *Novissima Verba* (July 17, 1897) (Dublin, Gill & Son, 1953, p. 57).
8. John-Paul II, *Redemptoris mater,* 21 (AAS 79, 1987, p. 389).
9. St. Catherine of Genoa, *Life,* 32 (Turin, 1962, p. 262).
10. See H. Rahner, *Symbole der Kirche,* Salzburg, 1964.
11. St. Ambrose, *On the Gospel of Luke,* II, 26 (CSEL 32, 4, p. 55).
12. P. Claudel, *La Vierge à midi,* in *Oeuvre Poétique,* Paris, Gallimard 1967, p. 541.

Index of Authors

Thematic Index